# HOUSTON

**COMPLETELY REVISED 6TH EDITION**

# HOUSTON

## COMPLETELY REVISED 6TH EDITION

### BY JOANNE HARRISON

**Gulf Publishing Company**
Houston, Texas

## THIS BOOK IS FOR ALL MY FAMILIES:

*For Jack and Helen Harrison of Charlestown;*
*For the Macdonalds of Poppasquash;*
*For my grandmother, who's seeing what comes next;*
*For the family of my heart in Houston;*
*And most of all for Joseph Patrick.*
*With love and thanks.*

*In memory of Gert Levinson, who had faith.*

Gulf Publishing Company
Book Division
P.O. Box 2608 ☐ Houston, Texas 77252-2608

10  9  8  7  6  5  4  3  2  1

**Library of Congress Cataloging-in-Publication Data**

Harrison, Joanne, 1948–
    Houston / by Joanne Harrison. — 6th ed.
        p.   cm. — (Texas monthly guidebooks)
    Rev. ed. of: Texas monthly guide to Houston. 5th ed.
    c1990.
        Includes index.
    **ISBN 0-87719-272-3**
        1. Houston (Tex.)—Guidebooks. I. Harrison, Joanne.
    Texas monthly guide to Houston. II. Title. III. Series.
    F394.H83H37
    917.6404′63—dc20                                    95-43886
                                                              CIP

*Texas Monthly* is a registered trademark of Mediatex
Communications Corp.

Printed in the United States of America.

# CONTENTS

Acknowledgments . . . . . . . . . . . . . . . . . . . . . . . . . . . . . . . . . . vi
Preface to the 6th Edition . . . . . . . . . . . . . . . . . . . . . . . . . . vii
You Are Here . . . . . . . . . . . . . . . . . . . . . . . . . . . . . . . . . . . . . . 1
Sam . . . . . . . . . . . . . . . . . . . . . . . . . . . . . . . . . . . . . . . . . . . . . 11
The Story of Houston. . . . . . . . . . . . . . . . . . . . . . . . . . . . . . 22
Things to See . . . . . . . . . . . . . . . . . . . . . . . . . . . . . . . . . . . . . 44
Calendar of Annual Events. . . . . . . . . . . . . . . . . . . . . . . . . 80
Arts . . . . . . . . . . . . . . . . . . . . . . . . . . . . . . . . . . . . . . . . . . . . 124
Sports and Fitness. . . . . . . . . . . . . . . . . . . . . . . . . . . . . . . . 152
Green Houston. . . . . . . . . . . . . . . . . . . . . . . . . . . . . . . . . . . 162
The Restaurant Guide . . . . . . . . . . . . . . . . . . . . . . . . . . . . 171
Clubs & Pubs . . . . . . . . . . . . . . . . . . . . . . . . . . . . . . . . . . . . 216
Hotels . . . . . . . . . . . . . . . . . . . . . . . . . . . . . . . . . . . . . . . . . . 228
Get Out of Town. . . . . . . . . . . . . . . . . . . . . . . . . . . . . . . . . 238
Galveston . . . . . . . . . . . . . . . . . . . . . . . . . . . . . . . . . . . . . . . 244
Clear Lake and the NASA Area . . . . . . . . . . . . . . . . . . . . 265
Read More About It . . . . . . . . . . . . . . . . . . . . . . . . . . . . . . 276
Index . . . . . . . . . . . . . . . . . . . . . . . . . . . . . . . . . . . . . . . . . . 288

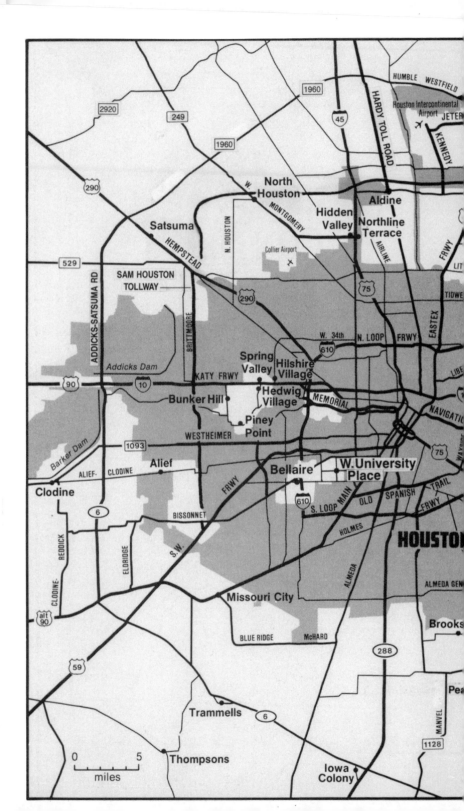

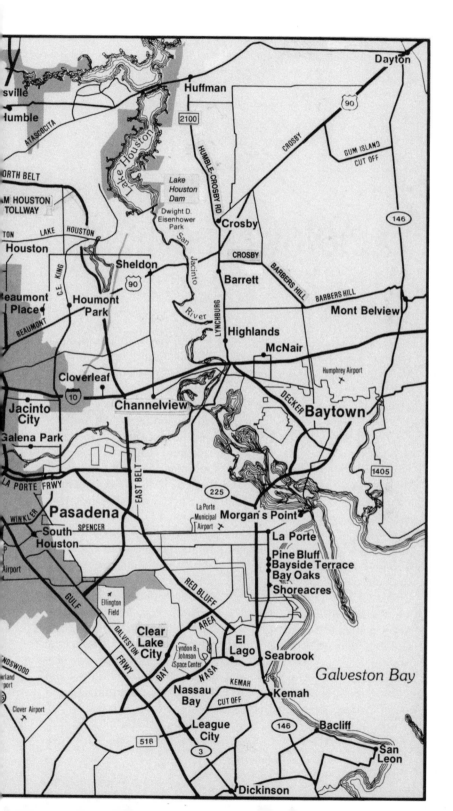

# ACKNOWLEDGMENTS

I'd like to thank all those who helped me with this project. Thanks to my editor at Gulf Publishing Co., Claire Blondeau, who really does understand; to my ace researcher Steve Englishbey; and to researching gardening maven Mike Peters—without them it wouldn't have been possible.

A special thank you to film critic Joe Leydon for all the material on the movies; to former "Proteus" impresario Don Harrison for club info; to Duffy Miller of the other Bellaire and his pal Jack Harrison down on the farm for all the fun to Jake Harrison for all the airport rides; to Ginny Carroll and Carol Jackson of *Newsweek* magazine's Houston Bureau for their patience; to troubadour Don Sanders for my fave, the *Bayou Song*, which I heard while writing this; to the staff of the late lamented *Houston Post* for their many fine articles about our town; and to the librarians at the Texas and Local History Collection of the Houston Public Library whose encyclopedic knowledge of the city deserves everyone's appreciation.

Most of all I'd like to thank my family of friends: Louis B. Parks and Susan Nenney; Mr. Mike; Debbie Fant; Mario Marques; Susan Ackerman; Marina Otis Spiropoulos; John Paul Barnich; John Davenport; Spencer; Rhona Schwartz and, of course, Ms. Chelsea; Andrew Williams; Gabrielle Cosgriff; Saul Levinson; Sherry Nelson; artist Edward Ross Miles, who taught me stick-to-it-iveness; and Sandy Sheehy and Tom Curtis, who taught me everything I know about writing. Thanks. I couldn't have done it without you.

*J.H.*

# PREFACE TO THE 6TH EDITION

Houston is my home. I love to talk about it, so that's what this book is: a one-sided conversation. Still, how can anyone, no matter how much in love with words, create a text picture of a living organism? (That's what a city is: a living thing that changes every time people think they've caught its essence.) So, at best this book's a snapshot. The city presented here, frozen in my flash, is Houston as I see it. Yours would be a different place.

Through five previous editions of the *Texas Monthly Guidebook to Houston*, one of them mine, other writers and editors each have described their own places. Some were tales of boomtowns, others saw shoppers' paradise. Some emphasized business opportunity; others, gracious living. This version is what I see: an amazing story. A place filled with the unexpected. A city of surprises.

Maybe that's because, like the majority of Houstonians including the founding Allen brothers, I came here from someplace else, not knowing what to expect. As a child in the cold Northeast, I thought Houston would look like a western movie. Cowboys. Cactus. Tumbleweed blowing through the streets. I thought I might see millionaire "awl" men in burnt-orange Cadillac convertibles, longhorns on the grille, lighting their "see-gars" with hundred-dollar bills. It didn't happen. Like Humphrey Bogart's Rick Blaine, who came to Casablanca for the waters, I'd been misinformed.

The first time I saw the Bayou City, summer hit me in the face like a hot, wet sponge. That was August 9, 1976. Caught heading into the sun on the Southwest Freeway in a car without air conditioning in the middle of evening rush-hour traffic, I wondered, as many an immigrant had before me, why on earth I had come to this strange place. Now I know the answer.

Italian film director Michelangelo Antonioni knew it. "I have never felt salvation in nature," he said. "I love cities above all." I love cities, too. I love their energy, their mystery, their layers of past lives, and their futuristic beauty. And Houston is both energetic and mysterious. Its past is a surprise and its obsession with the future a wonder.

In San Antonio, Boston, and New Orleans, history is all around. In San Francisco, a spun-sugar city decorating the tops of caramel-colored hills, urban beauty can take your breath away.

Houston isn't beautiful, and it keeps its past well hidden. Its freeways and its stories are never finished, abandoned in the city's headlong rush to reinvent itself each day. Houston has always been a city imagined. And the city imagined in this book is mine.

*Joanne Harrison*

# YOU ARE HERE

Welcome to Houston. We are the fourth-largest city in America —the current pecking order runs Los Angeles, New York, Chicago, then us, but we'll pass them up one of these days.

We are sitting on what the geologists call the Gulf Coastal Prairie at 95 degrees and 22 minutes west longitude and 29 degrees, 46 minutes north latitude, which means that when you look at a map of the earth we share the same east-west line with Cairo, Egypt; Kuwait City; Delhi, India; and Chongqing, China.

North and south, we're on a line with Winnipeg, Canada, and Vera Cruz, Mexico, but if you continue down all the way into the Southern hemisphere, you'll run smack into the Pacific Ocean. Houston is further west than Equador, Peru, and Chile.

The city of Houston proper takes up some 598.42 square miles, but because we have governmental powers of annexation, it's likely that we'll gobble up some more of the contiguous unincorporated areas.

Metropolitan Houston, which includes parts of eight surrounding counties, sprawls over more than 8,778 square miles. That's bigger than more than a dozen sovereign nations and about the same size as the entire country of El Salvador or Israel.

According to the 1990 census, there are 3,731,131 of us in the metro area. That's more people than live in the states of Alaska, Arizona, Arkansas, Colorado, Connecticut, Delaware, the District of Columbia, Hawaii, Idaho, Iowa, Kansas, Kentucky, Maine, Mississippi, Montana, Nebraska, Nevada, New Hampshire, New Mexico, North Dakota, Oklahoma, Oregon, Rhode Island, South Carolina, South Dakota, Utah, Vermont, West Virginia, or Wyoming.

In the city itself there are 1,630,553 folks, which is just a little bigger than the population of the southwest African nation of Namibia where a Houstonian (well ok, a Deer Park resident—close enough for government work) named Chelsi Smith won the Miss Universe title in 1995.

The people who measure these things claim that Houston is 48 feet above sea level, but they must have been standing on something when they dropped the plumb line.

During the daytime here, the sun shines about 57 percent of the time—which *isn't* bad. Everyone knows our summers are jungle hot, and the average relative humidity hits 90 percent in the early morning—which *is* bad. If they stayed outside, most folks who live here would have 365 bad hair days a year. That's why we are the world's most air-conditioned major city.

But heat and humidity aren't our only challenges. The rest of the weather here is pretty unusual as well.

## HOUSTON: WEATHER OR NOT . . .

Beware the Blue Norther! Like *Monty Python's* Spanish Inquisition, nobody in semi-tropical Houston expects suddenly freezing temperatures, but from September to May fronts from the north play seesaw with the warm, wet Gulf winds. In December and January, Northers bred in the Canadian Rockies can be downright arctic.

Yankees and other foreigners think we're making this up. We're not. While it's true that Blue Northers aren't as common in Houston as they are in some other parts of Texas, they happen here frequently enough to make us sit up and take notice.

It's really the suddenness that's so scary. A day that starts off balmy and beautiful can alter in an instant as a steel-blue tidal wave of clouds appears in the Northwestern sky. The temperature can drop by as much as 50 degrees in a few hours and the winds preceding the cloudwall do their advance work with as much skill as political operatives. Blustery and fickle, they can even reach gale proportions.

Nineteenth-century travelers compared being smacked by a Texas Norther to encountering Beelzebub himself. If you're inside, safe and dry, a Norther can be the best show in town. The wind screams, sweeping leaves, branches and loose articles of lawn furniture down the street; the sky turns from blue to molten metal, opens and then pours out rivers of rain; the lightning is incessant as thunder—and sometimes hail—pounds away on the soundtrack. Often, the whole thing's over in a few hours. The wind clocks around, and the lovely day picks up where it left off.

In winter—usually Houston's best season—Blue Northers have been known to blow in with a load of sleet and ice the city down for as long as two or three whole days. Once, in 1859, Houston actually had a meteorologically measurable snowfall. A few times since then we've had more than a dusting, all compliments of the Canadian Rockies.

Beyond creating aesthetically pleasing ice patterns, Northers actually have done some good in Houston's history. Back in the 1800s, before there was good drainage, sanitation, or mosquito control, Yellow Fever epidemics swept the city on a regular basis. Northers, which froze the standing water where mosquitoes bred, stopped two of the worst plagues cold.

---

**HOUSTON FACTOID:**

*The strongest ultraviolet light rays in the United States are supposed to be at Salton Sea, in the California desert and at Galveston, Texas*

---

While it's rarely unbearably cold in Houston, most people believe that it is normally unbearably hot. This isn't really true—though try telling that to the New York reporters, here for the Rockets 1994 basketball championship, who headlined our climate as the "Hellhole." Actually, it's only a hellhole about 12 weeks a year. The other 40 weeks, Houston's climate ranges from quite nice to really gorgeous. Why we continue to build and air-condition almost entirely in reaction to the relatively few unbearably hot weeks remains a mystery. Most of the time, even in summer, our evenings are wonderful: soft, sultry, and romantic with the scent of night-blooming jasmine, though even Houston's most ardent fans concede that our Augusts are generally unfit for human existence. The heat builds up until everybody and everything is ready to explode—it's hurricane season.

Hurricanes are the favorite topic of local TV and radio weather reporters virtually year-round. They do pre-hurricane season reports and post-season wrap-ups. It's hard to live in Houston without becoming some kind of hurricane expert.

No matter what else you've heard, cyclones and hurricanes really are the same thing. Cyclone is a description. (It's Greek for something that moves in a circle.) Hurricane is a description of a different kind. The West Indian Tiano people called their god of the winds Huracan. Below the Equator, the storms spin clockwise; above, they spin counterclockwise.

Either way, the basic storm facts are these: When things on our side of the earth just get too damn hot, nature needs to get rid of the heat, so it rises.

Above the Atlantic Ocean, off the western coast of Africa, all that heat and humidity in the summer atmosphere gathers itself into tropical waves and starts moving west. If nothing gets in the way, the tropical waves begin to form circulations, spinning across the warm waters gathering even more energy. The warmer the water, the more tightly the storm winds itself up, forming a kind of donut shape with walls of clouds around a clear center. The winds increase until they are upward of 75 miles per hour and the barometric pressure in the center keeps falling, creating a kind of vacuum effect. This can actually suck up huge amounts of water and carry it along in tidal waves. Envision a kid who's sucked up half a straw's worth of soft drink, then quickly put his thumb over the mouth end. "Barometric pressure" is what keeps the soft drink in the straw as the junior meteorologist waves the exhibit at his unimpressed parents.

If this spinning storm, with its torrential rains and sucked up tidal waves, manages to make it through the narrow passage from the Atlantic into the Gulf of Mexico, somebody in our neck of the woods is in *big* trouble.

Although the official hurricane season in the Gulf runs from June through November, the vast majority of storms churn up in late August or early September. That's when the monsters come.

In September 1900, the worst natural disaster ever to strike North America hit Galveston Island. In the days before named storms, it was called "The Great West Indian Hurricane" or just

"The Great Storm," and it had already killed hundreds of people in Haiti and Cuba before it struck Texas. It was a weekend, and the island was crowded with tourists when the storm began in the early afternoon. The winds were bad—about 85 mph when the wind gauge broke off—but the tidal wave was awful. By morning, between 6,000 and 10,000 people were dead. The true total will never be known, because whole families were wiped out and there was no one left to report them missing.

Nothing of that magnitude has hit us since. Hurricane *Celia,* which landed near Corpus Christi in 1970, had winds almost twice as strong as those of the Galveston storm, but no tidal wave. There was a lot of damage, but few deaths. The same was true of *Alicia,* a mid-range hurricane that hit Galveston and Houston in 1983. Damage was more than $3 billion, but there were fewer than two dozen deaths.

Several years can go by without a storm's hitting Texas, and this creates a fools' paradise for shorefront development, but sooner or later nature *always* returns to take back her beaches.

Weather in the Houston-Galveston area isn't *always* extreme, even though it sometimes seems that way, but those of us who live here have long since learned to adjust, and even to laugh at our predicament. To illustrate appreciation for our crazy climate, the late, great Texas folklorist and writer J. Frank Dobie told this story: An old Yankee meteorologist packed up and headed home in disgust because he was unable to predict local weather. On his way out of town he gave one last forecast: " . . . it will be hot as Hades, or cold as Flugens, as wet as a drowned rat, or as dry as a dried apple dam—just whichever whichway it damn pleases."

Of course, our weather isn't the only unusual thing about our terrestrial living space. The place we're sitting on is pretty strange as well.

## WHERE WE STAND

Geology is the study of the earth, and the earth under Houston is both mind-boggling and boring. Go figure. We don't live in the Rocky Mountains. We don't even live on the Balcones Escarpment. Nothing that dramatic. Geologically speaking, we live on the Gulf Coastal Plain, which sits underneath the entire Houston-Galveston area. For purposes of geology, the whole area is always lumped in together, and excluding offshore, the region covers almost 3,000 square miles—which is about three times the size of Rhode Island. This plain actually covers almost all of both southern and eastern Texas. In fact, it includes almost 40 percent of the state's entire area and runs from 150 to 250 miles inland from the coast, where there are, typically, lots of long barrier beaches, such as Galveston Island and Padre Island. The beaches front the Gulf, but are separated from the mainland by lagoons and marshes. Back from the marshes reaches the coastal prairie. A prime example is that endless stretch of nothing south of NASA that I-45 passes through on the way to Galveston.

Around here the coastal plain slopes almost imperceptibly toward the Gulf of Mexico. The highest point of land is only 90 feet up, (that's on top of a salt dome at the prison farm near Arcola) and there's so little incline—five feet or less per mile—that to sensible people the whole place just flat looks *flat*. This does make for great wide-open skies, but not much in the way of topographical interest.

The marshes along Galveston Bay are less than five feet above sea level, and every time it storms, they flood as nature (but not condo developers) intended. Buffalo Bayou, as well as Cedar Bayou, Clear Creek, Dickinson Bayou, Halls Bayou, Chocolate Bayou and Bastrop Bayou all form little valleys, a fact that can be appreciated when the water is low. The banks of Buffalo Bayou near downtown can be thirty feet high in places. And anyone who looks at bayou banks can see that most of what we're sitting on, soilwise, is now or at one time used to be sandy mud. Gardeners and folks with foundation problems also know it as #!@%! gumbo soil. And there's a lot more of it here than anyone suspects.

The "recent" geological story of the Houston-Galveston area is unusual in that it's been consistent. Back around the time of the dinosaurs, and long before, other places had volcanos and glaciers to liven things up. Under your driveway in West Texas, there could be the remains of a lava flow as stunning as anything in modern Hawaii. Under your driveway in Sugarland or West University, Spring, Santa Fe, or Pasadena, there's sandy mud, nothing but sandy mud. There are almost *unbelievable* quantities of it.

The ground we are sitting on is composed almost entirely of sedimentary deposits. Put some sugar in a glass of iced tea and watch it settle to the bottom. The sugar is the sediment, and that process demonstrated in your tea glass is pretty much what happened to the area that's now Houston. Since the interglacial periods of the Pleistocene era more than 30,000 years ago, sandy particles suspended in bayou outwash, floods, in heavy rain, and other runoff water have been settling to the bottom where they landed on other sandy particles, and so on . . . and so on . . . and. . . . Those particles just kept piling up. Today, downtown Houston sits on a depth of something like 50,000 feet of them. Transco Tower (the one with the beam of light on top near the Galleria) is 901 feet high. Now imagine a stack of Transcos—about 55 of them, one on top of the other—*THAT'S* how deep this stuff is.

There are a few other things down there. There are also stripes of sandy soil wider than a mile—some of them up to three miles across. They are the ghosts of ancient rivers that once flowed South and Southeast across our coastal plain, emptying into the Gulf.

Galveston Bay, Trinity, and East and West Bays take up more than 553 square miles, but left to their own natural devices, they're less than 12 inches deep. The Army Corps of Engineers' dredging operations make sure that the channels necessary for shipping stay a whole lot deeper.

There are only two natural passes connecting the bays to the Gulf of Mexico: Boliver Roads, which is heavily dredged and has become a kind of freeway intersection for ships, and San Luis Pass at the west end of Galveston Island, which is still wild. There is also a narrow, dredged channel or "fish pass" at Rollover Pass on Boliver peninsula, connecting East Bay to the Gulf. Got it? There will now be a pop quiz because next time there's a hurricane you'll be hearing all these names again in a much more dramatic context.

And high drama isn't confined to the geological features you can see. Wait 'til you find out what else is going on down there.

## HOUSTON'S FAULTS

In Houston we have our faults—but, thank goodness, they're not as bad as California's!

Geologically speaking, there are active faults in the Houston area. Faults are what geologists call the cracks in the earth's crust where the sections meet and move. Ours move a little more than one and one-half inches a year, which is about the same rate as California's famous San Andreas. What saves us from earthquakes is the local cracks' lack of seismic energy. There isn't really much built-up pressure behind them because we're sitting on sand, not rock.

The reason our faults aren't as well-documented as those in California—in addition to a sad lack of proximity to Hollywood—is that they're hard to find in the coastal plain, which is on the geological-interest scale little better than mush. We only recognize our faults when they slip and do damage to some manmade structure. By then, it's too late.

Some of our faults actually are visible. Most are stable—they haven't moved in eons—others are just dormant and are actually likely to wake up one morning. Trouble is, there's no good way to tell which is which, and when one of them slips, the result is an earthquake.

There really are earthquakes in Houston. There were measurable ones in 1926, 1958, and 1966, but even those were so mild that the only folks who noticed—aside from the guys with the Richter scales—were people with houses sitting on top of them.

For the most part, it's easy to dismiss our faults as a nuisance. They don't kill people, they just crack foundations and dislocate water and sewer lines. But while danger to life and limb is almost nonexistent, the darn things do cause several million dollars' worth of damage each year. For example, the Katy Freeway (I-10) just west of Loop 610 keeps cracking, and is forever being repaired, because it's sitting right on top of the Eureka Heights Fault. So next time you're stuck in a monster traffic jam on the Katy because road work has forced three lanes down to one, you'll know whose fault it is.

It's the Allen brothers' fault that all of us are here, but they wouldn't have been here themselves if it hadn't been for the most important feature of our natural environment.

## BUFFALO BAYOU

It doesn't look like much, but we wouldn't be here without it.

Buffalo Bayou is the reason the Allen Brothers put their would-be city here. Anyone who's ever seen the Mississippi or the Columbia or the Ohio knows that it isn't a great watercourse. It begins in the extreme northern part of Fort Bend county and flows east for about eight miles. Then it runs for some 38 twisting and turning miles through Harris County until it reaches San Jacinto Bay, Trinity Bay, Galveston Bay, and finally the Gulf of Mexico.

It isn't what Buffalo Bayou *is* that convinced people to settle here—although it is, technically speaking, a river—it's the direction of the bayou's flow. Look at maps of Texas and you will see that all the major rivers flow roughly north to south. In the days when water was the easiest—and often the only— route of transportation, it was crucial that Buffalo Bayou flowed from west to east. Without it, there was no ready access to the farms and ranches of interior Texas, and without their products, there was no sense in having a port.

The Allen brothers founded their port of Houston at the confluence of those two great waterways, the White Oak and the Buffalo bayous, and they probably had a hard time explaining their location to Yankee shippers.

The word "bayou" is a cultural attribution. For it you can thank the Cajuns—we think. (Actually, nobody's really sure where the word came from. We're just sure that, in New York, they don't call the water flowing around the west side of Manhattan Hudson Bayou.)

Why it's called Buffalo Bayou is another mystery. There are a number of possibilities, including the faux Indian legend version which goes: Once upon a time, when great herds of buffalo roamed over the prairie where the City of Houston now stands, there was a snow white bull who was the buffaloes' chief, and every day he led the herd down to where the water ran to drink. That shallow stream became known as Buffalo Bayou.

The native people in the area came to believe that the white buffalo was a messenger of the Great Spirit who brought them prosperity. But then the Europeans came, and because they did not know the Great Spirit or his messenger, they killed the white bull for his beautiful coat.

The people were distraught at the sacred animal's death, fearing that the Great Spirit would turn his face away from them. But suddenly, along the banks of the bayou, there appeared a beautiful new tree, decorated with huge, fragrant, white flowers. The great buffalo's spirit had become the "buffalo tree," the white-flowered magnolia, that grew and prospered along the banks of Buffalo Bayou.

There is the more prosaic buffalo version which just says there were at one time lots of the useful beasts in the area. And then there is the Stephen King version: The bayou is named for one of its major inhabitants—the buffalo gar.

The gar is a huge, ugly, marine creature more closely related in some ways to reptiles than to goldfish. Thanks to the bayou cleanup efforts of the past few decades, the nasty things, which are also known as alligator gar, once again rule the bayou as they have done since prehistoric times.

Up to 10 feet in length with elongated, beak-like jaws chock-full of long, sharp teeth, they are survivors of a primitive superorder of fish that was once abundant in North American waters. Now they live only in rivers along the Atlantic and Gulf coasts (with some cousins in the Great Lakes and along the Mississippi).

Drifting near the surface of the water, they look like logs, and their narrow, cylindrical bodies are covered with thick, armor plate. Because of these diamond-shaped scales made of bone and enamel, no other fish dares to attack them.

Their covering is so tough that in pioneer times, before the invention of the steel plow, people hunted gar for their skin, which was used to cover plowshares. Nowadays folks kill gar because the gar kill more desirable fish, but unless you really know what you're doing, gar fishing in the bayou should probably be avoided.

Since the Buffalo Bayou Coalition and other preservation groups have done such a good job of cleaning up what used to be one of the filthiest bodies of water in the country (it didn't catch fire like Lake Erie, but it did run full of River Oaks's raw sewage for many, many years), you can now see friendlier wildlife. Among them are some of the very species that inspired John James Audubon, the great naturalist painter.

The great blue heron, the green heron, and the kingfisher, to say nothing of the wood duck, all of whom became subjects in Audubon's masterwork, *Birds of America,* can be seen along the banks of the bayou today just as they were when Audubon sketched them more than 150 years ago when he traveled up the bayou with Sam Houston in the 1830s.

# SAM

The man Houston's named for was much more interesting than the guy you learned about in civics class. Everybody knows that he was the commander of the Texian army that won the battle of San Jacinto—and Texas' independence; and most people know that he was president of the Republic of Texas; but fewer know that he held the office twice; or that, after he managed to get the Republic annexed, he was elected our United States senator and also served as governor. He'd also been a United States congressman from Tennessee and served as governor of that state, but that was before he got smart and moved to Texas.

Sam Houston was truly larger than life. (He was also larger than his contemporaries. He was 6'2" in an era when the average man was about 5'6".) But he was also a complicated individual with serious personal problems, including what we'd call clinical depression, still he somehow managed to rise above all of it every time it really counted.

Samuel Houston was born on March 2, 1793, but not on the frontier. He was the fifth son of Major Samuel Houston, a well-to-do Virginia planter who'd served in the American Revolution and liked soldiering so much that he devoted almost all his time to the state militia, much to the detriment of the family's finances.

Young Sam's mother, Elizabeth Paxton, was from the most prominent family in the county, and despite bearing and trying to raise nine children, she somehow found time to run what was left of the family's business affairs.

Elizabeth tried to make Sam go to school, which he disliked intensely, but she managed to keep him at Liberty Hall Academy for only a grand total of something like six months. Lack of formal education was not uncommon in those days, even for wealthy children, but Sam did have a great advantage over the less well-off— his father had a huge library. There the boy devoured books on ancient history, which would become his lifelong passion, and read the classic works of literature. He claimed later that he memorized poet Alexander Pope's translation of the *Iliad*. As Houston was always noted for his prodigious memory, if this is an exaggeration it's not off by much.

Then, when Sam was 14, everything changed. After running the family into catastrophic debt, Major Houston decided to sell what he could in Virginia and settle on the nearest-in frontier. He put a down payment on 419 acres in eastern Tennessee, but while winding up his militia affairs, Sam Houston's father died.

The family home had already been sold. There was nothing else for it. The widow and nine children (along with five African slaves) piled into two wagons and headed west. Times were tough, but the family was never in *really* dire straits because Major Houston had two brothers who'd been prosperous farmers and merchants in the area since just after the Revolution.

Sam hated farming every bit as much as he'd hated school. All he wanted to do was sit around and read ancient history. This did not go over well with his hard-working family. They set him to work behind the counter of a dry goods store the family owned. He didn't like that either. The family was disgusted. His older brothers wanted to know what was *wrong* with that boy?

Sam Houston was, as he said himself many years later, "wild and impetuous." So at 16, lanky, rawboned, and almost 6' tall, he did an impetuous thing. He ran away from home. If his own family refused to understand him, he'd find one that would. And he did. Sam found Chief Oolooteka of the Cherokee.

The Cherokee were not like something out of a John Wayne movie. For one thing, they lived in their own towns, not in teepee camps. They were not warriors, they were farmers (though African slaves did most of the actual work). The seven clans of the Cherokee nation had their own laws and a sophisticated governmental system. They had their own courts of law, and their own alphabet. They published newspapers in Cherokee and English. Women had status in the community, took part in government, and land could be inherited only through female relatives. Their basic world view was tolerant. Sam Houston had found his true home.

Chief Oolooteka, who spoke several languages including English, gave the restless, fatherless boy a place in his family and eventually formally adopted him, giving him the name Colonneh, The Raven. Happy at last, Sam quickly learned Cherokee and adopted Cherokee dress and customs. All his life, he would consider himself a part of their nation as well as his own. He stayed with the Cherokee for three years. Today we'd say that in those three years he got his life together. But everyone knew he couldn't stay forever.

Returning reluctantly to "civilization," Sam Houston improbably taught school for a term (wearing Cherokee calico shirts and his hair in a long braid), and when the War of 1812 came, he joined the army. Both England and America recruited native tribes as allies, and Houston ended up in Andrew Jackson's command fighting the British army's Creek allies in Alabama. The severe shoulder wound he received at the Battle of Horseshoe Bend never really healed; it would plague him all his life. The thigh from which a Creek arrow was rudely yanked also was seriously scarred. After a post-war stint as an Indian agent, during which he testified in front of a startled Congressional committee wearing full Cherokee tribal dress, Sam went to Nashville to read for the law. Everyone told him it would take at least 18 months, if he could do it at all; six months later he passed the state examination.

Houston's law practice flourished—it didn't hurt that he was a protege of Andrew Jackson, the state's most powerful man— and pretty soon he was Tennessee's Attorney General. In 1823 he was elected to Congress, and four years later he came home to become governor. (These things were easier then. Everybody with clout knew everybody else, and most of the time the fix was in.)

Fixed or no, 36-year-old Houston was in the governor's mansion when he married 20-year-old Eliza Allen (no kin to the founders of our town). Less than three months later, she left him. These days, if a governor's wife deserted him under mysterious circumstances it would barely make the *National Enquirer.* At that time, it was enough to ruin a political career.

Nobody really knows why Eliza left Sam, though there has been LOTS of speculation (including an interesting historical novel edited by the late Jacqueline Onassis called *The Raven's Bride*). Houston himself never said a word except: "It is no part of a gentleman to make war against a woman. If my character cannot stand the shock, then let me lose it." Whatever happened, Tennessee lost a governor. On April 16, 1829, Sam Houston resigned, and went "home" to the Cherokee.

This is when he got the Cherokee nickname "Big Drunk." Although he did some work to further the tribe's interests, even visiting his mentor Andrew Jackson in the White House to have crooked Indian agents removed, he spent most of his time dead drunk in the home of a Cherokee widow, Tiana Rogers, whom he apparently married under Cherokee law.

Eventually, Sam came to his senses and returned to politics—this time as Jackson's operative in a secret scheme to see if the restless Mexican territory of Texas could be brought into the Union. Houston, a powerful orator, also spent time on the lecture circuit talking about Texas. It was during one of these speaking engagements, at an exposition of new inventions in New York City, that he met the Allen brothers. John Kirby and Augustus Allen, whose business in New York was in bad shape, were fascinated by Houston's tales of the Mexican province where there was plenty of opportunity—but also plenty of political chaos.

Politics in Mexico at that time were so complicated that only scholars can keep it all straight. The *Reader's Digest* version is that there were almost constant revolutions and counter-revolutions in the decades after Mexico won its independence from Spain, but almost all of the fighting had been confined to interior Mexico.

At the same time, Texas, which might as well have been the dark side of the moon as far as most Mexican politicians were concerned, had been attracting ever larger numbers of Anglo settlers. As matters in Mexico became more and more chaotic, this Anglo minority became frightened.

By the 1830s, things were going from bad to worse. When Mexico City took away any trace of Texan autonomy and made the area a sub-territory of the Mexican state of Coahuila, then proposed to make Texas a penal colony for Mexico's worst offenders, the Anglos decided to act.

Because he was one of the few residents with any big-time political experience, the Texans asked Sam Houston, who'd been living in Nacogdoches only a few months, to draw up a constitution making their province an autonomous Mexican state, and giving them full rights as Mexican citizens. He did, and everyone, himself included, labled the document brilliant. Stephen F. Austin took the proposal to Mexico City, where the powers that be read it and promptly threw the Texan in the slammer.

As it turned out, the new man in power, General Antonio Lopez de Santa Anna, who liked to call himself the Napoleon of the West, had no intention of keeping the Anglos Mexican. He wanted to get rid of them. His plans for the rest of Mexico's citizens were none too benign either. He abrogated the Mexican consitution and began to rule as absolute dictator. Many Mexicans were outraged at what he'd done and actively opposed his regime, so he did away with all Mexican state governments, and ruled by the sword.

As Santa Anna sent troops north to occupy possible opposition strongholds, and to force the Anglos out of Texas, it soon became obvious even to the pro-Mexico faction lead by the now-free Stephen F. Austin that peace was impossible.

Santa Anna made sure of it. His hand-picked military governors began to confiscate arms and property. The Texans put together a provisional government and began to enlist an army. They appointed Sam Houston major general, but he had little actual authority. Some of the local militias took matters into their own hands and attacked the Mexican force at San Antonio. After a five-day battle, the Texans won. Houston knew better. The defeated commander at San Antonio was Santa Anna's brother-in-law. The Napoleon of the West wasn't likely to let such an insult pass by.

As the militiamen occupied the stronghold they'd won—a mission known as the Alamo—Houston sent orders to remove the 14 Mexican cannons and any other useful arms, and then blow the place sky high because it was a death trap, strategically indefensible. The militas refused to obey. Under Texas provisional government law, they didn't have to: Each unit was independent and could choose its own strategy. Some 200 men hunkered down inside the old mission. Only seven of them were native Texans; the rest were adventurers from around the world. The way they figured it, they'd beaten the Mexicans once, and could do the same thing again.

Frustrated with a military that did as it pleased, Houston waited for the governing council to come to its senses about the way to run an army. Meanwhile he met up with his old friend Johnny Goyens, the multilingual free black man who was the uncrowned king of the Texas-U.S. borderlands. The two went to negotiate a treaty of neutrality with the native tribes. Sam Houston, understood—as others did not— that it was just a matter of time before

Santa Anna and his army turned up in Texas; he didn't want to end up fighting a two-front war.

The war wasn't long in coming. On February 23, 1836, Santa Anna arrived in front of the Alamo with an army of more than 1,000 men. The Mexican force quickly grew until, it was said, it reached 6,000. The battle of the Alamo took 16 days. In the end, all of the Texans died.

On March 2, 1836, Sam Houston's birthday, Texas officially declared its independence. Two days later, Houston was appointed commander-in-chief of the army.

A few weeks later, the Mexican army surrounded the small force of Colonel James W. Fannin near the town of Goliad. The outnumbered Texans surrendered. Santa Anna had every one of them shot.

The countryside was in hysterics. The only thing standing between the settlers and the depredations of Santa Anna's army was Sam Houston and about 1,400 volunteers. The government kept ordering him to fight, but with his ill-trained, ill-equipped force, Sam used the tactics he'd read about so often in his beloved histories of the ancient Romans. He delayed. He shadowed the Mexican army, waiting for his opportunity. He was called a coward and worse. Provisional president David Burnet wrote him: "The enemy are laughing you to scorn . . . you must retreat no further." Demands were made to replace him, but by then the cabinet was running for its life and replacing Houston was not high on the priority list.

Santa Anna hoped to capture the government (the rebel traitors in his eyes), and he almost had them at Harrisburg. They escaped just ahead of his advance guard. Frustrated, he burned the town to the ground and then made camp nearby, at the San Jacinto River. He knew Houston was somewhere in the vicinity, but Houston had been shadowing him for weeks, so the Mexican general didn't take Sam's presence as a serious threat.

This was the opportunity Houston had been waiting for. The Texans had the better of the geography. They were hunkered down behind a rise and partly hidden in a grove of live oaks. The Mexicans were camped on a rolling field. It was dry ground—but there was marsh on one side and a muddy bayou on the other. The Texans understood what the terrain meant. They had destroyed the bridges and heavily fortified the only road. Now, there was no way out—except through them. And still, Houston waited.

Maybe Santa Anna assumed that Sam was just shadowing him again, or maybe he was "laughing Houston to scorn." Whatever he assumed, Santa Anna allowed his army to settle down for the regular mid-afternoon siesta. And *then* Houston attacked.

The battle proper lasted only 18 minutes. It was a rout—630 Mexicans died. Another 208 were wounded and 730 were taken prisoner. Many of the Mexican dead were those hunted down in the mud of the bog and the bayou; the killing lasted well into the night. Texan losses were only 6 killed and 25 wounded. One was General Houston, whose ankle had been shattered by a musket ball.

In the confusion, Santa Anna himself disappeared. He was found the next night wearing silly-looking civilian clothes and trying to slog away through knee-deep mud. Instead of shooting him, Houston ordered the Napoleon of the West held hostage until his underlings in Mexico City officially recognized Texas' independence.

In the weeks that followed, some, especially those who'd lost friends or family to Santa Anna, thought Houston should have been killed for not having Santa Anna killed. Others declared Sam Houston the greatest general since Alexander the Great.

Houston wasn't listening to any of them. He was in a coma in a New Orleans hospital. His shattered ankle had become so badly infected that the smart money was on his death. But as usual, he did the unexpected. He recovered.

Sam Houston's election to the presidency of the fledgling republic (with its grand total of 65,000 citizens) was a mortal lock. He was sworn in on October 22, 1836, and adjorned to the two-room presidential mansion made of logs.

Houston City, he boasted, had grown rapidly from a single hut to a town of 1,500 souls and, the president said, "I have not seen a drunken man since my arrival." Evidently he wasn't looking very hard.

President Houston had to keep a special in-basket on his desk for all the challenges he received to settle matters with duels. (Well, that kind of thing can happen when you call your predecessor, the provisional president, a "hog thief" and less-august citizens a whole lot worse.)

Matters of honor notwithstanding, Houston is credited with having gotten the Republic on its feet by establishing the justice system and getting government departments working, though the legislature refused to ratify boundary treaties with the Cherokee, and there was never enough money.

But the Republic's consitution had a term limits clause, and Sam knew his time was short. The president was not allowed to serve back-to-back terms, and that was just fine by Mirabeau B. Lamar, Sam's vice president and leader of the anti-Houston faction. When the other two contenders both committed suicide (where's *Unsolved Mysteries* when you need it?), Lamar's succession was a done deal. Sam was disgusted. He spent his last few months in office dead drunk, gave a three-hour farewell speech at Lamar's inaugural, and promptly left for the United States ostensibly for an extended visit with his pal, ex-president Andrew Jackson.

On the way back home to Texas, he met and a few months later married Margaret Lea of Alabama. Her family was *not* happy about their young belle's marrying a 46-year-old drunkard who never darkened the door of a church. They didn't care *how* illustrious his career had been. But Margaret was strong-minded and promised to reform him, so off to Texas they went. Everyone gave it six months. Everyone was wrong. The happy marriage produced eight children and lasted until Houston's death.

In his arch enemy's absence, Lamar had not only moved the capital to what Sam described as "the most unfortunate site upon earth for the Seat of Government" (that is, Austin), he also drove the government into virtual bankruptcy by pursuing quixotic schemes such as attempting to annex Santa Fe, New Mexico, by force.

The citizens were happy to see Sam back. In his second term, he put the government on a financial diet and even—*mirabile dictu!*—cut his own salary in half. But the Republic's problems were almost overwhelming and Sam knew that the only reasonable solution was annexation by the United States. Trouble was, the legislature didn't see it that way. The *legies* and Sam battled all the way to the end of Houston's term in 1844, and right up until he managed to get lame duck U.S. President Tyler to sign the annexation resolution on his way out the door of the White House.

Texas officially became the 28th state on December 29, 1845, and a few weeks later Sam Houston was elected to represent it in the U.S. Senate. There his startling attire—with Indian blankets, leopard-skin vests (explaining that leopards never change their spots), and Mexican sombreros—shook up his self-important colleagues. His speeches had much the same effect.

He spoke vigorously in favor of the less-than-popular war with Mexico, and his speech helped the official declaration of war to pass the Senate. In gratitude, President Polk offered the 53-year-old

Houston a field command with the rank of major general. Fortunately, he had the good sense to turn it down; the United States won
anyway. After long and difficult peace negotiations, Mexico agreed
to recognize the Rio Grande as the southern border of Texas. Sam
was not pleased. He figured the U.S. could have gotten more.
This attitude played well in Texas, but not in the rest of the
country where the Mexican War had been very unpopular and
most people were just glad to see the end of it. Still, his Texas chau-
vinism helped Sam get elected to a second term, where he faced
an increasingly strong pro-slavery faction in the Senate. It's not as
if Houston was personally an abolitionist—like most men of his era
and class he owned slaves—but he, like his mentor Andrew Jackson, always put the union first.

Because he did, he reluctantly backed Henry Clay's Compromise of 1850, which was supposed to settle the matter by letting
both sides keep their own ways of life, but only because, he said (in
a line that Lincoln would later make famous), "A nation divided
against itself cannot stand."

Sam Houston was considered a serious, if as-yet-undeclared can-
didate for president in the run-up to the election of 1852. He had
been making the 19th century equivalent of the rubber chicken
circuit for quite some time, and he had a lot of political markers
out. His supporters had organized "Houston Clubs" in many
states, and his desire for the office was so obvious that *The New
York Times* was prompted to write that he would "do anything to
get the presidency."

But that didn't happen. He was too flamboyant for some and
had made too many pro-Indian and pro-union speeches for others.
At the Democratic Party convention, he was passed over. The nomination ultimately went to an obscure New Hampshirite named
Franklin Pierce—who won the White House.

In the increasingly divided Congress, Houston's was the only
southern opponent of the Kansas-Nebraska Bill, which would
destroy the compromise holding the Union together. Houston
stated prophetically " . . . if you tear it up and scatter it to the winds,
you will reap the whirlwind . . ."

The Texas legislature passed a resolution condemning the hero of
San Jacinto. Newspapers denounced him as a Northern toady, and
old friends, who called him a traitor to the South, turned their
backs on him, but he carried on and for the next several years

devoted most of his attention to improving the military, even though, he said: "I think our military system is all wrong." When the state Democratic convention nominated a radical secessionist for governor, Sam had had enough. Anticipating the LBJ law by about a century, he kept his Senate seat but announced for governor anyway. He had no campaign fund and no organization. Almost every newspaper in Texas opposed him. Even the stagecoach refused to take him as a passenger. (A buggy salesman agreed to carry him around as an advertising gimmick.) The campaign was vicious with the secessionists calling Houston a "traitor-knave" and drumming up a campaign to have him tarred and feathered. Sam gave as good as he got, accusing his opponents of being embezzlers and of having escaped to Texas only one step ahead of the law, but he lost the election.

Now 66, Houston left the Senate and made one more try for the governor's mansion, campaigning as "a Democrat of the Old School and an Old Fogey in politics." By now he was known as Old Sam and something like the Tony Bennet factor was at work—he had been a public figure for most Texans' entire lifetimes—and, perhaps out of sentiment, this time they elected him.

And he promptly went to war with the rabidly secessionist legislature. As if that weren't enough to keep him busy, he briefly ran for the Democratic presidential nomination. But the politics of Union and secession were getting uglier and uglier. Sam withdrew his candidacy and went back to spending full time trying to keep Texas out of the secessionist camp. It didn't work.

South Carolina seceded in December 1860, and the Texas legislature was foaming at the mouth to follow suit. Sam stumped the state giving pro-union speeches. His life was threatened constantly and hecklers threw rocks at the old man.

In the new year, the Southern states tumbled over one another in the rush to secede, and the Texas legislature voted to join them. "Let me tell you what's coming," Sam said. "Your fathers and husbands, your sons and brothers will be herded at the point of a bayonet. You may, after the sacrifice of countless millions, win Southern independence . . . but I doubt it." No one would listen. Houston tried to postpone the inevitable by demanding a popular referendum before such a drastic step. The legislature agreed because the reps knew their constituents. The people voted more than 3 to 1 for secession, and the secessionists resolved that Texas was now a Confederate State.

Sam Houston would have none of it. He had taken an oath to uphold the Constitutions of Texas and of the United States. He rejected any legislative committee's power to change that. The legislature rejected him. They demanded that the old man take an oath of loyalty to the Confederate government or lose the governorship. They scheduled the ceremony for the Capitol at high noon on March 16, 1861.

As the ceremony began, they called the names of the state officials one by one. At noon they called out the name Sam Houston. Again and again and again. Down in the basement, where he kept an office, Sam sat behind his desk, whittling. He kept on whittling until the sun went down. Then he got up, closed the door, and went home.

Once the war had started, he stood by Texas. "I can but cast my lot with theirs, and await the issue," he said. Sam Houston died on July 7, 1863. He didn't live long enough to see his namesake city grow up.

# THE STORY OF
# HOUSTON

*"Houston,*
Tranquility Base here. The Eagle has landed."
— *July 20, 1969*

In the first word ever spoken from the surface of another world, Astronaut Neil Armstrong called out our name. No other city will ever be able to make that claim. This is our chief claim to fame, but the rest of our history has, itself, been a long strange ride.

In the beginning, there was nothing here but the primeval ooze. What's now Houston was nothing but unexplored, untamed marshland. You couldn't give it away. Even the indigenous, nomadic Karankawa people, on those rare occasions when they visited from their seasonal wanderings along the coast, felt the need to smear themselves with alligator grease and mud in a vain attempt to ward off the clouds of mosquitoes that ruled the area of Buffalo Bayou.

The few Anglos who ended up here did so by accident. The reputation of the Karankawa as cannibals did nothing to attract settlers, and the killer climate scared off the rest. Although both Spain and France made blustery claims to the area, neither did anything much to make those claims stick.

A few brave souls ventured in from the Gulf or up from Mexico to trade with the Indians or to trap the plentiful local game, but they were rare exceptions. *Nobody* came the land route south or west because it was a nightmare of mud and dense undergrowth. The few streams and small rivers were snarled and shallow. Only small canoes and rafts could make any headway, and that didn't include whatever trouble they'd encounter with snakes, alligators, and bufflalo gar.

Throughout the period when what's now central Mexico, coastal California and part of the eastern United States were being explored and ultimately settled, this part of the world was known as a nasty, foreboding place, hospitable only to insects, reptiles, cannibals, and outlaws.

The first European who visited here and lived long enough to tell about it was a Spaniard named Alvar Nuñez Cabeza de Vaca. This unfortunate fellow was shipwrecked along with a boatload of other folks near Galveston Island. That was in 1528. The survivors were imprisoned by the Karankawas, who used them as slaves. Eventually he escaped and spent five years trading with friendlier Indians, exploring the swampy coastal regions of inland east Texas, and trying to figure out how to get the hell out of there.

When he finally did, what he had to say kept other tourists away for the better part of two hundred years.

But by the late 1600s, the lure of the region's natural wealth was attracting French traders. These brave and greedy fellows were working out trade routes west of the Mississippi, buying game and pelts along the way and then selling their merchandise in settlements. The trade became lucrative enough to inspire a French official, Louis Juchereau de St. Denis, to create a royal road from Louisiana to the Rio Grande. It is better known by its later Spanish name, the Camino Real. (Today, Almeda Drive in Houston follows the route of the Camino.)

In the never-ending rivalry between the 18th-century rulers of France and Spain, even the remote reaches of Texas had to be contested. As the French sent out explorers into the Gulf Coast area, the Spanish rulers sent out Capt. Joaquin Orobio y Basterra to see whatever there was to see in the uncharted coastal area between the Guadalupe and Sabine rivers. He was also supposed to keep an eye out for the French.

He didn't run into any other Europeans, but the Bidais and the Orcoquisacs tribes, who roamed the area, told him that *they* had seen Frenchmen—though how these people that even the Karankawas considered primitive would know a Frenchman from a Ukranian remains a mystery.

Throughout much of the early 1800s, the Europeans kept themselves busy at home fighting the Napoleonic wars. In fact, by 1803 Napoleon was so desperate for cash with which to pursue his military adventures that he proposed to sell the Louisiana Territory, which he considered virtually worthless, to the young United States. The French ruler figured that, as long as his arch-enemies Britain and Spain didn't control it, he could always send an army to take it back later if he felt like it.

When President Thomas Jefferson suggested that the Louisiana Purchase should include all the land west and south as far as the Rio Grande, Napoleon said sure. He wasn't the one who'd have to duke it out with Spain about who really owned what. Besides, Napoleon was in the process of making his brother the king of Spain, and his brother would do whatever he told him to. The upshot of all this was that, until about 1819, both the United States and Spain claimed title to what's now Houston. Neither side did much about it and the area became a kind of no-man's land.

The Texas coast just down the bayou from here became infamous as an outlaw hideout. Renegades, who ignored what little bit of law there was, came from all nations and thumbed their noses at both of the governments who claimed the territory.

Jean Laffite, who wrote his name several different ways, though all of them spelled P-I-R-A-T-E, was one of the most flamboyant bad guys. He looted Gulf shipping and, in defiance of the 1808 federal law that banned importation of slaves directly from Africa, established his own slaving operation.

He had a ready market. Louisiana cotton and sugar plantations had an insatiable demand for labor. This steady market for contraband Africans made smuggling slaves from his Texas base into Louisiana a highly profitable enterprise.

In one of those weird twists of fate too bizarre to have been made up, it was Laffite's economically successful trafficking in slavery that first drew the U.S. government's attention to the potential of the Galveston area as a major trade center. In 1818, the government bureaucrat sent to roust the French slavers found himself morally outraged but economically dumbfounded by the dollar volume of Laffite's illegal trade. Clearly, he reported back to Washington, there was money to be made just down the bayou from what's now Houston.

Soon, Washington saw the potential of the region. Cartographers demonstrated that a network of navigable streams existed, even though all seemed to run in the same direction, northwest to southeast. Still, it was also obvious that a chain of barrier islands, stretching south from Galveston all the way to the Rio Grande, formed a protected canal keeping the ravages of Gulf storms away from shipping. This was *very* important.

All of this was big news in an era when water routes were the freeways of the day. Roads, where they existed, were only for the very brave. All were bone-jarring and most were subject to regular raids from opportunistic bandits and outraged natives, both of whose territories they crossed on the route west.

It's hard to explain today the lure of the west in the early 1800s. For some it was the notion of independent living far away from any kind of civilization that attracted them, but these were the exception. For most, the west meant land. And the idea of land had its own magic.

Many immigrants to America were fleeing European governments that had forbidden them to own land. The Irish, for example, were kept landless by their English conquerors; Jews in many parts of Eastern Europe were unable to buy real property; and landless peasants from all over the continent were delighted at the prospect of being able to afford something that only nobles could own back home.

Pressure on the young United States government to open up the west was both sudden and intense. No matter what prudence the government cautioned, officials knew that land-hungry people—and those who planned to make a buck off them—were going to rush in wherever there seemed to be economic promise.

One of those who headed west was Dr. James Long of Mississippi. In 1819, he led an expedition of 300 settlers into the disputed territory of Texas. Envisioning himself a kind of military adventurer, he built trading posts on the Brazos and Trinity rivers, but the posts were marginal at best. He set up a small fort closer to the Louisiana border, left his pregnant wife, Jane, there to hold it, and set off to have more military adventures. He never came back, but she did give birth to the first Anglo child in Texas, thus going down in pre-multi-cultural era seventh-grade history books as the "Mother of Texas."

Even though Long and most of his party were killed or driven off by the Spanish, his notion of an empire for the taking in Texas

inspired others. Moses Austin, a gentlemanly type from Massachu-
setts, arrived in 1820 and dickered with the Spanish governor at
San Antonio for the right to settle 300 Anglo-Americans in the
province of Texas.

The Spanish thought the old man was crazy. What would it profit them to allow 300 Protestant, English-speakers to settle in
Catholic, Spanish-speaking Texas? They wouldn't fit in, and
besides, they were probably some kind of advance party for the
Americans.

Moses Austin was ready to pack it in when he ran into an old
friend, Felipe Enrique Neri, Baron de Bastrop, a Dutch soldier of
fortune who was then renting his sword to Spain, and Bastrop inter-
ceded for him. When the governor relented, it was a major concession because Spain was still trying to keep foreigners out of Texas.

Austin didn't live long enough to appreciate his victory, and the
mandate to colonize the Texas coast passed to his son, Stephen F.

It's hard to believe now, but with the exception of nomadic
tribes such as the Karankawa, almost *nobody* lived in Texas at that
time. Spanish settlement was confined to a few villages surrounding earlier Catholic missions, and the government in far-off
Madrid had zero interest in developing the area.

Then, in 1821, everything changed. Mexico won independence
from Spain. The government was now in Mexico City—a whole lot
closer to Texas. And it (though the leaders changed constantly)
wanted the Anglos *out*. But the Anglos had no intention of going
anywhere. They were, in fact, scouting the best riverbank farmlands
where colonists from the South could grow cotton and sugar cane.

At first, they bet on the Brazos, talking themselves into seeing it
as the Mississippi River of Texas. But like most other Texas rivers it
had too much water some of the year and not enough the rest.
Besides, the underbrush and snags made navigation next to impossible. And would-be entrepreneurs began to look elsewhere for a
water route to the interior. Eventually, they noticed Buffalo Bayou.

Almost unique among Texas rivers, it ran east and west, roughly
perpendicular to the Brazos. It also offered decent navigational
possibilities all the way south to Galveston Bay, where there was a
harbor to shield ships from Gulf storms.

So the Anglos set to work. In 1822, Nathaniel Lynch built a small
fort near where the bayou merges with the San Jacinto River (Yes,
the site of the present Lynchburg ferry), and the next year John

Richardson Harris, for whom Harris County is named, opened a trading post upstream where Buffalo Bayou merges with Braes.

Harris plotted out a city and named it Harrisburg in his own honor. He was convinced that he had chosen the best available site. He owned the "head of navigation." Above his city, Harris knew, the bayou was just a narrow, brush-snarled stream. Below it, there was smooth sailing all the way to Clopper's Bar (now Morgan's Point), a shifting sandbar several miles downstream. He would be king of the river.

By 1829, it looked like he was. His family's port was a gold mine. Ships arrived every week from the United States bringing new settlers and goods for trade. Harrisburg was well on its way to becoming the commercial center of the region, but everything was thrown into disarray when the founder died of yellow fever while on a business trip to New Orleans. His estate was tied up in the Mexican courts for many years.

At around the same time Harris turned toes up to the dandelions over in Mardi Gras central, the Texians, as the settlers called themselves, and the Mexican authorities began to have more and more misunderstandings. Part of this was natural fallout from the power struggle going on in central Mexico for control of the government. From out here on the frontier, it was hard to tell who was on first, let alone what paperwork they wanted filled out.

The story of how Texas separated from Mexico and became a Republic is extremely complicated. There are many fine books on the subject. The TV sound-bite version is that, done dirty by Mexican strongman Antonio Lopez de Santa Anna, the Texians fought, and with Sam Houston's victory at San Jacinto (see "Sam" chapter), won their independence.

Many people sacrificed much to achieve this. Many fought for it. The Allen brothers of New York, a couple of twentysomething land-title speculators, were not among them. While they did outfit a ship at their own expense and sent it to defend the coast, they were in Texas to make a buck, not to get shot at, so they made sure they didn't.

In the aftermath of the fighting, property titles were really muddled. No one was really sure of who owned what because the paperwork was still largely in the hands of the Mexican authorities. Anyone who wanted to buy land usually ended up caught in protracted legal wrangles.

And the Allen brothers wanted to buy land. They had figured out that if they could set a town (which, of course, they would own) in a place that would make it a commercial center for the new farmlands now opening up, they could make a fortune.

They tried to buy several different locations, including Galveston Island. When that didn't pan out, they looked further inland. They recognized quickly that John Richardson Harris had chosen the prime water location upstream from Galveston Bay, but the thought of endless probate litigation scared them off.

Augustus Chapman Allen and John Kirby Allen decided to look elsewhere. Eventually they bought a parcel of land further up the Buffalo Bayou, and then spent the next decade claiming that *IT*, not Harrisburg, was the real head of navigation.

They decided to name their swampland "Houston" after the hero of San Jacinto, whom they'd once met briefly at an exposition in New York. They figured that Sam's name gave the place cachet, and—if they were lucky—they might actually pursuade him to spend some time there.

So these are Houston's "founding fathers," though it would probably be more accurate to call them the founding frat boys. They were *very* young. (John Kirby was only 23 and his brother a few years older when they came to Texas).

Nowadays, kids in their twenties are considered ideal junk bond traders because they have infinite chutzpah and practically no understanding that actions have consequences. Today, the Allen brothers probably would have been in business school, or on Wall Street creating an empire of paper, not out claiming to have founded a city.

Maybe that's why their city had a beginning like no other. Traditionally, interior American urban centers grew up on the banks of great rivers or around trading posts, military encampments, or water holes, but Houston began life as a newspaper ad.

On August 30, 1836, only four months after Sam Houston whupped the Mexican army at San Jacinto, an unusual advertisement appeared in the *Telegraph and Texas Register,* an ancestor of the late lamented *Houston Post*. This infomercial was the first word Texans had of the town of Houston.

"... situated at the head of navigation, (*WRONG*) on the west bank of Buffalo Bayou, is now for the first time brought to public notice because until now, the proprietors were not ready to offer it to the public, with the advantages of capital and investments. (There were none. They barely had enough to make the note). The town of Houston is located at a point on the river which must ever command the trade of the largest and richest portion of Texas. By reference to the map, it will be seen that the trade of San Jacinto, Spring Creek, New Kentucky and the Brazos, above and below Fort Bend, must necessarily come to this place, and will at this time warrant the employment of at least ONE MILLION DOLLARS of capital, and when the rich lands of the country shall be settled, a trade will flow to it, making it, beyond all doubt, the great interior commercial emporium of Texas."

Sounds good. Unfortunately, the Allen brothers neglected to mention in their ad that the city of Houston existed only on paper.

But according to the advertisement in the *Telegraph,* Houston also offered these other advantages: "Vessels from New Orleans or New York can sail without obstacle to this place . . ." (That would take the construction of the ship channel.)

"There is no place in Texas more healthy, having an abundance of excellent spring water, and enjoying the sea breeze in all its freshness. . . . (Note that this ad appeared in August. Need I say more? As if that weren't enough, for the better part of half a century, annual Yellow Fever epidemics regularly carried off large numbers of the citizenry. This doesn't even count those lost every year to typhus, typhoid, and dysentery.)

"Nature appears to have designated this place for the future seat of government. . . . " (Actually, the brothers planned to make Sam and the other officials of the Republic an economic offer they couldn't refuse).

This mendacious notice appeared in newspapers as far away as Washington and New York, to say nothing of the versions that appeared in Germany and what's now the Czech Republic. Land-hungry people wanted to believe it every bit as much as TV viewers now want to believe infomercial miracle diets, and so they headed for the miracle metropolis on the bayou. Fortunately for the brothers, they brought their capital with them.

So, the Allen brothers ended up outsmarting everybody. They had conjured a city out of printers ink and imagination—and their spiritual descendants in Houston have been doing the same thing ever since.

The brothers didn't just want a town, they wanted an *important* town, and in making this happen, they had another ace up their collective sleeve. While Augustus ran the business side of things, John Kirby got himself elected to the Congress of the Republic, and as a member of the Texas Congress, he used all his influence—plus offers of free land—to have the town of Houston named the temporary seat of government. The hard sell worked. The government agreed to come.

Promoters less self-confident than the Allen brothers might have panicked at this point. The would-be capital of the Republic was still a stretch of prairie constantly mired deep in mud and plagued by mosquitoes. Hostile Indians still roamed the area, and 12-foot alligators lurked in the swamps just off what would be Main Street.

## GAIL BORDEN

Yes, this is the same Borden as in Borden's milk, but Gail Borden was a lot more than that. For one thing, he was a world-class eccentric. For another, he was an inventor of considerable repute — and, while living in Galveston, he rode a cow instead of a horse.

Gail Borden was born in New York state in 1801 and moved to Indiana as a child. There he had the only formal education he would ever have — a grand total of about a year and a half's worth. Like many people in the 19th century, Borden had bad lungs, and as a young man moved to Mississippi for the warmer climate. Somehow he'd managed to acquire enough knowledge to support himself there by teaching school and doing surveying work.

When he moved to Galveston in 1829, he did some farming and ran some cattle in upper Fort Bend county, and worked on his various inventions. Neighbors found him an odd and interesting character with his head in the clouds much of the time; it was no surprise when Borden's farm and cattle operations didn't work out. Soon he joined his brother Thomas as surveyor for Stephen F. Austin's colony and became involved in the early politics of the area. He drew up

*continued on next page*

the very first topographical map of Texas and was one of the founders of our first real newspaper, the *Telegraph and Texas Register,* which spent much of its first few years of publication on the run from Santa Anna's army.

In 1836, Gail Borden's firm drew up a layout for the then-barely existing village of Houston. The grid pattern of the downtown streets we drive on today was Borden's creation.

In later life he sold his interest in the newspaper and devoted his attention to the Texas Baptist Education society, which founded Baylor University, and to his inventions. He experimented with an early form of air conditioning as a way to ward off yellow fever, and a vehicle that would move on both land and water, and then got into the food business. His first product, a "meat biscuit," drove him into bankruptcy. His next, condensed milk, would change the world.

Before Borden, it was impossible to transport milk any great distance. There was no refrigeration beyond blocks of ice, and pioneers heading west, to say nothing of both armies in the Civil War, needed some way to keep up nutrition. Borden found it. By packing condensed milk in air-tight cans, he created something that would keep indefinitely. He also developed processes for condensing fruit juice and coffee, founded schools, and did other good with his fortune.

Undaunted, the Allens hired Gail Borden's surveying firm and mapped out a grand town of 62 blocks.

They set aside town squares for a capitol building, as well as a courthouse and a church. But they knew that until the jungle-like swamps that comprised most of the townsite were drained and cleared, none of this was going to happen. African slaves and former Mexican prisoners of war did most of the back-breaking labor. They had to fight snake bites, insect bites, impure water, and disease, but the swamps slowly became streets.

The government settled in a collection of tents and log cabins while the Capitol was being built. The "presidential mansion" consisted of two rooms with a mud floor, but Sam Houston held forth in it just as if he were in Washington City. And as all those having business with the government, as well as those attracted by the Allens' ad, flowed into town, the city grew.

It did so well that it soon became known far and wide as "the greatest sink of dissipation and vice that modern times have known." The streets, such as they were, were lined with saloons, and the saloons were filled with rowdy drunks just about 24 hours a day. Outraged moralists attempted to get these establishments to close during church services on Sunday. Some of them actually did.

The wooden Capitol building itself, painted a modish shade of "Peach Blossom," stretched out on Main Street and along Texas Avenue where the old Rice Hotel now stands. Unfortunately, when the first Congress declared itself open for business on May 4, 1837, the roof wasn't anywhere near finished. Pretty soon a spring norther whipped through and poured down torrents of rain. The wind tore away the canvas that had roofed both the Senate and House "chambers"—rooms at opposite ends of the building—and pretty soon the place was ankle-deep in water. The desks and all that proposed legislation were soaked, leading local wits to opine that there'd been no harm done because Senators and Representatives were all wet anyway. Things didn't improve appreciably for the government and Houston's fame, as the Capital of the Republic didn't last long.

Three years after its founding, the city's mud and yellow fever sent the wagons bearing the Texas archives scuttling out of town to Austin.

Some of this can be chalked up to politics. Under the Republic's constitution, Sam Houston couldn't succeed himself as president, and his bitter rival, Mirabeau B. Lamar, was elected in his place. Lamar *hated* Houston, both the man and the city. He prided himself on being a cultured individual and as such had no intention of living in a pestilential swamp named for his greatest foe.

People actually chased the government wagons, begging them to turn around, but the drivers weren't listening. Once the government left, taking about half the population with it, Houston began to look more and more like a ghost town. Many another frontier town had dwindled and died, and Houston's prospects for survival looked gloomy indeed.

The one thing Houston had going for it was the makeup of the population. This was not an agricultural center. The citizens of Houston were not farmers—they never had been. These were city folks. Enough of them were well-traveled, enterprising, educated, and cultured (as well as more than occasionally unprincipled) enough to figure out something that would take up the slack left when the wagons rolled west to Austin.

They held councils of war to figure out what to do. The biggest potential source of income came from the Brazos Valley. There in the rich bottomlands planters were harvesting great crops of cotton and sugar that could only be brought to market in Galveston with great difficulty. The roads ranged from awful to non-existent. The Brazos River was impossible to navigate reliably, and once downriver, goods then had to be shipped east to the island. Now here, the entrepreneurs of Houston thought, was an opportunity.

In January of 1839, they commissioned a steamboat named *Laura M* to prove that Buffalo Bayou actually was navigable. Houston itself was too small to be noticed from the bayou. The vessel poked and pushed its way slowly through muck and debris until it had chugged three miles past the stakes marking the trail from the bayou to the city. The captain would have missed it on the return, too, except for the anxious welcoming committee standing on the bank.

Amazingly, within a year, Houston was shipping mules, cattle, cotton, and sugar cane from the Brazos Valley. Part of the Allens' sales pitch that Houston would become "the great interior commercial emporium of Texas" was beginning to come true.

The city parents pushed ahead. The first local dock was built on Buffalo Bayou in 1840, and in 1841 they passed a city ordinance establishing the Port of Houston.

Houston's first fortunes were built on "white gold." Cotton receipts became the measure of the town's prosperity and financed much of Sam Houston's second presidential campaign.

By the mid-1840s, politics of the Republic revolved almost entirely around whether or not Texas would join the United States. Various European powers, including England, which was getting a good deal on Texas cotton, did everything they could to keep us out of the Union. Mexico, too, didn't want to see its former province join the United States. But in the end, the annexationists prevailed. Other than the land office business the celebration brought to the numerous saloons that lined Congress Avenue, statehood brought Houston little more than some degree of military security and economic stability. It made few major changes in people's everyday lives.

In May of 1846, America's national pride caught up with Texas. Amid waves of jingoism, President James K. Polk declared war on

Mexico. Though the immediate causes of the war were at best obscure, Texas, which had long-simmering disputes with its former master, was delighted. Houstonians were more than happy to enlist. The conflict actually brought a certain amount of prosperity to Houston as the price of cotton rose. But the real beneficiary of the war was Galveston, the Bayou City's long-time bitter rival.

Galveston, which Houstonians saw as little more than the southern terminal of their own trade route, saw Houston as a back-country hellhole nicknamed "Mudville," and was winning the economic race.

Its population was many times that of Houston, and it was close to becoming the dominant economic center for the entire region.

It didn't help that Houston, meanwhile, had developed a nasty reputation for lawlessness. Saloons far outnumbered churches, and killings in the street were daily occurrences.

Its less-than-upstanding reputation notwithstanding, Houstonians knew that money solved many problems, and they set out to create their own transportation hub, one to more than rival Galveston.

The solution seemed to be for the city to establish itself as a railroad center. The State of Texas had very little cash money, but it was generous with land grants for railroad rights of way. Houston applied for every grant going, and by 1856 it had become the city "Where Eleven Railroads Meet The Sea." This slogan is the origin of the goofy city seal with the old-fashioned locomotive in the center.

But the coming of the railroads was not universally accepted. Some Houstonians argued that the city should develop other forms of transportation so it couldn't be held economic hostage by the railroad companies. Although products could be shipped to Galveston faster and more cheaply by rail than they could on Buffalo Bayou, some were afraid that bayou transportation might become obsolete. It took constant effort and regular expenditure of city funds to keep the river route open. Erosion and pollution also were constant problems.

The Houston Navigation Company, which had been co-founded by William Marsh Rice, controlled travel on the bayou. But by the late 1850s, the Galveston Wharf & Cotton Press Company, a.k.a. "The Octopus of the Gulf," had all but strangled water traffic up to Houston. Trade war between the two towns was heating up when the real thing, the Civil War, intervened.

Farmers withheld their cotton, fearing a Federal invasion. The Yankees did blockade Galveston, which prompted many of the island's citizens to flee to Houston, and others to become blockade runners, a highly profitable activity.

Houston became the military headquarters for the Confederate District of Texas, New Mexico, and Arizona, though flat as it was, it would be difficult to defend. The closest it ever came to a real fight was the escapade of barkeep Dick Dowling, who together with many of his Irish customers fought off the Federals at the economically crucial river and railroad junction of Sabine Pass. All then repaired to Dowling's bar to celebrate.

The Union army made no further progress on the Texas coast, but won the war anyway.

After the Civil War, Houston was broke and, to add to its woes, a yellow fever epidemic devastated the city in 1867. Still, the spunky Houstonians continued to do business. They opened lumber operations, ice plants, and foundries. The population grew to 23,000, but outside opinion wasn't appreciably better. One visitor called it "an insignificant town possessing a malodorous bayou and intolerable mud."

During the post-war period, the Houston-Galveston rivalry picked up where it left off. Galveston, which called itself "The Queen City of the Gulf" and had designs on becoming the biggest city in Texas, had no intention of giving up her title to an upstart town with muddy streets and no class.

All through the Gilded Age, the two towns were neck-and-neck. Houston built the first version of the Ship Channel, dredging a route navigable for smaller vessels all the way from the Gulf to the city. This did not please the oligarchy that controlled the Galveston wharfs. They were plotting revenge when nature took the whole thing out of everyone's hands.

On Saturday, September 8, 1900, the worst natural disaster ever to strike the North American continent hit Galveston Island. It was a killer hurricane that, in the days before named storms, came to be known with simple accuracy as the "Great Storm." It struck with such force that Galveston was practically wiped off the face of the earth. A huge tidal wave washed over the island from the Gulf side to the bay. More than 6,000 people died. The disaster was so awful, and word of it spread so rapidly via the new telephone technology, that people from as far away as North Dakota Indian reservations and the court of the German Kaiser took up collections for the survivors. But the infrastructure of the island port had been totally destroyed. Galveston never recovered from the devastation; Houston's only economic competition was gone forever.

The next year seemed to confirm its place as America's city of destiny. In Beaumont, which was economically tied to Houston, a gusher of oil, the like of which no one had ever seen, exploded out of an underground salt dome at a place called Spindletop. It errupted with such force that it took weeks before the flow of oil could be staunched.

The Spindletop gusher changed Houston forever. Before it, oil was hard to extract, expensive and far away. After it, Texas, the nation and the world experienced the changes that cheap, plentiful oil could bring.

The oil boom was on! In 1904, the Humble Field came in not far from where Intercontinental Airport now stands. At 12,000 acres, it was the largest field in South Texas. By 1906, there were more than 30 oil companies headquartered in Houston, along with seven banks and 25 newspapers!

While much of the new money came from oil, the old fortunes were still built on timber and real estate. Unlike other places where old money refused to socialize with new, Houston's group of elite entrepreneurs, led by lumberman and builder Jesse H. Jones, worked together. Whatever they thought of one another personally—and in some cases it wasn't much—they had the foresight to see the importance of a real, deep-dredged Houston Ship Channel. Without it, all of them knew, there was no inexpensive way to get their products to a worldwide market.

Although the cotton market collapsed in 1914, the city's 100-year-old dream came true the same year. Officially opened, the Houston Ship Channel snaked its way fifty-one miles to the Gulf just in time to help Houston profit from the war in Europe. This city has always profited from wars, and World War I, which was the first fought with gasoline-burning engines, gave the new oil-based economy a big boost. The cotton market recovered as well, once the United States entered the conflict in 1917. Houston was on a roll.

They'd been here all along, but suddenly people noticed the beautiful trees that lined the bayou. People planted them on the grounds of their lavish new homes, and Houston became known as the Magnolia City. It also became known worldwide as a great place to hustle a fortune. (Tell me something every Houstonian didn't already know!)

## GEORGE THOMAS "MICKEY" LELAND

Of all the people who knew the late member of Congress, there were probably very few who knew that Mickey Leland's real name was George Thomas—that is, until they put it on the new federal building downtown.

In life, Mickey Leland was a controversial character. He was born in the Fifth Ward, the son of a strong-minded teacher and the husband she kicked out of her house when Mickey was just a kid. She made sure he went to college, though: He graduated from Texas Southern University with a degree from its prestigious pharmacy program and promptly joined the civil rights movement. By 1970 he was a well-known activist, but decided to change the system from within. Thanks in part to the support of Jean de Menil, who was something of a father figure for him, Leland was elected to the Texas House in 1973.

There he livened things up considerably. He wore a purple and orange dashiki, platform shoes and an Afro the size of the Astrodome on the floor of the Lege. Redneck reps were apoplectic, but even his political enemies agreed that he became a terrific legislator—and that his (bleeding) heart was in the right place. Every Christmas day, he quietly spent time with prisoners — in memory of his own civil rights demonstration time in jail. And he made hunger his main cause.

Long after his election to Congress, it still was his main cause—and that's how he died in 1989, on a mercy flight to famine-stricken Ethiopia. The International Building at Houston Intercontinental Airport is named in his honor.

Sinclair Oil built the first oil refinery here and now the city expanded into the "upstream" end of the petroleum business. No longer was oil just a natural resource to be pumped out of the ground and sold like a crop. Now, Houston business types realized, it was a product, and it could be refined into other, more lucrative products. The petrochemical industry was born, and Houston spread like an oil slick.

During the era of rapid growth between 1915 and 1929, the whole look of the city began to change. The wooden frame houses that had lined downtown streets since the days of the Republic were torn down. Folks with money wanted to look like folks with money. They built pretentious homes (like the Kirby mansion at the corner of Smith and Gray, which once boasted a huge indoor swimming pool) on what were then the edges of the city. Meanwhile, in the center of town, "skyscrapers" of 15 to18 stories began to rise.

Houston was the ideal place for "young men in a hurry," and they flocked to town by the thousands with their good ideas, good products, and good scams. Residential real estate values went crazy. The Hogg brothers developed River Oaks so all that nice new money would have a place to roost.

By the time the Great Depression hit the rest of the country, 40 oil companies were operating from Houston, and largely because of them, Houston never experienced the economic tragedy that devastated the rest of the nation. Not a single Houston bank failed in the Great Depression (it took the savings and loan crooks of the 1980s to inflict that on us). While more than a quarter of all American workers were jobless and other ports were suffering, Houstonians kept their jobs and tonnage at the Port of Houston dropped off only slightly.

With an eye ever on the main chance, Houston's Congressional delegation, with ex-Congressman Tom Ball as their *eminence griese,* landed one of the federal grants meant to relieve economic misery through public works. They used it to deepen the Ship Channel to 34 feet.

By now, our port was one of the busiest in the nation, and when World War II began Houston's economy went into overdrive. While it's certainly true that the American armed forces fought bravely and skillfully, the thing that really won the war was production. America, the well-named "Arsenal of Democracy," just flat out outproduced the Nazis, and Japan; Houston was in the forefront of that production. Thousands of concrete barges, steel merchant ships, and medium-sized war vessels were built in and around the Houston area. Chemicals, used in everything from bombs to nylon stockings, were much in demand. As a result, the value of Houston-produced chemical products skyrocketed from $30 million in 1939 to $750 million a few years after the end of the war in 1949.

That same year, Houston was the site of a hotel-warming party unlike any other in history. Glen McCarthy, the man known as "King of the Wildcatters," opened his Shamrock Hotel. It cost an unheard of $21 million, and the interior was painted 63 different shades of green in honor of his Irish heritage. He hired a train to import Hollywood stars for the occasion, and a crowd of more than 50,000 Houstonians turned out to gawk. The booze was free and pretty soon the whole thing became a brawl. McCarthy's opening day party was so *Texas* that it has become legend—literally. Novelist Edna Ferber used it as a set piece in her bestseller *Giant,* and Hollywood made a movie version in which a thinly-disguised McCarthy was played by James Dean.

The Shamrock came to symbolize Houston's new money. Dinner for two in The Emerald Room (exclusive of drinks and tip) cost $30 at a time when poverty level for a family of four was about $1,000 a year. There were waterskiing exhibitions in the hotel's huge pool and debutante balls every spring. Through the Shamrock, the nation had come to associate Houston with wild Texas excess, and the city did nothing to discourage the idea.

Five years later, on August 3, 1954, Houston threw itself a monster party to celebrate the much-ballyhooed "M-Day" when the population of the metro area finally went over one million.

The post-war years here were economically stable and confident. The "boys" were home and they were marrying and settling down in new suburbs such as Spring Branch. They were also finding jobs in the oil business.

More than 194,000 barrels of oil a day went down the Ship Channel to the Gulf. Wool, grain, lumber, cattle, and cotton from the farms of the interior did, too, just as the Allen brothers imagined they would.

From high above downtown, in Suite 8F at the old Lamar Hotel, a group of wealthy, powerful men looked down at the city they had, to a large extent, created and they certainly still controlled—and they thought it good.

The city's awkward urban sprawl, its dependence on the automobile, and its bent toward pollution didn't bother them. They had a sense of pride in the heavy industry that was moving into the Ship Channel area. They saw no need to stop industrial waste from being dumped into the filthy water. Pollution was a cost of doing business, and business was good.

The "8F Crowd" saw to it. Suite 8F was known, and with good reason, as "the unofficial capitol of Texas." There was a lot more power concentrated there than in the Capitol in Austin. The owner of the Lamar, and Suite 8F, was Jesse Jones, who also owned most of what is known as "old downtown." His cronies in the Crowd included Judge James A. Elkins, who controlled the city's largest law firm and First City National Bank; George R. Brown and his brother Herman, who owned the gigantic construction firm Brown & Root, as well as one of the world's largest pipeline companies, Texas Eastern Transmission; and Gus Wortham, who owned American General Insurance. There was one other crucial character present, Lyndon Baines Johnson, the rising politician who had once been a Houston schoolteacher. During the glory days of 8F, he was little more than the Crowd's "hey-boy," doing whatever political dirty work they needed done—but LBJ was a quick learner, and his day was coming.

---

### HOUSTON FACTOID:

*Lyndon Johnson lived at 435 Hawthorne in the Montrose area. He taught at San Jacinto High, now the main building of Houston Community College Central Campus.*

---

Even after the major 8F players passed from the scene, the 8F mentality continued to dominate Houston. Rather like the benevolent despots of the Enlightenment, the city's "big men" did what they thought best for the citizens. Often enough, they were right. For example, many of the 8F-ers were on the board of the M.D. Anderson Foundation, and through them the M. D. Anderson Foundation created The Texas Medical Center. Now virtually a city within a city, it was the oligarchs willingness to spend lavishly on the very best medical talent that began to put Houston on the world's medical map.

Although it was the brainchild of an outsider, Judge Roy Hofheinz, the Harris County Domed Stadium enjoyed behind-the-scenes support from the Crowd and went on to make history for Houston. The Astrodome opened pretty much on schedule in

1965 despite tremendous controversy over its grass-killing opaque ceiling. The subsequent invention of AstroTurf is a typically Houstonian use of lemons for money-making lemonade.

Back in the 1960s, it was dubbed the "Eighth Wonder of the World" and set off a frenzy of dome construction nationwide. Although it is now the world's oldest and smallest domed stadium, it will always be first in Houston's heart.

President John F. Kennedy never really was. He was too Boston and Harvard to set well, but when he came to town for a testimonial in honor of Congressman Albert Thomas, Houston rolled out the welcome mat anyway. The president and his wife, Jackie, were given the royal treatment and they retired to their rooms, the International Suite at the old Rice Hotel, for dinner. (The menu was: crabmeat cocktail, Chinese bird's-nest soup, quail, and chateaubriand from a Texas Black Angus.). In the morning, the president broke away from his Secret Service agents to shake hands with some of the crowd of well-wishers in the lobby, then he and Jackie got in the car for the ride to the airport. They were meeting Governor John Connally at Love Field in Dallas for a motorcade through downtown. It was November 22, 1963. Houston was the last place JFK ever stayed.

By the end of the 1960s, Houston encompassed some 450 square miles and, like a teenager, it was still growing. City officials began a massive annexation program of surrounding communities while stubbornly rejecting any zoning ordinances. They liked to point out that the traffic flow was as efficient as any city that had attempted to control growth patterns through zoning. (And if you believe that . . . .)

Developers were then, as they had been since the days of the Allen brothers, a sacred species. They are still allowed to build with a relatively free hand, which accounts for many of the streets that dead-end unexpectedly in apartment complexes or industrial parks. If developers want to take part of a public street, and they can pay for it, hey, no problem. It's the Houstonian way.

The Houstonian way of arranging large matters behind the scenes reached its zenith when Congressman Albert Thomas, the heirs of 8F, and the man who had learned his lessons well, President Lyndon Baines Johnson, arranged to locate the nation's most prestigious government project, the headquarters of the National Aeronautics and Space Administration, in the middle of a pasture about 20 miles south of Houston.

Of course all the usual suspects profited financially, but so did the city. The decision to locate NASA at Clear Lake was the most important single event in the modern history of Houston. It was also the swansong of the old Crowd system. As the city expanded, it also attracted more and more people from around the nation and the world. They weren't used to a major metropolis that functioned politically like a small Southern town—as late as 1972 a black woman politician and a black labor leader were refused service in a private club here because of their race— and they began to raise money and run for office. The acknowledged end of the Crowd system came with the mid-1970s election of "Mayor Fred," Fred Hofheinz, son of the outsider who'd built the Astrodome.

By the end of the decade, when Kathy Whitmire—who would become Houston's first female mayor—was running for office, the world oil market was going crazy. Political upheaval in the Middle East drove the price of a barrel of oil through the roof, and Houston was right along for the ride.

Those were heady days. People were moving in at the rate of 1,000 a week hoping to get a piece of the oil boom. Multimillion-dollar corporations were invented on paper napkins in fast food restaurants (Compaq Computer Corporation for one); real estate prices doubled and then doubled again. Ordinary people played Monopoly with suburban homes. There was no end to it. In Houston, anyone could get rich *quick,* and every telephone pole sported a "business cards in 10 hours" sign to prove it.

That's why the bust was such a shock. Everyone in Houston was talking $50 a barrel and then maybe more. Everyone else in the industrialized world was working and praying for cheap oil. By the mid-1980s, the industrialized world won and the Houston economy, utterly dependent on oil, collapsed.

Banks, really *big* banks, went bankrupt, merged or changed names—something that hadn't happened even at the depth of the Great Depression. The savings and loan fiasco of the 1980s only made things worse. The federal government had bone-headedly deregulated the S&Ls, while continuing to insure the deposits. A legion of morally rudderless business types, many of them right here in Houston, saw this confluence of stupidities as their golden opportunity to buy S&Ls, make bogus loans to all their pals, and then go out of business knowing that the Feds—meaning the rest of us—would have to make good. Their shenanigans cost the taxpayers billions, and almost all of them walked away scot-free. But they left plenty of wreckage behind them.

There were empty shopping centers all over the surburbs, with weeds growing high between the broken concrete slabs in their parking lots.The real estate market imploded. Desperate middle-class people "walked" their homes as foreclosure became the order of the day.

Apartment complexes attempted to lure tenants with free move-in, free rent, and no leases required. It didn't work. Many became ghost towns, infested with drug dealers. Loyal employees fared no better. Petroleum engineers, landmen, even roughnecks with years of service found themselves suddenly jobless. The largest city in Texas, the fourth largest city in the nation, was in a state of shock.

As if things weren't bad enough, on a cold January morning in 1986 the *Challenger* Space Shuttle, pride of the nation, bearing an ethnically diverse crew of seven that included the first "Teacher in Space," exploded just after liftoff. NASA, shining symbol of the city of the future, was devastated and thrown into a prolonged period of self-examination.

When the Shamrock fell victim to the wrecking ball because its new owner, The Medical Center, needed a parking lot more than it needed to keep the city's signature venue functioning, it was a fitting symbol that Houston would never be the same town again.

And it isn't. It's older and wiser, with a much more diverse economy. It'll never be that much fun again, but it will never be that desperate again either. As the turn of the millenium approaches, Houstonians have stopped talking about becoming the biggest city in the world, once the town's ambition for the year 2000. Now we talk about other things, about making this a better, more stable place to live. The tidal wave of people attracted by the boom has receded leaving those who really *want* to be here.

The story of Houston is much like the story Ray Bradbury told at the end of his classic work of science fiction, *The Martian Chronicles*. In it, a family born in another place, another world, has settled on Mars. After many trials and serious misunderstandings with the now all-but-vanished indigenous inhabitants, they are, at last, at peace.

In the story, the family goes on a picnic during which the children look down into the slow, dark vertigo waters of a Martian canal. "Daddy," they ask, "where are the Martians?" And the father points toward the bayou-like waters from which, staring back, the one-time immigrants see only their own reflections. Welcome to Houston.

# THINGS TO SEE

To tell the truth, Houston doesn't really have much in the way of conventional, one-of-a-kind tourist attractions. There's no Mount Rushmore, no Golden Gate Bridge, no Hollywood anywhere near here. We do have NASA, which is absolutely unique, but otherwise our attractions require a bit of flexibility to be appreciated. They're not the kind of things that leap immediately to mind when you're looking for a destination. But think about it. It's boring and conventional to tour big-name attractions. It requires spunk and imagination to find and enjoy the unusual, and there are lots of unusual things around here to see and do if you take the time to investigate. Be adventurous. Travel widely close to home and discover the hidden treasures Houston holds for *UN*conventional tourists. (W = wheelchair access.)

## ALKEK VELODROME

**19008 Saums Road in Cullen Park • 578-0858 • Open daily Admission**

About once every four years, when it's time for the Olympics, America really pays attention to bicycle racing. Many of the folks who frequent the Velodrome, the only facility of its kind in Texas, think about speed all day every day. They are some of the country's very best track riders, but that doesn't mean you have to be to use the place. In fact, you don't even have to ride a bike. There are sessions for skaters as well. Helmets and wrist guards are required. Call for information as the track is reserved for different activities at different times, although there are also open sessions.

## AMERICAN COWBOY MUSEUM

**11822 Almeda on Taylor-Stevenson Ranch • 433-4441**
**W variable • Admission**

For six generations, the Stevensons have preserved their black cowboy heritage. Now they share it with the public at their private, nonprofit exhibition. The history of African-Americans in the west is rich, varied, and unfortunately too little-known. The ranch tries to remedy this situation by showing children the stories of people like William Goyens, who was so important to Houston's early history. The Stevensons also preserve the heritage of Hispanic and Native American cowboys as well as arranging touring exhibits. Tours of the ranch are by appointment; call for reservations.

## AMERICAN FUNERAL SERVICE MUSEUM

**415 Barren Springs Drive (near Intercontinental Airport. From I-45, exit Airtex. Take Airtex west to Ella Boulevard, turn right and proceed to Barren Springs. The museum is on your right.) Houston, Texas 77090 • 876-3063 • Open: 10–4 Mon–Sat; Noon–4 Sun. Closed New Year's Day, Thanksgiving, and Christmas Admission**

It sounds strange, but it is actually one of Houston's hidden treasures. The Funeral Service Museum features the "Funerals of the Famous Gallery," where you can see artifacts and information on the funeral ceremonies of political and celebrity figures such as Presidents Eisenhower, Kennedy, and Nixon; Martin Luther King, Jr.; Jacqueline Kennedy Onassis; actors Rudolph Valentino and John Wayne; coach Vince Lombardi; and the King himself, Elvis Presley. There is also a collection of antique, horse-drawn hearses, and memorabilia from President Abraham Lincoln's funeral and historic train procession, including an exact replica of his coffin, one of only two in existence, as well as a full-size, gilded replica of Egyptian King Tut's Sarcophagus.

## WILLIAM GOYENS

You can make a good case that Houston wouldn't have existed without William Goyens, but few Houstonians have ever heard of him.

In the 1830s, William Goyens was something like the king of Nacogdoches, Texas. He owned the only inn and trading post on the most important trade route from Louisiana into Texas. He was a blacksmith and wagon manufacturer, he spoke English, Spanish, French, and several native languages—and he probably saved the life of John Kirby Allen, who was on his way to found Houston at the time.

What makes all this especially interesting is that William Goyens was black. He'd been born free in North Carolina. In fact, his father, too, was a free man who'd fought in the American Revolution. William Goyens (there are various spellings of his name, including Goings) moved to Texas about 1820 following various awful misadventures with slave rustlers who refused to take his free status seriously. Goyens always ended up getting the better of them and, upon escaping, often sued them for damages.

When the Allen brothers were on their way to Texas with all their goods, they were involved in a serious steamboat accident. Twenty-five people were killed, John Kirby Allen was seriously injured, and the brothers lost everything. William Goyens' daughter, a skilled native healer, treated J. K. Allen, and her father resupplied the two New Yorkers on credit.

Goyens and John Kirby Allen remained close friends until Allen's early death, and both served the Republic. Among other things, Goyens was General Sam Houston's interpreter in negotiating the all-important treaty that kept the Cherokee neutral in the Texas War of Independence.

Honored for his service to the Republic, Goyens continued to prosper, becoming a real estate mogul in the Nacogdoches area and building himself and his wife, a white woman, a lavish two-story mansion on a hill at the edge of town, where he died in 1856.

## AMERICAN MUSEUM OF ARCHITECTURE AND DECORATIVE ARTS

**Houston Baptist University • 7502 Fondren • Houston, TX 77074 774-7661, Ext. 3311 • Open 10–4 Mon–Fri, 12–4 Sun • Free**

Another of Houston's great hidden attractions. The Museum of Architecture on the Houston Baptist University campus has a fine, small collection of art and architectural designs from Colonial America, as well as various artifacts from the different ethnic groups that settled the Republic of Texas. Seeing the very things that these folks used to decorate their homes brings you closer to them.

## ANHEUSER-BUSCH BREWERY

**775 Gellhorn Drive at I-10 East • 670-1696 • Open 9–4 Mon–Sat, excluding holidays; Closed Sun • W variable • Free**

See how they make your favorite brew. Afterward, sample some suds. The gift shop, where the brewery offers lots of logo-covered merchandise, is open from 9 to 5. Self-guided tours are available continuously, and during the summer, guided group tours set off on the hour from 11 to 3. No reservations needed unless you plan to bring a group of 20 or more.

## ARMAND BAYOU NATURE CENTER

**5600 Bay Area Boulevard, approximately 20 miles southeast of Houston. Exit Interstate 45 at Bay Area Boulevard, head east approximately 12 miles • 474-3074 • Open Wed–Sun; Closed Mon–Tues. • W variable • Free**

Armand Bayou lets you see the Houston area as it was before civilization. In the 2,000 or so acres of reserve are forest, prairie, and marsh environments, with educational material available on each. In addition to the trail system, boating on the bayou is popular. Visitors can either bring their own boats or take advantage of a free group ride. (Also see Clear Lake section.)

## ASTRODOME

**Kirby Drive at South Loop • For tours, enter west gate on Kirby 799-9544 and 799-9595 • Tours daily at 11, 1, and 3 (5 p.m. tour during summer when no night event is scheduled; no tours on**

days when afternoon event is scheduled) • W variable • Admission
$4/kids under 3 free • Parking $4

Now the world's oldest and smallest domed stadium, the
Astrodome (formally the Harris County Domed Stadium) is one of
the best-known attractions in the city. It is home to the Houston
Astros (baseball), the Houston Oilers (football), and the University
of Houston Cougars (football), but the Astrodome also has hosted
bullfights, lacrosse matches, and motorcycle races. It is the site of the
annual Houston Livestock Show and Rodeo. Opened in 1965, this
brainchild of the late Roy Hofheinz was the victim of a Bud Adams-
induced renovation that consigned the exploding scoreboard—a
bizarre civic treasure if ever there was one—to the junk heap.

## ASTROWORLD

**9001 Kirby Drive (at South Loop) • 799-8404 • W variable
Schedule and price varies with season**

Just across the freeway from the Astrodome, the 75-acre park is
part of the sprawling Astrodomain complex. Thrill seekers who
keep up with the latest in amusement-park rides have a lot to
choose from at Astroworld. The Texas Cyclone, a traditional wood-
en monster, is rated as one of the best roller coasters in the country, and Thunder River sends a raftload of screaming people
careening through simulated river rapids. An extravagant stage
show entertains the less active.

## BATTLESHIP TEXAS

**San Jacinto Battlegrounds. From southeast corner of Loop 610,
take Texas 225 east approximately 15 miles to Texas 134,
then follow the signs • La Porte • 479-2411 • Open 10-5 daily
W variable • Admission $4/kids $2**

After extensive renovation, the Texas is once again open to visitors, many of whom are amazed to find it painted dark blue. The
guides, some of whom actually served aboard the ship, gallantly
insist that this is the correct color. You decide. Commissioned in
1914, (note the World War I vintage wooden decks) the battleship
also saw extensive action in World War II. After the renovation, large
areas of the below-deck space were opened for the first time, and it
is fascinating to see how people lived in those dangerous eras. The
Texas is now permanently moored on the Ship Channel at the bend

---

**HOUSTON FACTOID:**

*There is a Texas Navy, and the Battleship Texas, moored near the
San Jacinto Monument, is its flagship.*

---

where it skirts the San Jacinto Battlegrounds. When the weather is
fine, it is a pleasant walk from the San Jacinto Monument. The self-
conducted tours and displays onboard show the ship's history, and
there are souvenirs available in the dockside gift shop.

## BAYOU BEND
**One Westcott Street • 639-7750 • Tues–Fri, 1½-hour tours every 15
minutes from 10 to 11:45 and 12:45 to 2:50; Sat, 1-½-hour tours
every 15 minutes from 10 to 11:45, depending on the season**

The late philanthropist and civic leader Ima Hogg had a love of art
and a love of Houston. As a result, the Museum of Fine Arts inherited her collection of American decorative arts from the seventeenth
through nineteenth centuries. Hogg's 28-room home, a carefully
maintained antebellum-style mansion on Buffalo Bayou, houses
some of the finest examples of American furniture, paintings, metals,
ceramics, and other artifacts from Puritan days to the Victorian period. Tours of the home and extensive gardens are conducted in
groups of four, but no one under 14 is permitted. Children are welcome during family tours of the grounds and first floor of the home
on the second Sunday of every month except March and August.

## BAYOU PLACE AT THE ALBERT THOMAS
**500 Texas Avenue • Open daily • Admission**

Bayou Place, located in the refurbished Albert Thomas Convention Center, is Houston's answer to the RiverWalk in San Antonio
or the West End of Dallas. Opening in 1996, it will house more
than a dozen nightclubs, including everything from a Sports Bar to
a karaoke club. One cover charge will get you into all of them, and
the restaurants will have separate, streetside entrances. The whole
complex in the heart of the Theater District will connect to the
Bayouside park behind Wortham Center.

## MISS IMA HOGG

No matter what you've heard to the contrary, Miss Ima Hogg, late grand dame of Houston society, did NOT have a twin sister Ura. That is a Yankee canard. Proof that you're a real Houstonian comes when the name Ima Hogg doesn't sound weird anymore. The real Miss Ima was the only daughter of James Stephen Hogg, who, in a typically Texan Horatio Alger story, had been raised in an orphanage and gone on to become the state's first native-born governor. Widowed early, he, too, died young leaving his four children a good name and the Varner Plantation, which became their fortune. Not long after Governor Hogg's death, the West Columbia oil field gushed into the family's front yard. With her eldest brother, Will, administering all that oil money, Ima was free to pursue her love of music and art, studying at the University of Texas as well as in New York and Europe. When she came back home to Houston from Germany about 1910, she taught piano and music theory for a while to talented young scholarship students. She also paid for the musical education of many others. But Miss Ima was a high-energy kind of gal, and she was bored—and so she set about getting a muddy small town its very own Symphony Orchestra, and darn if she didn't do it. Her next project was to get women appointed to the school board in a day when women didn't even have the vote and working outside the home was considered pretty scandalous. That worked out quite nicely, too, thank you very much. Every time rough-and-tumble Houston needed money for a major civic project, or for some charitable enterprise, Miss Ima would "get her brothers interested," and the next thing you knew it was done. Memorial Park, Symphony Young People's Concerts, funding for the then terribly unfashionable field of mental health were only a few of their projects.

Just before the First World War, Ima developed an interest in antique furniture. She'd realized that there was no serious collection of American antiques anywhere in Texas, so she

*(continued on next page)*

decided to create one for the state, and to locate it here in Houston. In a 10-year period, between 1920 and 1930, Ima and her brother Will assembled one of the most remarkable collections of American antiques in the country—but they had no place to put it. She had enough money to build a museum, but Ima was practical as well as generous, so she commissioned Houston society's favorite architect John Staub (designer of Shadyside, near Rice University) to build a mansion which would house both Miss Ima, her three brothers, and the antiques. The result was Bayou Bend. Her brothers soon moved to their own homes, but Ima lived in the graceful, antebellum-style building for the rest of her long life. Bayou Bend was always supposed to be a gift to the City of Houston, and Ima spent many years planning the arrangement of the collection and working with the Museum of Fine Arts to train docents, but that wasn't enough to keep her busy. She ran for and won a seat on the Houston School Board; she oversaw the works of the Hogg Foundation, especially in the education and training of mental health professionals; she was a charter member of the River Oaks Garden Club and helped to set up the annual Azalea Trail, highlighted by her own spectacular garden at Bayou Bend. Nothing could keep her down. At age 93, she took off for England to hunt antiques for the collection and to take in some concerts. She never came back, but her last words did: "Whatever happens, remember that it is the way it was meant to be. I'm doing what I want to do. I'm where I want to be. I have no regrets."

## BAYOU WILDLIFE PARK
**Between Dickinson and Alvin on FM 517, 6 miles west of 1-45**
**337-6376 • Open 10–5 Tue–Sun; Closed Mon • W variable**
**Admission; Group rates**

Take the guided tram tour through this prairie wildlife preserve. There are 86 acres of exotic birds and wild animals. There's also a picnic area, as well as a petting zoo and barnyard for the little ones.

## ALBERT THOMAS

A Nacogdoches boy who graduated from the then-Rice Institute in 1920, Albert Thomas went to the University of Texas, became a lawyer, and got himself elected to Congress in 1936. In the days before the notion of term limits became popular, he made legislating his career and represented Houston's interests in Washington for the next 30 years. Because he had accumulated so much seniority in the era when seniority counted, and so much clout as a committee chairman and as a power in the Democratic party (there *weren't* any Republicans in Texas then), Albert Thomas was an important running buddy of Lyndon Johnson. And in the early 1960s, this paid off for all of us. At the time, the United States figured it was behind the old Soviet Union in the so-called "Space Race" and was prepared to throw big bucks into remedying that. The manned space program was in its infancy and needed a headquarters. That's where Albert Thomas, Lyndon Johnson, and some very fancy real estate dealings came in. As a result, NASA's Manned Spacecraft Center was located in Houston, we became Space City, and a grateful city named the convention center in his honor.

## HERMAN BROWN PARK

**Mercury Drive, north of Interstate 10 and east of Loop 610 East 673-2191 • W • Free**

Named for one of the founders of Brown & Root and brother of George R. Brown, whose money financed a number of large-scale civic projects such as the Convention Center, the park is comprised of some 840 acres of playgrounds, basketball and tennis courts, and hike-and-bike trails. It's one of the major green spaces on the east side of town.

## BURKE BAKER PLANETARIUM

**1 Hermann Circle Drive inside the Museum of Natural Science in Hermann Park • 639-4600 • Open daily • W • Admission**

The planetarium offers something for everyone. There are the regular "Stars of the Season" shows for tyro astronomers, and laser

## GEORGE R. BROWN

When George R. Brown was born back in 1898 in Belton, Texas, no one suspected that he'd turn out to be one of the biggest philanthropists in Houston's history. His middle name was Rufus, which must have been hard on him in grade school, but didn't matter once he'd become a multi-millionaire.

George Rufus was the younger brother of Herman Brown, who, together with his brother-in-law Dan Root, had founded Brown & Root engineering and construction firm. When young George finished his college education at Rice Institute and the University of Texas, he went to work as a mining engineer, but was badly injured in an accident. Once he was feeling better, he went to work for his big brother and Dan Root.

The three men became pals of a rising politician named Lyndon Baines Johnson. This certainly did their business no harm. In fact, through a combination of expertise and heavy-duty political influence, Brown & Root soon was awarded a slew of huge government contracts, including lucrative "cost-plus" agreements to build U.S. facilities in Vietnam during the war there.

They built the enormous Rice Stadium—then called Houston Stadium—at cost using no union labor.

These and other jobs made all three principals multi-millionaires. After his brother died in the early 1960s, George sold out, making him one of the wealthiest people in Texas. He then embarked on his third career: philanthropy.

George R. Brown raised millions for Rice University, where he was a trustee, and before he died in 1983, he set up the Brown Foundation, which continues to fund civic projects that benefit his adopted city.

sound and light shows such as *Laserpalooza, Laser Zeppelin, and Laser Floyd: Dark Side of the Moon*—where rock music and even comedy routines accompany the heavenly display—for the less scientifically inclined.

## CHILDREN'S MUSEUM OF HOUSTON

**1500 Binz • Open Tue–Sat 9–5; Sun noon–5; Free Thurs 6–8; Closed Mon • W variable • Admission: $5, $4 ages 65 and older, children under 2 and members are free**

Nobody here is ever going to say "don't touch." Touching and exploring and learning are what the Children's Museum is all about. The colorful building alone is worth the trip.

## COCKRELL BUTTERFLY CENTER

**1 Hermann Circle Drive at the Museum of Natural Science in Hermann Park • 639-4600 • Open daily • W • Admission**

Butterflies are free in their three-leveled, transparent plastic home at the Cockrell. They flutter around visitors who enter their world through a nifty underground cave and come up behind a 40-foot-high waterfall. This is supposed to simulate a limestone sink-hole surrounded by a tropical rainforest and it does a good job. For the more scientifically inclined, there are other exhibits in which butterflies can be seen emerging from their chrysalises. In the Brown Hall of Entomology, there's an educational feature that shows several thousand spectacular butterflies, moths, and beetles, and explains the roles of insects in the environment.The Cockrell is one of the most spectacular take-ins in town. Bring the kids.

## CONFEDERATE MUSEUM

**2740 FM 359, Richmond, TX • 342-8787 • Open Tues–Thurs; Sat–Sun by appointment only. Closed Mon, Wed, Fri • Admission**

Housed in three small buildings is a fine collection of Confederate memorabilia including currency artwork, furniture, and costumes from the era of the War Between the States. It's best to call ahead, as there are sometimes scheduled events.

## DOWNTOWN TUNNEL SYSTEM

There's something growing underneath downtown Houston, and it shows no signs of stopping. But people who work downtown don't seem to mind at all. The tunnel system, which runs under most of the major buildings downtown, allows pedestrians easier passage between buildings without their having to brave the elements or traffic. Underground restaurants and shops do a heavy business during the lunch hour. With its various branches, the system is more than five miles long, and the city has plans to add more tunnel routes. Access is possible from the lobbies of several major buildings, including Pennzoil Place and Allen Center. Charity tunnel-hike walkathons, costumed treasure hunts, and other civic events make fun use of the system on weekends.

## FORT BEND MUSEUM
**500 Houston Street, Richmond, TX • 342-6478 • Open 10–4 Tue–Fri; 1–5 Sat–Sun; Closed Mon • W variable • Admission**

At one time there really was a fort on a bend of the Brazos River; it eventually became Richmond, Texas, and this fine, small museum complex tells the story. Exhibits include memorabilia from Stephen F. Austin's original colony; Mirabeau B. Lamar, second president of the Republic; and from the Confederate era. The Long-Smith Cottage and the John H. Moore Home, both nearby, are part of the museum. (Also see Get Out of Town section.)

## FUNPLEX
**13700 Beechnut • 530-7777 • W varies • Admission varies**

This is a huge amusement park under glass with attractions and distractions for the whole family. In summer, the air-conditioning is a godsend for parents with tiny ones in tow. There's junk food, of course, and everything from bowling and mini-golf to a laser ride and a monster climbing gym for small kids. Three cinemas show movies suitable for kids and teens, and there are more video games than any human needs. Be sure to wear socks if you plan to bowl or roller-skate. Bring quarters!!! Admission is free, but nothing else is. Call or write for hours and prices.

## THE GALLERIA I, II, AND III
**5015 Westheimer • 622-0663 • Open daily • Admission free • W**

This is Valhalla for Houston's shop-aholics, but The Galleria also has transcended mere malldom becoming both a bona fide,tourist attraction and the city's agora. This huge space with its glasslike roof is modeled after the original centuries-old Galleria in Milan, Italy. Houstonians and visitors from all over the world gather here to enjoy the indoor skating rink, dozens of restaurants, fast food outlets, and people-watching cafes. In addition to the major stores—Lord and Taylor, Macy's, Marshall Field, and Neiman Marcus—there are scores of specialty shops.

## MIRABEAU BUONAPARTE LAMAR

Today it doesn't look like much, just a small wooden sign stuck into a patch of green on a side street near a Half Price Books and the Montrose Post Office (77006), but at one time this was one of the most prestigious places in Houston. This was the Lamar plantation, home of Mirabeau B. Lamar, second president of the Republic of Texas, bitter political enemy of Sam Houston, and an all-around piece of work. Lamar High School is named for him, as are any number of other institutions, but the honor he coveted most, serious recognition for his poetry, justifiably eluded him.

Born in Georgia in 1798, in the days when the real Napoleon was still a hero, not a dictator, Mirabeau B. was the son of a wealthy planter. Educated as a Southern gentleman, he was an accomplished horseman and fencer as well as a poet and painter. After dabbling in politics and partisan journalism in his native state, Lamar moved west to recover emotionally from the death of his young wife.

Arriving in Texas just in time for the Revolution, he helped to build Fort Velasco at what's now Richmond, Texas, and contributed patriotic poetry to local papers. He joined the Texas army as a private, but on the eve of the Battle of San Jacinto, he was commissioned colonel. Good thing. His quick thinking and leadership of the cavalry helped to win the day, and ultimately he became the Republic's Secretary of War.

In the Republic's first election he became vice president, but spent most of his time back in the United States partying and doing what amounted to public relations for Texas. Sam Houston didn't think much of his veep's activities, and the bad blood between them deepened. In the next election, the anti-Sam party had three candidates; Lamar and two others. In one of the great mysteries of early Texas history, the other two candidates both conveniently committed suicide before election day, leaving the field clear for Mirabeau B. Lamar.

His term as president was not a success. He reversed Houston's policy of conciliation with the Cherokee and

*(continued on next page)*

Comanche, and spent millions of dollars the Republic didn't have to drive them out. He also moved the capital to Austin, something for which Houstonians will never forgive him. Lamar's great legacy, however, is the Texas education system. He convinced the Congress of the Republic to set aside public lands to finance public schools and the universities that would become the University of Texas and Texas A&M. After leaving office, he had a long and colorful career in the pro-slavery politics of the U. S., but eventually retired to his plantation near Richmond, Texas, and died there in 1859.

## GEORGE OBSERVATORY

**Brazos Bend State Park (one hour southwest of Houston on U.S. 59) • 242-3055 • Open 3–10 Sat • Admission**

Although used by serious scientists during the week, on Saturdays the observatory becomes part of the Challenger Learning Center. In memory of the lives of the seven Challenger astronauts, the center teaches students teamwork and problem solving through simulated shuttle missions. There are also "Discovering Science" programs that offer a hands-on opportunity to observe the sun with solar telescopes and to visit the observatory's exhibits. In the late afternoon you can get one of the $1 passes that allow you onto the floor of the main dome where the 36-inch telescope is located. Admission is by the carload. Bring friends.

## GLENWOOD CEMETERY

**2525 Washington Boulevard • 864-7886 • Open 7–5 daily • Free**

This is one of the city's oldest burying grounds. The cemetery goes back at least 150 years and when it was built on what passes for a hill, this quiet spot was *way* out of town. It's a lot bigger than it seems from Washington Avenue, covering 65 acres of what now amounts to parkland. The view of Buffalo Bayou and the downtown skyline are just spectacular, and at the center is a unusual German gingerbread-style house that serves as the caretaker's office. Nearby is one of Houston's great morbid curiosities, the grave of Howard Hughes. Howard was a local boy whose Daddy's money came from the oil drill bit he'd invented. Howard inherited lots of money at a very young age and went on to other things, not the least of which was becoming a galactic-class eccentric. Old and sick, he was on his way home to Houston (by chartered jet from Acapulco to the Texas Medical Center) when he died, thus setting off avalanches of litigation. Legions of lawyers fought for years about jurisdiction and about who'd get the fortune. As if that wasn't complicated enough, there was the flap about the "Mormon Will," which inspired the goofy, wonderful film *Melvin and Howard.* Rent the video, then go visit the real Howard in Glenwood Cemetery. His grave site is open to the well-behaved public.

## GREATER HOUSTON PRESERVATION ALLIANCE WALKING TOURS

**712 Main Street, Suite 110 • Houston, TX 77002 • 216-5000 Call for dates and times • Admission.**

In its ongoing, valiant attempt to foster the preservation and appreciation of Houston's historic structures, neighborhoods, and sites, the Society offers walking tours of some of the city's most interesting places. There are regular, monthly excursions around the downtown Market Square area, but there are also visits to little-known neighborhoods such as Broadacres, the residential area of North and South boulevards, which was founded in 1922 by James A. Baker and his father, Capt. James A. Baker, the man who saved the Rice University fortune by solving the murder of William Marsh Rice. The Society has also done tours of Houston's African American heritage and of the Old Wards.

## GULF COAST RAILROAD MUSEUM

**Railwood Industrial Park, 7390 Mesa Road • 631-6612 for information • Open 11–4 Sat • Admission**

Houston's city motto (which *nobody* knows) is: "Where 11 Railroads meet the Sea." In honor of our Iron Horse heritage, the Gulf Coast Chapter of the National Railway Historical Society has put together this tribute to a bygone era. It features historic railroad cars, both passenger and freight, built between 1915 and 1955. The Visitors Center, which is housed in a Santa Fe baggage car, offers interpretive exhibits of railroad artifacts.

## GULF GREYHOUND PARK

**FM 2004 off I-45 South • (409) 935-7171 • Open daily during racing season • Admission**

This is the world's largest greyhound race park, all 315,000 square feet of it. The grandstand is quite posh with four levels offering clubhouse seating (read "air conditioning") as well as full-service dining. For those anxious to put down a bet, there are 318 teller windows.

## HERITAGE MUSEUM OF MONTGOMERY COUNTY

**1506 I-45 North Feeder Road, Conroe, TX • (409) 539-MUSE Open 9–4 Thurs–Sat • Free (donations appreciated)**

In a small, green oasis beside busy I-45, the Heritage museum is housed in a white-painted, old-timey house. The exhibits trace the development of Montgomery County, but the best is our version of Betsy Ross, a copy of the original drawing of the Lone Star Flag by C B. Stewart. While you're there, stop in at the little tourist information cabin for info on other places of interest in the county as well as at Lake Conroe.

## HERMANN PARK

**Fannin at Hermann Drive • W variable • Free**

Hermann Park is the traditional heart of Houston. Within the park's 388 acres are the Houston Zoo, the Museum of Natural Science, Burke Baker Planetarium, Miller Outdoor Theatre, a golf course, the Houston Garden Center, and a miniature train that takes passengers on a leisurely circuit of the park.

## CONRAD HILTON ARCHIVES

**University Hilton on the campus of the University of Houston, Entrance 1 off Calhoun • 743-2430 • Open Mon–Fri, 8–noon, 2–6 W • Free**

There are some pretty strange attractions in Houston (see Houston Sports Museum and American Funeral Museum, for two) but this is one of the best. It features more than 3,000 photos having to do with Hilton's life and the hotel business, as well as an assortment of awards and plaques. But the real reason to visit is to see one of actress Elizabeth Taylor's many original wedding albums—this one from her 1950 marriage to Conrad "Nicky" Hilton, Jr. The archive is on the second floor of the campus hotel in the south wing.

## GEORGE HERMANN

Hermann Square is indeed the official name for what looks like City Hall's front yard. But, no matter what you've heard, it is not Martha Hermann Square. *And,* no matter what you've heard, drunkards are not safe from arrest on that space.

It is, however, the plot on which city benefactor George Hermann, a world-class eccentric if ever there was one, was born, and at one point in the 1800s he supposedly maintained it as a kind of private drunk tank for his ranch workers in town for a Saturday-night carouse. Hence, the safe-from-arrest legend.

In any event, around the time of Texas independence, Hermann's parents had emigrated from Switzerland to Houston—why is a mystery. Mrs. Hermann was a strong-minded woman who'd sold her jewelry to finance her husband's business venture—the fledgling city's first bakery. Fortunately, it prospered and the family used the profits to buy the land near what's now City Hall. They built a 2-story house, bought some cows, and went into dairying.

While George was serving in the Confederate army, both his parents and his only sibling died, leaving him little but the land. Alone in the world, he went into the cattle business with the Settegast brothers, and made his first fortune. The next two came from real estate and the oil folks found underneath it.

In his own lifetime, George Hermann was well known for squeezing every nickel until the buffalo screamed. He refused to marry because, he said, "Wives are too expensive." He lived as a border in one room of a house he owned, and always wore cheap work clothes.

When he got sick in the spring of 1914, Hermann gave the city 285 acres of land just outside of town for a public park. It still is one—Hermann Park, home of the zoo and Miller Outdoor Theatre.

*(continued on next page)*

George Hermann died of stomach cancer in October 1914, and everyone knew he'd written a will leaving everything to the city—but nobody could find it. Police opened his safe. City Council members tore up his one-room domicile. The mayor ransacked his desk. Officials opened his safe deposit boxes and questioned his friends. Nothing. Finally, a clerk at South Texas Bank found the will in some old boxes that had been earmarked for the trash.

The relieved city administration discovered that Hermann had left Houston another 278 acres of parkland, $2.5 million (a king's ransom in those days), and his beloved homestead in downtown. Hermann was buried, as he requested, wearing a cowman's suit, new boots, and holding a 10-gallon hat. The grateful town gave him a royal sendoff, with a packed funeral service in the City Auditorium. Today, there is a life-sized statue of George Hermann at the southwestern corner of Hermann Park, facing Hermann Hospital.

## HOLOCAUST EDUCATION CENTER AND MEMORIAL MUSEUM OF HOUSTON

**401 Caroline • Houston, TX 77004 • 789-9898 • Call for information**

Exhibits of original artifiacts, photography and art show the story of the Holocaust, arguably the greatest crime in modern history. More necessary now than ever because the generation that experienced such terrible suffering in the Nazi death camps is passing away, the museum serves as an educational center for the whole Gulf Coast area. Rent the video of *Shindler's List*, and then come here. You will be amazed to discover how many of your neighbors experienced this horror first hand, and you, too, will vow "Never Again."

## HOUSTON ARBORETUM

**4501 Woodway • 681-8433 • Open daily • W • Free**

More than 150 acres of green space is dedicated to nature in a neighborhood where concrete and steel get most of the attention. While traffic drones on the Loop and Memorial, visitors can disappear into the world of the arboretum's winding trails. The peaceful sighing of the wind, the call of the birds, and the smell of the vegetation are enough to make the most jaded city dweller content. This is the oldest wilderness education program in Houston, and there are guided tours as well as self-guiding booklets for both adults and kids. There is also an extensive educational program.

## HOUSTON FIRE MUSEUM

**2403 Milam at McIlhenny • 524-2526 • Open 10–4 Tue–Sat; Closed Sun and Mon • Admission**

Housed in the former Fire Station No. 7, which was built in 1898, the museum opened in October 1982 with a collection of historic equipment, uniforms, and memorabilia. It shows the history of the Houston Fire Department from its early 19th-century volunteer days (when the city burned to the ground on a regular basis) to the present, when it leads the way in developing some of the world's most sophisticated arson investigation techniques.

## HOUSTON MUSEUM OF NATURAL SCIENCE

**One Hermann Circle Drive in Hermann Park • 639-4629 Open Mon–Sat 9–5, Sun–Mon noon–5 • W • Admission**

In some ways, this place is like Houston's collective attic. There is something old-fashioned about its approach, especially in the case of exhibits from the days when the oil industry was still new and wonderful. The Hall of Medical Science is interesting to kids, and the space-exploration exhibits are a good introduction to the subject. The Isaac Arnold Hall of Space Science contains artifacts from the Mercury, Gemini, and Apollo space programs. Elsewhere in the museum, a 70-foot-long dinosaur skeleton dominates the two-story main exhibit area. Dinamation, the touring near-life-size animated-dinosaur show, frequently makes an appearance. Next to the museum is the Burke Baker Planetarium. A series of special presentations re-creates the heavens on the planetarium's domed ceiling and analyzes different aspects of the universe, from planets and stars to comets.

## HOUSTON SPORTS MUSEUM

**4001 Gulf Freeway (inside Finger Furniture Center) • 221-4441
for information • Open 10–9 Mon–Sat; Closed Sun • W • Free**

No. The location of the museum is *not* a joke. It really *is* inside a
furniture store—but there's a good reason. Once upon a time, the
Houston Buffs baseball team, a mainstay of the old Texas League,
played their home games on this site. In one of those wonderfully
Houstonian mixtures of commerce and whimsy, the museum was
built around the stadium's home plate. Other exhibits include
memorabilia from the World Champion Houston Rockets basketball team, the Houston Oilers, Aeros, and a baseball Hall of Fame.
One of the most interesting features is a special exhibit on Houston's baseball history from the early Texas League to the Astros.

## HOUSTON ZOOLOGICAL GARDENS

**1515 Outer Belt Drive in Hermann Park (off 6500 block of
Fannin) • 523-5888 • May–September, open daily 9:50–5;
October–April, daily 9:50–6 • W • Admission, except on city
holidays**

The zoo is a treat. Right near the main entrance is the Kipp
Aquarium, which features a living coral reef that contains a rain-
bow of gorgeous tropical fish. There are also exhibits with the
many examples of marine and freshwater life from around the
world. The zoo is home to one of the nation's top breeding programs for exotic birds, and it boasts a fascinating collection of reptiles including rare albino snakes and dragon-like Chinese alligators. The Children's Zoo, complete with petting area, is a special
favorite with the little ones.

---

### HOUSTON FACTOID:

*The Kellum-Noble house downtown in Sam Houston Park was
the home of the city's first zoo.*

---

## JAPANESE GARDEN

**Hermann Park near the Sam Houston statue • 520-3283**
**Open daily 10–6 • W variable • Admission**

This six-acre landscaped garden is of special interest to those with a green thumb. It houses more than 1,800 trees including pine, oak, Japanese maple, dogwood, pink-flower cherry, peach, plus seven species of azaleas, 30 types of flowering grasses, and Japanese irises. There are several traditional Japanese garden accoutrements including a tea house. The garden was created by famous designer Ken Nakajima as an oasis of tranquillity—and it is.

## JESSE H. JONES PARK

**Eight miles east of Interstate 45 or two miles west of U.S. 59 behind Kenswick • Take the FM 1960 exit off I-45 or U.S. 59 845-1000 • Open daily • W • Free**

See the timeless flora of the Gulf Coast. Four cypress swamps can be seen from the boardwalk and overlook deck. A fern trail on the prairie's 154 acres leads to a white, sandy beach on Spring Creek, where anglers can get in some fishing. Guided tours can be reserved in advance, or visitors can use one of the self-guided trails.

### JESSE JONES

Although he was born in Tennessee, Jesse Holman Jones was known as Mr. Houston. He was the stud duck around here for more years than most people could count, and you still see his name on many important civic monuments such as Jesse H. Jones Hall for the Performing Arts.

Jesse Jones came to Texas at about the age of nine when his father, William Hasque Jones, a prosperous man with interests in tobacco and lumber, moved the family to Dallas from Tennessee. When young Jesse came of age, he joined the family lumber business in the offices of his uncle M.T. Jones and was appointed manager of the Dallas operation. A few years later he moved the offices to Houston and then

*(continued on next page)*

established his own firm, The South Texas Lumber Company. It would become the foundation for his business empire.

Soon he branched out into real estate and banking; he also bought and served as publisher of the *Houston Chronicle* and settled down to running his multitudinous business interests with the social help of his new wife, Mary Gibbs of Mexia.

At one time in the 1930s, Jesse Jones owned most of downtown Houston. He liked to run his hands over the stone facades of the buildings he owned as he passed by on his way from the Lamar, one of the hotels he owned (site of Jones' famous 8-F suite, where the fortunes of Texas politicians such as Lyndon Johnson were decided), past the banks he owned, to the *Houston Chronicle*, which he owned and from which he disseminated all the news he thought fit.

A man with this firm a grip on the levers of power was a natural for appointive politics. Jesse Jones' first governmental position came in 1932 when President Hoover named him to the board of the Reconstruction Finance Corporation, which was trying to deal with the ravages of the Great Depression. When Franklin D. Roosevelt took office in 1933, he kept Jones on and later appointed him to numerous other New Deal offices dealing with finance. His work saved hundreds, if not thousands of businesses, and despite Jones' personal politics, which ranged from ultra-conservative to totally reactionary, a grateful Roosevelt named Jesse Jones Secretary of Commerce in 1940. But their philosophical disagreements ran deep and Jones ended up leading the anti-Roosevelt faction in the Democratic party. The president demanded his resignation in 1945, and Jones then broke completely with the Roosevelt-Truman group.

In the early 1950s, Jesse and Mary Gibb Jones set up a major charitable foundation, the Houston Endowment, Inc., which has funded scores of artistic and civic projects over the years.

A non-profit organization with all the attendant tax advantages, it also owned and operated the *Chronicle*. Many competitors claimed, with considerable justification, that this status gave the paper an unfair advantage. After a protracted court battle, the Foundation divested and sold the paper to the Hearst Corporation in the 1980s. By then the founder, Jesse Jones, wasn't around to see it. He died on June 1, 1956.

## LYNDON B. JOHNSON SPACE CENTER

**NASA Road 1, three miles east of Interstate 45, 25 miles southeast of Houston • 483-3111 • W • Open daily 9–4 • Free**

This is the number one attraction in the Houston area. While the Disney-built Space Center Houston gets most of the attention these days—and it certainly is well deserved—the Space Center itself is worth an extra visit. There, on Rocket Row, you can see the actual craft that took America into space. Of special interest is the *tiny* Mercury-program rocket and the first space capsules, which were dubbed (with complete accuracy) the Man in a Can. Virgil I. Grissom, who was one of the original seven Astronauts, flew in a Mercury can. When asked, as a guy with the "Right Stuff," if he'd been scared, he is supposed to have said: "How would you feel sitting on top of 3 million separate parts, each one made by the lowest bidder?" See for yourself what he was talking about. There is nothing else like NASA—except perhaps for Star City in the former USSR, and it's a lot easier to get to Clear Lake. (See also listings for NASA/Clear Lake.)

## KIDDIE WONDERLAND

**7800 South Main • Houston, TX 77030 • 667-0813 • Open: daily Admission**

Kiddie Wonderland is a funky time warp. It's been there on South Main in the vicinity of the Astrodome since long before there *was* a Dome. There is no actual admission charge, but to participate, buy a strip of tickets. The vintage, child-sized amusement rides, which only very young children find exciting, are not some preservationist's idea of a museum, they've just *been* there since the 1950s. So have the ancient ponies. These come in fast, medium-fast, and slow varieties; the child gets to choose. Generations of Houston children have enjoyed Wonderland's simple pleasures. Parents and grandparents do, too.

## KING'S ORCHARD

**FM 1774 between Plantersville and Magnolia • (409) 894-2766 Open 8–5 p.m. Tues–Sun (March–September) • Free.**

Pick your own fresh fruit. There are strawberries, blackberries, raspberries, blueberries, nectarines, peaches, plums, figs, and apples in season. They don't charge you to get in, but the fruit is sold by the pound. Allowing for age and attention span, kids love it. Call for directions.

## MEMORIAL PARK

**Memorial Drive between Westcott and Loop 610 • 845-1000 • W Free**

The main attraction of 1,466-acre Memorial Park is its three-mile jogging trail, complete with exercise stations along the course. The upwardly mobile love to meet here after work and on weekends. On Fridays, the trail is more crowded than a singles bar. The park also has a tennis center, a golf course, and softball fields, which are the site of most city league games.

## MERCER ARBORETUM

**22506 Aldine-Westfield Road, north of FM 1960 • 443-8731 Open daily • W • Free**

Nature has received more help from people here than in other arboretums, but the trees and shrubs that have been planted manage to recall the densely wooded Big Thicket in East Texas. In addition to trails and a greenhouse, the Mercer Arboretum has a meeting room and resource library for public use.

## EDITH L. MOORE NATURE SANCTUARY

**440 Wilchester • 932-1639 • Open daily • W • Free**

Anti-concrete crusaders rejoice. The Houston Audubon Society has preserved almost 20 acres off Memorial Drive for flowers, trees, and animals. Inside the lush green sanctuary, tension falls away as visitors watch birds, fish, and other critters in their native habitat. The deck at the sanctuary's pond is a particularly good vantage point for watching life along and in Rummel Creek, which runs through the property. The late Edith L. Moore's log cabin, complete with a screened-in porch, now serves as the visitors center.

## MUSEUM OF PRINTING HISTORY

**1324 W. Clay Street • Houston, TX 77019 • 522-4652 Open 10–4 Tue–Sat**

It isn't easy to find, but it's well worth looking for. This tiny museum offers several surprises including the oldest printed piece in the world and the only known copy of the rules of colonization of Texas. There are also German Renaissance engravings and other unique artifacts that illustrate the importance of printing in government, education, art, and religion.

## JOHNNY NASH INDOOR ARENA

**6200 Willardville Road off I-45 South • 991-0671 • Open Fri nights • Admission**

Friday nights there's the "Bulls and Barrels Rodeo" featuring do-it-yourself contests for those with more medical insurance than sense. There are also live bands, barbecue, and dancing. Special events, such as not-ready-for-the-WWF wrestling on Saturday nights or when scheduled. Call for information and directions. The place isn't easy to find.

## NATURE DISCOVERY CENTER

**7112 Newcastle in Russ Pitman Park • 667-6550 • Open 10–5 Sat; noon–5 Sun; noon–4 Tue–Thurs; Closed Mon and Fri • Free (but donations are appreciated)**

The Center offers numerous activities to those in the West U-Bellaire area. There are family nature rambles and nature story time for pre-schoolers, as well as ecologically themed exhibits and a new Vertebrate Room located in the museum space on the second floor of a restored 1925 home. There is a charge for some exhibits, and children under 10 must be accompanied by an adult.

## OLD TOWN SPRING

**I-45 North/Spring Cypress Road • 353-9310 • W variable • Free**

Old Town Spring is a semi-restored version of an early 1900s Texas railroad town. Many of the buildings are original, and others of the same period were moved to the site, some 20 miles north of Houston. The quaint little settlement has craft-and-gift shops by the dozen, in addition to a couple of restaurants and bakeries and lots of "antique" emporiums. Some visitors find the whole thing too cute for words, others love its unpretentious charm. Christmas brings out the best in Old Town Spring. Families enjoy the festive holiday atmosphere. Shopping hours are Tuesday–Saturday 10–5. Some stores are open Sundays.

## ORANGE SHOW

**2401 Munger • 926-6368 • Open Sat and Sun, noon–5. Group tours during the week, $2.50 per adult; nonprofit or school group tours free; $1 for adults, children under 12 free**

To say that the late Jeff McKissack was a fan of the orange would be a serious understatement. In the early 1950s, McKissack, who had trucked oranges across most of the southeastern United States in his youth, cleared out a nursery he had been tending and began to work on what would become the Orange Show. In 1979, 26 years later, it was opened to visitors. McKissack died in early 1980, but his colorful monument to the orange lives on as a widely recognized example of folk art. In the spirit of its founder, the Orange Show sponsors quite a number of eccentric events. Among the best are the tours of examples of McKissack-like whimsy including Weird But Wonderful sights such as The Beer Can House, 222 Malone (north off Memorial Drive a few miles west of downtown). This is the home of a retired upholsterer who spent decades drinking beer, then flattening the cans and covering his house with them. He used the pull-tabs to create huge garlands that decorate the trees. Another special place on the Orange Show's list is "The Pig-dome." This is what Victoria Herberta calls her intensely purple frame house at 4208 Crawford near downtown. It is surrounded by colorful plastic flowers and decorated with signs and license plates extolling the virtues of hogs. The house, which is also Herberta's home, once also housed her pet pigs. The 800-pound Priscilla became nationally famous for rescuing a retarded child from drowning, and "baby" 200-pound-plus Jeffrey Jerome was the spokespig for the homeless. The pigs ended up homeless as well when a heartless city government ruled that downtown Houston cannot be a haven for hogs. Nevertheless, Herberta soldiers on, welcoming visitors who bring nonperishable canned goods for the homeless, and showing off her pig memorabilia and her amazing collection of soft-drink bottles. Who else is going to show you things like this? Call the Orange Show for upcoming events.

## PASADENA HISTORICAL MUSEUM AND THE STRAWBERRY HOUSE

**201 Vince in Memorial Park, Pasadena, TX • 477-7237 Open 9:30–2:30 Mon–Fri; 9:30–5 Sat; 1–5 Sun • Free**

Once upon a time Pasadena, Texas, was the strawberry capital of the country. It's fruit harvest was eagerly awaited as far away as

Chicago. The historical museum collection of local history and memorabilia tells the story. The Strawberry House, which is located behind the museum, shows what a Pasadena home would look like in three periods of history—early 1900s, 1920s, and the 1940s. (Also see Calendar section.)

## POLICE MUSEUM

**17000 Aldine-Westfield Road • 230-2360 • Open Mon–Fri 8–3:30 Free**

Are your kids fascinated with cop shows on TV? Have police officers just visited school? This often-overlooked attraction is a great follow-up for children with any interest in police work. Adults will be fascinated, too, by the exhibits of weird weapons confiscated from bad guys, police uniforms from all over the world, and a police helicopter. Interactive sessions give children a chance to "ride" in a police car and check out the gun collection under the supervision of an officer. The museum is located at the Police Academy, about 35 minutes north of downtown in the vicinity of Intercontinental Airport.

## PORT OF HOUSTON

**Board tour boat at 7500 Clinton Drive, Clinton exit off East Loop 670-2416 • Tours: Tues, Wed, Fri, and Sat at 10 and 2:30 p.m.; Thurs and Sun 2:30 Closed Mon • Free**

The Port of Houston, more than 50 miles inland from the Gulf of Mexico, is one of the primary reasons for Houston's commercial success, and none of this would have happened without the machinations of Member of Congress Tom Ball, patron saint of the Port. Thanks to his efforts with the Ship Channel, Houston is number one in the United States in foreign trade and the third-largest U.S. seaport in total tonnage. Close to 5,000 ships per year call at the port. Ninety-minute tours aboard the inspection boat *Sam Houston* give visitors a close-up look at the port's facilities, including the Turning Basin and more than 40 wharves. There is always a lengthy waiting list, and even though the boat is air-conditioned, if your turn comes up in August, think twice. On hot afternoons, the Ship Channel does *not* smell pretty.

## TOM BALL

Tomball the town was named for Tom Ball the person, who in his own day needed no introduction.

Thomas Henry Ball was born in Huntsville in 1859, became a lawyer and, of course, immediately moved to Houston. He was a big wheel in Democratic Party politics—then the only kind of politics there was in Texas. He ran for governor as a Prohibitionist, but that's not why they name towns after people. Tom Ball was elected to Congress, and he learned where all the political bodies were buried. That's why, when he came home to serve on the Port of Houston Commission, he knew exactly what to do.

The city of Houston, as everyone knows, is 50 miles from the Gulf. And, in their natural state, most of those 50 miles are too shallow for deep draft, ocean-going ships, the only kind it's profitable for a port to deal with.

Around the turn of the century, city bigwigs figured out that a ship channel could be dredged from Harrisburg to the Gulf—but it would cost the earth. Enter ex-member of Congress Tom Ball. Ol' Tom figured out that if Houston's city fathers could raise some of the dredging money up front, he could persuade his former colleagues in Washington to appropriate money for the rest. They did. He did. And the rest is history. You can thank Tom Ball for inventing the concept of Federal Matching Funds.

## ROUND-UP RODEO

**FM 1093 in Simonton (45 minutes west of Houston) • 499-1546**
**Open Saturdays only • Admission**

The City Parents take visiting political delegations here. (You should have seen the ancient leaders of the People's Republic of China in cowboy hats back in the 1980s!) But most of the time this is the place where young cowboys prove their macho. The open rodeo is followed by country-and-western dancing for anyone still able to move. There are a restaurant and concession stands on the premises. Call for directions.

## SAFARI-LAND OF TEXAS

**McClellan Road • 359-1946 • Open 10–5 Tues–Sun; Closed Mon**
**W variable • Admission**

Take the one-hour tram tour staffed by professional guides through 120 acres of wilderness near Kingwood. Here exotic wildlife roams freely and visitors can safely feed hundreds of exotic animals and birds. There's also a wildlife museum and a petting zoo for kids as well as patio picnic areas. Call for directions. It's not easy to find.

## SAINT ARNOLD BREWING COMPANY

**2522 Fairway Park Drive • 686-9494 • Open Sat only • Free**

Saint Arnold, who looks kind of like Santa Claus, is the patron saint of beer. When the local folks created this microbrewery in the face of all that national competition, they figured they needed all the help they could get. It seems as if Saint Arnold looks after his own. The company's brew is a success, and they are happy to show you how they make it. Tours every Saturday afternoon. Free tasting afterward. Call for directions and details.

## SAM HOUSTON PARK

**1100 Bagby (downtown) • 845-1000 • Hourly tours Mon–Sat 10–4;**
**Sun 1–5 • W Variable • Admission**

In the shadow of Houston's downtown skyscrapers, Sam Houston Park is a reminder of the city's past. The park is a collection of 19th-century structures that have been moved to a grassy area near City Hall and the Central Library. The collection is what they call in the museum trade a "lifestyle exhibit": Its reason for existence is to demonstrate how ordinary people lived. Among the buildings open to the public are the Kellum-Noble house, which the Heritage Society saved from the wrecking ball in 1954. Good thing. At the time, it was the only home left in Houston that had been built while Texas was a republic. "The Old Place" is a cabin moved from near where NASA stands today; it dates from *before* the Republic. Among the others are the San Felipe Cottage, which was the home of Houston's first professional fire chief, and the Pillot House, which was in the same family for almost 100 years. The Jack Yates House was built in 1870 by a freed slave who became one of Houston's civic leaders; and the Staiti House, built in 1904, was modified after a 1915 hurricane. The church of St. John was built in 1892 by members of the congregation. After the tour be sure to visit the Museum, the Yesteryear Shop, and Melange, the Society's Tearoom. It serves fine, simple fare in a historic setting.

## SAN JACINTO MONUMENT

**5500 Park Road La Porte (From the southeast corner of Loop 610, take Texas 225 east approximately 15 miles to Texas 154. Follow signs.) • 479-2421 • Open daily 10–6 • W • Museum is free; admission to tower elevator and multimedia show**

Of course it's taller than the Washington Monument. This is Texas! The 570-foot high, star-topped obelisk stands on the site of the Battle of San Jacinto. And *it* is the most important conflict folks outside of Texas never heard of. Here, in 1836, the forces of General Sam Houston defeated the same Mexican army that only a month before had captured the Alamo. If Sam hadn't won, everything that is now the western United States would be part of Mexico today. In the lobby of the monument is the San Jacinto Museum of History, a collection of artifacts from Texas' past. A state-of-the-art 150-seat theater houses *Texas Forever!! The Battle of San Jacinto,* a multimedia shows that interprets the battle and other Texas historical events. It does not mention that Senator Joe McCarthy, about the closest thing America's had to a home-grown fascist, gave the address at the dedication. From the observation deck near top of this largest masonry monument in the world, you can watch the ships sail up the channel to Houston.

## SOUTHERN EMPRESS

**Texas 105 West (Lakeview Marina) at Lake Conroe; 7.5 miles west of I-45 North • (800) 324-2229 or (409) 447-3002 • Open Fri, Sat, and Sun only • W variable • Admission**

This is one of the truly terrific things to do on Lake Conroe. The *Empress* is an old-timey sternwheeler that steams around the lake as you dine and enjoy on-board live entertainment, or just take in the view. It's relaxing to drift past the piney woods in the Sam Houston National Forest, and around the coves of the lake waiting for the daily sunset spectacular. Be warned: admission, which includes meals, is not cheap. (Also see Get Out of Town section.)

## SPACE CENTER HOUSTON

**Nasa Road 1 at Second Street, on the Johnson Space Center campus • (800) 972 0369 or 244-2100 • Open 10–5 Tue–Fri; 10–7 Sat–Sun; Closed Mon (except during school holidays) • W Admission**

This is the really big show. It's magic. It's a treat for the imagination. Houston is a city based on imagination—it was, after all, imaginary when the founders advertised for residents—but the Space Program was the ultimate act of imagination, and Space Center Houston's design, by Walt Disney Imagineering, does the voyage out from Earth proud. The exhibitions take visitors through the past, present, and future of NASA's Manned Space Program though spectacular interactive exhibits, and IMAX giant-format films. You can interact with real, live astronauts and see demonstrations of the latest equipment. You can also take a behind-the-scenes tram tour of Johnson Space Center, and see the podium President John F. Kennedy used when he made his "Go To the Moon" speech. Wear a space helmet. Land an 85-ton orbiter. Touch a rock brought back from the moon by one of our neighbors. Inspire the future astronauts in your family. Inspire *yourself*. Go!

## SPLASHTOWN USA

**I-45 North in Spring • 355-3300 • W variable • Admission**

For folks in the Woodlands and FM 1960 areas, this is the water amusement park of choice. It sprawls over 45 acres and features some 35 wet-and-wild rides In addition to the water slides, wave pools, and kiddie puddles, Splashtown offers a variety of special events, such as the annual laser light show.

## TEXAS GOLF HALL OF FAME

**1800 S. Millbend, The Woodlands (behind the 18th green, off the Tournament Players Course) • 364-7270 • Open 10–3 daily • Free**

A fascinating collection of antique golf memorabilia and tributes to the legends of the sport. Some of the greatest golfers in the history of the game came from around here, and you can learn about them—and more—in the museum's 15-minute film.

**TEXAS MEDICAL CENTER**
**Visitor Information Center • 1522 Braeswood • 790-1136**
**(Assistance center) • Tours 10 and 1 Mon–Fri; reservations**
**necessary; afternoon tours available for groups of ten or more**
**W • Free**

The Medical Center, a huge complex of buildings, is one of the world's great monuments to healing. Back in the 1960s and 1970s, it was best-known as the home base of the dueling celebrity heart surgeons Denton Cooley and Michael deBakey, but it exists at all largely because of someone who's little known, M.D. Anderson, for whom the famous cancer research center is named. (Also see Bibliography section.)

**TRANQUILITY PARK**
**Downtown in the block bounded by Smith, Walker, Rusk, and Bagby • W • Free**

Yes. They do spell it with one "L." That's the extraterrestrial spelling. In any event, the grassy embankments and gently sloping paved walkways of this park across from City Hall lure many downtown workers to lunch outside or simply to sit in the sun while the rest of the city buzzes by. The park is built around the pools and metallic columns of the Wortham Fountain. Named for the Sea of Tranquility, it honors the site of the first moon landing in 1969.

**TRANSCO TOWER AND WATERWALL**
**2800 Post Oak Boulevard • W • Free**

At 909 feet, this gorgeous, neo-Deco skyscraper by famed architect Philip Johnson is the tallest suburban office building in the world, and the 7,000-watt revolving light on top is visible from all over Houston. The building also has a 51st-floor observation deck, which is open during business hours. The view is interesting, but not as spectacular as the Waterwall across the green. This huge fountain sits behind a stone "scaenae frons," just like the ones you'd see in an ancient Roman theater. Lighted at night, it is a favorite of small children, romantic couples, and visitors of all descriptions.

## M. D. ANDERSON

Monroe Dunaway Anderson knew opportunity when he saw it. Although born in Jackson, Tennessee, in 1873, he got to Houston as soon as he could. Actually, M. D. was a banker just like his daddy, but he wasn't sure that banking was the business for him. So, around the turn of the century, young Monroe, along with his brother Frank and their boyhood friends the Clayton brothers, Ben and Will, headed west and went into the cotton business in Oklahoma.

Anderson, Clayton and Company soon moved to Houston, where it became the biggest cotton brokerage in the world, and made each of the partners pots and pots of money.

Monroe Anderson never married and didn't go out and about very much. Nobody outside the business community knew him well, but everybody knew his name after his will was read in 1939. The reclusive businessman had left his entire fortune—a then-staggering $19 million—plus a large parcel of land on the southern side of downtown, to the foundation established in his name and to the University of Texas.

Mostly, the foundation's trustees did simple good works like buying eyeglasses for indigent schoolchildren, and building the main library at the University of Houston. But in the 1950s, when the legislature decided that Texas needed a cancer research center, they voted to match the state's funds—*only* if the state would locate the center here in Houston, and coordinate with the then-imaginary Texas Medical Center.

In fact, without the Anderson trustees, it's doubtful that the Medical Center would exist. The same might be said of present-day Rice University. The Anderson Foundation made it possible for Rice to buy the interest in the Rincon oil field that accounts for a sizable share of the university's endowment. This huge sum keeps tuition low and Rice near the top of the nation's best buys in college education.

## WALLER COUNTY HISTORICAL MUSEUM

**906 Cooper, Brookshire, TX • 934-2826 • Open Wed and Fri 10–4; Sat 9–noon • Free (donations appreciated)**

This is a good introduction to the hard lives of early Texas pioneers. The museum houses furnishings and costumes of 19th-century rural people as well as medical instruments of the period (ouch!).

## WATERWORLD

**9001 Kirby Drive at South Loop, adjacent to Astroworld 799-1234 • W variable • Times and admission vary with season**

Waterworld is Astroworld's very own 15-acre beach. Why drive to Galveston when the wave machine at Waterworld creates waves up to four feet high for rafting and body surfing? One of the park's water slides can get riders going up to 40 miles per hour before "splashdown." There is also a lagoon swimming area and a children's area.

## WORTHAM CENTER TOUR

**Texas Avenue at Smith Street (downtown) • 546-0281 • Open 10, 11, and 2 Mon–Fri; 10 and 11 Sat; Closed Sun • W variable Admission**

Learn about the fascinating world behind the curtains through the Wortham's 45-minute backstage tour. See the 437,000-square-foot, $74 million (on time and under budget) performing arts center the way few others have. You need to make reservations 24 hours in advance, but after you've taken the tour you'll never look at a performance the same way again.

## WORTHAM IMAX THEATRE

**One Hermann Circle Drive • 639-4629 • W • Admission**

This is as close as most of us are ever going to get to outer space, the deepest rainforests, undersea coral reefs, or any of the other spectacular venues now being filmed by the special IMAX process. The giant screen, spectacular sound system, and 70-mm films are true wonders. Unfortunately, the entire city seems to have snapped to this fact. Call *well* in advance for reservations.

## GUS WORTHAM

Gus Wortham was born into a well-to-do Mexia, Texas, family in 1891. His father, John had been the Texas Secretary of State and served on the state prison board in Huntsville, where young Gus got to know J. A. Elkins, who was then the County Judge. Both would eventually move to Houston and become major players, but before that, the Wortham family spent some time in Dallas where John was in the lumber business and Gus became friends with another lumber tycoon, Jesse H. Jones. The pieces were all in place.

After attending several colleges including the University of Texas, Gus Wortham kicked around for a few years, eventually "finding himself" by working as a cowboy on a west Texas ranch owned by a family connection. He came home and went into the lumber business with his father, married Lyndall Finley, had two daughters, and then struck out on his own—sort of.

Having moved to Houston (as had Jesse Jones and J. A. Elkins), Wortham decided to go into the insurance business, another of his father's interests. In 1926, Wortham, Jones, Elkins, and J. W. Link, who had developed the Montrose area, each put up $75,000 and began the American General Insurance Company. Wortham devoted the rest of his working life to the company, which was worth $2.3 billion when he retired in 1972, and to civic activities.

With Jesse Jones increasingly away on government business during the 1930s and 1940s, the Houston establishment needed "one of their own" to represent their interests in state politics and to lead the way in civic boosting. The consensus heir to Jones, known as "Mr. Houston," was Gus Wortham.

He became the chairman of the Chamber of Commerce and served on the boards of just about every major Houston institution. He was instrumental in the construction of the Astrodome and numerous other civic projects, and was especially devoted to furthering the performing arts. He devoted much time and money to the Houston Symphony, Society for the Performing Arts, the Museum of Fine Arts, and Theater Under the Stars.

On his death at age 85 in the mid-1970s, his family requested donations be made in his memory to TUTS, the University of Houston, or to civic beautification.

## MARVIN ZINDLER
### KTRK-TV (Channel 13) • Evening newscasts

If you live in Houston—or have ever lived in Houston—you've heard of Marvin Zindler. Wearing a startlingly white wig and blue-tinted glasses, he appears nightly on the evening newscast shouting in a voice that any carny barker would envy. What he does is hard to classify. He came to fame by shutting down the "Best Little Whorehouse in Texas"—the original, not the musical based on his exploits. But nowadays he champions the underdog. On his *Action 13* segment, he proclaims "It's hell to be poor" as he cajoles doctors into fixing impoverished kids' cleft lips. He lists restaurants cited by the health department for "Slime in the Ice Machine," as the audience sings along with the "slime" theme song. On Fridays he wishes everyone "Good golf, good tennis, or whatever makes you happy." And that's why Marvin should be named a Houston civic treasure. There's nothing else like him anywhere. There probably isn't another city on earth that would appreciate him, and that's the whole point. In Houston, anything is possible, and anyone can be a star. Just ask Maaaaaarvin Zindler, EYE wit-niss news.

# CALENDAR OF ANNUAL EVENTS

Hey, come on. This is Houston. There's no excuse to sit at home. Somewhere in the Houston area there is something interesting happening just about every day of the year. Some of these festivals and performances come around on a regular basis, others are catch-them-while-you-can propositions. But be warned: Even the regulars sometimes happen on a slightly different date, so if you're interested in something, it's worth calling to check. Also keep an eye on the newspapers, both daily and weekly. Enjoy! (NOTE: All phone numbers are area code 713 unless otherwise stated.)

## JANUARY

**Dance Month at the Jewish Community Center of Houston.** Everything from local jazz dancers to traditional Israeli folk ensembles and African groups perform throughout the month. Many are world renowned. Because many events sell out, it's important to make reservations pronto. Prices vary, and both series and single tickets are available. Call 551-7255 for tickets, dates and times.

**Houston International Boat, Sport & Travel Show.** For all those who'd rather be sailing—or just on vacation—the International is your chance for a mental getaway. The show, which has been attracting crowds for more than 30 years, is the largest of its kind in the Southwest and will draw well over half a million visitors to the Astrohall/Astroarena/ExpoCenter complex during its run. Admission is about $5/less for kids. Call 526-6361 for days and times.

---

## IMAGES OF HOUSTON

*When Venetians come to America, they head straight to Houston. They feel comfortable here, our bayous remind them of their great canals. A lot of people in this world live with the roar of the ocean, in Venice and Houston we hear the more subtle music of the canal and the bayou.*

Max Apple
Houston novelist and screenwriter

---

**Bridal Extravaganza.** Unless you're planning to get married, or marry off your progeny, this might seem goofy. It isn't. It is a kind of one-stop shopping center for all those wedding essentials. More than 500 companies show off their wares—everything from the latest fashions to ice sculptures for the reception—under one roof at the George R. Brown Convention Center. Admission is about $7. Call 995-9206 for details.

**Houston Auto Show.** More than 500 examples of the hottest wheels in the world are on display at the Astrohall. Have a look at the latest cars, trucks, and vans as well as futuristic concept cars, and meet the numerous celebrities imported for the occasion. Admission is about $5/less with promotional discounts. Kids 12 and under free when accompanied by an adult. Call 799-9500 for dates and times.

**Dr. Martin Luther King, Jr. Day.** For those of us old enough to remember, it's shocking to note how young he would be still. Celebrate this great American's life and his famous dream with the MLK Birthday Parade through downtown and all-day festivities at Miller Outdoor Theater in Hermann Park. Free and open to all.

**The Marathon.** By now this annual event has become one of the premier long-distance races in the country. Largely because of the overwhelming community support, which includes bands, dancers, decorations, and lots of cheering spectators lining the route, the race draws thousands of entrants from all over the world. A favorite on the running circuit, the Houston-Tenneco Marathon has been a qualifying event for several nations' Olympic teams. Enjoy the "Hoopla," which was pioneered right here. It's a mixture of professional and not-ready-for-prime-time performers, ranging from jump-rope squads to rap singers to belly dancers, all trying to keep those runners heading toward that finish line. Entry fee for runners. Spectating is free. Call 757-2164 for day, time, and entry info.

**Winter Star Party.** Johnson Space Center Astronomical Society sponsors this family event at Challenger 7 Park near NASA. It's designed to introduce partygoers to our celestial neighbors. Spectacular views of the moon, Jupiter, and other planets may be seen through the society's telescopes, and there are videos, games, and prizes for the kids. Admission is free. Call 332-5157 for date and details.

**Houston Charity Cat Show.** If cats are your favorite furries, this show is just Purr-fection. You can visit with more than 700 kitties ranging from pampered pedigrees to household pets. There are training demonstrations. (Training? Cats? Alert the media!) There are also kitty costume contests and trick-cat competitions as well as vendors selling everything from grooming accessories to jewelry. Proceeds benefit animal charities. At the George R. Brown Convention Center. Admission about $5/less for kids and seniors. Call 776-8827 for days, times, and details.

**Super Bowl Sunday.** This is the biggest day of the year for couch-potato sports addicts. There are private Super Bowl parties all over town, and of course sports bars do a land-office business. Most will provide a fun atmosphere in which to watch the game, but look for the one at Wild West on Long Point. Proceeds from the cover charge there go to the Muscular Dystrophy Association. Call 465-7121 for details.

**Tour of Houston's Glenwood Cemetery.** The Greater Houston Preservation Alliance is deadly serious about its walking tours of the city. Glenwood, on Washington Avenue, was Houston's first private cemetery. It is also the final home of billionaire Howard Hughes; Charlotte Baldwin Allen, wife of Houston founder Augustus Allen; at least one governor, and several former mayors; to say nothing of flamboyant Shamrock Hotel developer Glenn McCarthy. Tickets are about $7. Call 236-5000 for date and time.

---

### IMAGES OF HOUSTON

*I am sitting now, writing this, under an unfriendly sky, color of cold granite, on a black iron bench meant to resemble a bower of ferns. I am in a crook in the elbow of the Allen Parkway and Montrose, where it is perpetually noisy—I imagine that at three in the morning cars still pour by with the distant sound of fast-running water.*

Rosellen Brown
Houston novelist

---

**International Piano Festival.** World-famous pianists join Houston's own Abbey Simon and winners of the Cliburn Prize at the University of Houston School of Music's exquisite piano festival. Master recitals are held in the Dudley Recital Hall, UH Central campus Entrance 16 off Cullen. Tickets about $12/less for students and seniors. Call 743-3167 for dates and performance schedule.

## FEBRUARY

**Lunar New Year.** Because Houston has a huge and diverse Asian community, the lunar new year has become quite a celebration. Many of this city's posh Asian restaurants offer magnificent multi-course banquets (reservations required), and there are children's events, dragon dances, and parades in several Asian shopping areas.

**Valentine Sea Turtle Open House.** The Kemp's Ridley sea turtle, a native of the Gulf, is in danger of extinction. Each Valentines Day, to help save the critters, the National Marine Fisheries Service releases hundreds of turtle hatchlings out in the Gulf in the hope

## HUGH ROY CULLEN

Hugh Roy Cullen's name, and the names of his family members, can be seen all over civic Houston. Cullen was a major philanthropist who started out in the classic Horatio Alger fashion as a poor country boy.

Born in 1881 in Denton County, Hugh Roy Cullen had very little schooling—which is ironic because he was the grandson of Ezekiel W. Cullen, known as the father of education in the Republic of Texas (and namesake of the E. Cullen Building at UH, home of the galaxy's longest registration lines).

When he was 16, Hugh Roy went to work for a cotton broker and learned the business. He left to start his own business a few years later. About that same time he married Lillie Cranz, and the two moved to Houston and began to raise their family of four daughters and a son.

Business prospered; soon Hugh Roy was speculating in real estate as well. In 1918, he went into the oil business where he specialized in drilling high-risk deep wells. He was so successful (among others, he brought in the Humble field and the O'Connor field) that he soon became known as the king of the wildcatters. He was co-owner of the South Texas Petroleum Company and founded the Quintana Petroleum Company. While working on one of these rigs near Edinburgh, Hugh Roy Cullen's only son, Roy Gustave, was killed in 1936. The family never really recovered emotionally from this terrible loss, and it was then that their philanthropy began, much of it in the form of memorials to the dead young man (such as the Roy Gustave Cullen building at the University of Houston).

Still, Hugh Roy Cullen remained a major, if backstage, player in Texas politics for almost 30 years. A militant opponent of the New Deal and supporter of the segregationist Dixicrat movement, in later life he backed Republicans, including Dwight D. Eisenhower.

Even his interest in politics couldn't compare to Cullen's interest in philanthropy. According to almost every reckon-

*(continued on next page)*

ing, by 1955 he had given away 90 percent of his fortune. In that year he set up the Cullen Foundation, and funded it with $160 million of his own money. He gave additional gifts of more than $10 million each to the University of Houston, which had been little more than a minor junior college when the Cullen family begain to donate these huge sums, and to various Houston hospitals. Hugh Roy Cullen died here on July 4, 1957.

that they will live long and prosper. To celebrate, the fish folks sponsor a day of festive events including name-the-turtle contests, food, kids games, and demonstrations. It's all at the National Marine Fisheries Service on Avenue U at 50th Street in Galveston. Call (409) 766-3523 for dates and details.

**Texas Home, Lawn & Garden Show.** If you have a home, there's something here to interest you. This monster show boasts booths, lectures, demonstrations, contests, and giveaways. Contractors, architects, decorators, landscapers, fire-ant killers, you name it. If it's somehow domestic, it's here at the George R. Brown Convention Center. Call 853-8000 for info.

**Houston Livestock Show & Rodeo.** In many ways, this is the biggest event of the year in Houston. For more than two weeks each winter, the city celebrates its western heritage in a really big way. It begins with the trail rides. Since 1952, when four men rode horseback from Brenham to Houston for what was then called the Fat Stock Show, the trail rides (there are now 8 of them) bring whole families on horseback from as far away as Cold Spring as well as visitors from all over the world. All the riders gather in Memorial Park, and the next morning parade through downtown in the Rodeo kick-off parade. The big event itself takes up the entire Astrodomain Complex and includes everything from a carnival, cattle exhibitions, and pig races to appearances by some of the biggest names in music. Admission is about $10/less for kids, but numerous promotional discounts are available. Call 791-9000 for information.

## IMAGES OF HOUSTON

*Houston Rodeo & Livestock Show ain't never seem the same since we come riding in from Arcola. All colored and correct. Long-sleeved shirts, cowboy hats, chaps, spurs, covered wagons, and a place all our own in Memorial Park. Ain't never seen that many niggahs in Memorial Park no way, least not at 4:30 in the morning. Perking coffee over open fires and warming each other with bourbon and one rodeo yarn after another.*

Ntozake Shange
Playwright and poet

**Mardi Gras.** The starting date of Mardi Gras varies with the Easter moon, (the real Fat Tuesday is always 41 days before Easter), but for celebratory purposes the calendar of Mardi Gras events usually kicks off in late February and runs for several weeks. Unlike the rowdy, drunken New Orleans version, most of Galveston's Mardi Gras is festive family fun—and it keeps getting bigger every year. In fact, to detail everything the Mardi Gras offers would take pages. Best bet is to contact the Galveston Convention and Visitors Bureau for a schedule of events. Admission to most is free. Call (800) 351-4236 or (409) 763-4311.

## MARCH

**Azalea Trail.** The surest sign of spring in Houston is this longtime tradition. For several weeks, generally in mid-March, Houston is glorious with azaleas. The River Oaks Garden Club takes advantage of the season to stage this two-weekend charity fund-raiser. It includes tours of Bayou Bend's fabulous gardens, the R.O. Garden Club's Forum of Civics garden, as well as the gardens of various private homes. Tickets may be purchased through local nurseries or the usual ticket outlets. Call 523-2483 for information.

**Saint Patrick's Day.** Even though the late, lamented Shamrock Hotel is history, March 17 is still the day when everyone is Irish. Official Houston celebrates with a grand parade on the weekend

closest to the date and unofficial Houston—mostly bars—celebrates all week. Downtown, at Allen's Landing, the Texas Army
fires cannons and bands play Irish music as the traditional "green-
ing" of Buffalo Bayou takes place. This involves more than just
dumping green dye in the water. The Parks Department gives away
free tree saplings to all who attend. Downtown restaurants feature
special menus (some with green beer) and at Grif's in Montrose,
the traditional two-day bash continues with a free bus ride to the
big parade along the Richmond Strip from Rice west to Unity. Call
528-9912 for details.

**Astroworld Opening Day.** If the kids (of all ages) are on spring
break, it must be time for Astroworld to open. Every year the
amusement park introduces at least one new major attraction,
which is unveiled on opening weekend. Spring break activities
include special concerts and contests. After the school holidays,
the park opens weekends through Memorial Day, then daily
through summer. Admission is steep, about $30/almost $20 for
kids, but numerous promotional discounts are available. Call 799-
1234 for info.

**Texas Brewers Festival.** Ever since small breweries returned to the
Lone Star state, "craft beer" has been growing in popularity. Now
the microbreweries—including Houston's own St. Arnold Brewing
(which was named after the patron saint of beer)—are celebrating.
The weekend-long event, held downtown on Market Square, offers
suds, grub from local restaurants, and music to chow down by. Call
686-9494 for information.

**Party on the Plaza Seasonal Kickoff.** Every spring and fall, there
are concerts on the plaza between Jones Hall and the Albert
Thomas Convention Center. Good regional bands of all sorts play,
and both food and drink are available. The crowd is after-work professional and a good time is had by all. Admission free. Call 621-
8600 for details.

# APRIL

**Baseball Season Opening Day.** The evil strike notwithstanding, for
many people this is the real New Year's Day. Hope for the Astros
still springs eternal. In April, at least, the World Series is still a real

## GLENN McCARTHY

Glenn Herbert McCarthy, one of Houston's most colorful characters ever, was born in the Spindletop oil field on Christmas Day in 1907. He weighed 12 and ¾ pounds. Clearly, he'd started as he meant to go on—*BIG!* One of his grandfathers' names was Lucky. He wasn't especially. Glenn's father was oil field trash and proud of it. A driller, he taught his son the trade.

When the family moved to Houston, Glenn lived at 1308 Welch and attended Lanier Junior High, where he was a hell of a football player. His pigskin career continued at a number of high schools and colleges including Rice, Tulane, and Texas A&M, all of which threw him out for drinking, fighting, or other "inappropriate" behavior. He was a born wildcatter.

By age 26, McCarthy had made $700,000 in the oil business. He spent every nickel on building a mansion. Pretty soon he was so deeply in debt that his creditors couldn't afford to let him go broke. But, not *complete* fools, they refused to let him write even a $5 check without a countersignature.

Undaunted, McCarthy kept drilling and by age 31 he was back on top again. By age 42, he was worth $212 million and was known worldwide as the "King of the Wildcatters."

Even that title wasn't enough for him. On St. Patrick's Day, 1949, McCarthy opened the Shamrock Hotel. It cost some $25 million to build and was a triumph of will and promotion over good business sense. Located "way out Main Street" on an empty prairie, it was made world-famous on opening day by the exploits of its owner/promoter.

To ensure a memorable event, McCarthy leased airplanes to fly in the press from all over the country. He invited—and got—more than 100 multimillionaires to attend, *and* he leased a special 16-car Santa Fe railroad train to haul in more than 100 Hollywood celebrities (including Dorothy Lamour, Erroll Flynn, and Pat O'Brien) to his three-day bash.

The opening was as crowded as the New York subway at rush hour and soon disintegrated into a huge, drunken brawl.

*(continued on next page)*

Nationwide radio programs, which were broadcasting live from the event, were knocked off the air. The stars were too drunk to talk and the millionaire oil men having fistfights in the lobby had unplugged the cables. Movie people passed out in the ballroom. The press had a field day, and author Edna Ferber used the affair as a pivotal setpiece for her novel, *Giant*, in which the character Jett Rink is a thinly disguised Glenn McCarthy. The movie version, starring James Dean as Jett/Glenn is worth watching for the Shamrock opening alone.

The real Glenn McCarthy died some years ago, and in one of those awful cases of Houston's self-inflicted amnesia, the Shamrock was torn down by a soulless Medical Center. The site is now, for the most part, a parking lot.

possibility. The ever-popular Hat Night promotion is often held in April, too. Call 799-9555 for schedule and ticket info.

**Doug Sanders Celebrity Golf Classic.** Each spring, local golf celeb Doug Sanders brings dozens of his famous pals to Houston to raise money for charity and to have fun playing golf. Past participants have included Clint Eastwood, Bob Hope, and several ex-presidents. Watching the high jinks is almost as much fun as playing. The tournament moves around among several locations. Call 864-3684 for details.

**Texas Crawfish Festival.** In Old Town Spring, they usually boil up more than 40,000 pounds of crawfish, then serve 'em with all the trimmings. While mudbugs are the featured attraction, there's also a carnival and lots of things to keep the kids happy. All the shops are open, so adults don't have to fight boredom either. Admission is about $3/less for kids. Call 353-9310 or (800) OLD-TOWN for further info.

**Houston International Festival.** This is the big daddy of spring festivals. Every year it salutes a different country, and for ten days it sprawls across the city involving everything from schools to the Museum of Fine Arts. Downtown along the banks of Buffalo Bayou, the festival grounds feature a number of stages offering musical performances of all kinds. Most are local groups or folk troups imported from the honored country, but there are always a handful of appearances by really big names. Admission is about $3/kids free, but there are a number of promotional discounts. Call HIF-0202 for event info.

---

### HOUSTON FACTOID:

*In 1850, forty-eight French people lived in Houston.*

---

**The Art Car Parade.** One of the most popular features of the Houston International Festival is "Roadside Attractions: The Artists' Parade." In this wacky event, cars, bikes, trucks and lawnmowers— anything on wheels as long as it's decorated to the max—wind through downtown, usually on the last weekend of the fest. Past entries have included one car entirely covered with hair (in curlers) and another that was, literally, on fire. Brave souls who prefer the best possible view of this lunacy can book reviewing-stand seats for about $8. Streetside spectating is free. Call HIF-0202.

**Japan Festival.** In the lovely Japanese Garden at Hermann Park, Houstonians can enjoy Japanese games for children, cultural arts demonstrations, as well as art exhibits and dance performances. There's also Japanese food for sale. Call 963-0121 for further information.

**Houston Women's Tennis Championship.** Some of the very best players in the world appear right here in the Bayou City at one of the premier tennis events in the United States. Past champions have included everyone from Chris Evert to Steffi Graf. If you want to see the big names going for the real points, this is the only sanctioned professional tennis tournament in Texas. Traditional site is the Westside Tennis Club. Call 953-1111 for details.

**Spring Westheimer Art Festival.** The Westheimer Colony Association, which has been sponsoring this strange, twice-a-year do for decades, keeps moving it around. Still, it always turns up somewhere in the vicinity of lower Westheimer and it always offers the best in bizarre people watching. The artists, potters and jewelry makers who exhibit their wares are really just an excuse to get out on a lovely spring afternoon. Call 521-0133 for info.

---

### HOUSTON FACTOID:

*The first recorded Japanese settlers in Houston came from a Japanese-sponsored rice farming program set up in nearby Webster in the early 1900s.*

---

**Pasadena Strawberry Festival.** Every year, on the weekend closest to San Jacinto Day (April 21), Pasadena hosts this t-riff down-home festival in honor of Sam Houston's victory and the strawberry harvest. Hard as it is to believe nowadays, Pasadena once was better known for its agriculture than its industry, and the town supplied much of the midwest with strawberries. Now the fest offers strawberry tastings, contests, games, rides, and lots and lots of food. Fun for the whole family. Call 472-1211 for details.

**Buffalo Bayou Regatta and the Anything That Floats Contest.** This is supposed to be Texas' largest long-distance canoe and kayak race, which is something of a miracle when you consider the location. For years, Buffalo Bayou was one of the most polluted bodies of water in the nation. Now, thanks to the Buffalo Bayou Coalition, which benefits from the regatta, it is clean enough to play on. To prove it, they stage this contest with divisions for both serious canoeists and for families just having fun, and the regatta also features a Corporate Cup Challenge for teams from local businesses. The parade of entries in the goofy "Anything That Floats Contest" is held just below the Sabine Street Bridge near downtown. Prizes are awarded. Call 520-3022 for entry fees and information.

**"Buck-a-Book Sale."** Under whatever its official name this time around, this is *the* event of the year for bibliophiles. Staged every

---

## IMAGES OF HOUSTON

*I set out to sail Buffalo Bayou on a four-by-eight sheet of three-quarter-inch plywood powered by eight mighty Weed-Eaters, and I saw many strange and wonderful things. I saw an egret and then another egret and a turtle and a refrigerator without a door on it and a heron and a possum and an upside-down '52 Pontiac. And I said to myself, this blessed stream contains many strange and wonderful things.*

Donald Barthelme
Houston writer

---

spring to benefit the Houston Public Library, the event offers thousands of books, donated both by the library and by its friends. All are available at bargain prices. Rare books are auctioned off at an admission-only event the night before the sale proper. Lately, the sale has been held at the Astroarena, but it has been held in several other locations. Call 247-2222 for dates and details.

**WorldFest/Houston International Film Festival.** If you love movies, this is your event. The film festival has gone through many changes, but it is still here thanks in no small part to founder Hunter Todd, who miraculously kept it going through some very lean times. Presenting 50 or so foreign and American independent films over the course of 10 days, it gives Houstonians a chance to see works unlikely to play the local multiplex. The venue has changed a number of times, so check for this year's site. Both individual screening tickets and festival passes are available. Call 965-9955.

---

## MAY

---

**Cinco de Mayo.** Once upon a time, in a misguided fit of imperialism, Emperor Napoleon III of France tried to take over Mexico. Naturally, this did not please the Mexican people. And on May 5, 1862, they defeated the French forces in the Battle Puebla. Ever since then, Cinco de Mayo has been celebrated. In this country, Mexican-Americans stage numerous festivities on the weekend

---

## IMAGES OF HOUSTON

*I quite like these warm baths, these warm* walking *baths.*

actor Alan Bates, star of *Unnatural Pursuits,*
which was filmed in Houston,
(on working outdoors in the Houston summer).

---

nearest the fifth of May. There's a parade through downtown and an evening of song and dance at Miller Outdoor Theatre in Hermann Park, to say nothing of concerts, dances, fiestas, and food fairs in Hispanic neighborhoods. There's also a big do at the George R. Brown Convention Center. Admission is usually free. Call 853-8000 for details.

**Pan African Cultural Festival.** The sights and sounds of Africa and the African diaspora are on view at Hermann Park's Miller Outdoor Theater. Everyone is welcome to this family-oriented event. There will be music, and traditional storytelling, as well as art displays, games and special events for the kids. Admission is free. Call 520-3290 for details.

**Texas National Handcar Championship.** Handcars are usually seen only in silent-film comedies. This is your big chance to see the real thing—and in action, too! Bands and other entertainers keep things lively as teams from businesses and civic organizations compete for bragging rights on the trolley tracks in Galveston's historic Strand District. The winners get the chance to compete in the national championships held later in the year in California. Galveston's Railroad Museum, which is sponsoring the event, gets the participants' entry fees. Spectator admission is free. Call (409) 765-5700 for information.

**Galveston Historic Homes Tour.** For two weekends in mid-May, some of the lovely, historic homes on Galveston island are open to the public. These range from simple bungalows to elaborate Victorian splendor. The Galveston Historical Foundation, which sponsors the event, provides information at its headquarters on the

---

**HOUSTON FACTOID:**

*The motto on Houston's city seal is "Where 11 Railroads Meet the Sea."*

---

Strand, and tickets may be purchased at each of the participating homes during the tour, and at the Strand Visitors Center, or Ashton Villa. Admission is about $15. Call (409) 762-TOUR for details.

**Wildflower Season.** Now appearing on roadsides and fields near you. Every time you see this gorgeous natural display, remember to thank Lady Bird Johnson. Through her inspiration, Texas leads the nation in beautification with native flowers. By early May there are blossoms everywhere, but the schedule does vary with the weather. On a fine spring weekend, urbanites flock to the countryside around Houston to revel in the blooming of bluebonnets (the state flower), margaritas, and Indian paintbrushes. A drive northwest of Houston on U.S. 290 will give you an excellent opportunity to stop and smell the flowers. While it is not illegal to pick them, it is illegal to trample on private property to do so. The Department of Public Safety has info on wildflowers every spring. Call (512) 465-2080 for details.

**Historic Heights Home Tour.** Spend Mother's Day weekend seeing where and how mothers and their families lived at the turn of the century. Some of the tour is guided, and other parts—including the designer showcase location where noted interior designers' and architects' room vignettes are on display—are self-guided. Call 868-0170 for admission fee and information.

---

**HOUSTON FACTOID:**

*News anchor Dan Rather grew up at 1432 Prince Street in Heights Annex.*

---

**Spring Opera Festival.** Houston Grand Opera has a well-deserved national reputation, both for the quality and the audacity of its productions. If you can't afford to see them in the splendor of the Wortham Center, this is your opportunity to enjoy one of HGO's lavish spectacles. Every spring, the Opera stages eight performances at Miller Outdoor Theatre in Hermann Park. Admission is free. Bring a picnic blanket and sit on the hill.

**Memorial Day.** It's the semi-official start of summer, and there are celebrations all over town. But it's a good idea to remember what we're celebrating. The former Decoration Day is a legacy of the Civil War, but has come to be the commemoration of all U.S. war dead. That's why there's a wreath-placing memorial service at the *Battleship Texas* and a service at the Houston National Cemetery. Call 479-2411 for times and information.

**Pin Oak Charity Horse Show.** For more than 40 years, this has been the highlight of the year for the equestrian set. Entries from across the United States and some foreign countries compete in events for saddlebred, hunter-jumper, walking, and other types of horses. Almost a quarter of a million dollars in cash and prizes are given and proceeds benefit children's charities. Call 578-PONY for dates and ticket prices.

---

### HOUSTON FACTOID:

*The mysterious death of equestrienne Joan Robinson Hill, a Pin Oak competitor, became known as the* Blood and Money *case, the most notorious mystery in modern Houston history.*

---

## JUNE

---

**Spring Music Festival.** In Old Town Spring, the reconstruction of a turn-of-the-century railroad town that's become a considerable tourist attraction, there are a couple of places, such as Wunche Bros., that regularly present some of the best in local music, so musicians know the town well. In early summer, the best of the best in local country singers and rock-and-rollers turn up for this ever-growing event. Of course there are crafts, T-shirts, and lots of eats, too. Call 353-9310 for dates and times.

**Thunder on the Brazos.** Now here's an interesting excuse for a festival. The Battle of Fort Velasco took place near Surfside on June 26, 1832. The Texian colonists fought with Mexican forces in a run-up to the Texas Revolution. The fest is both a celebration of the area's heritage and a fund-raiser for a historical reconstruction of the fort. Featuring a barbecue cookoff, contests for kids, and casino nights for adults, there also will be a carnival and a petting zoo. Admission is free. Call (409) 233-1531 for dates and times.

**Juneteenth.** Slavery was over in Texas, but people didn't know it until Union General Gordon Granger read the Emancipation Proclamation on June 19, 1865, in Galveston. Since that day, African-Americans have celebrated the day as "Juneteenth." While for many this is a family holiday celebrated with picnics and reunions, Houston also hosts a wide range of public Junteenth events. In the morning, the Juneteenth parade winds through downtown to City Hall. And there are daylong celebrations in and around the Miller Outdoor Theatre in Hermann Park. Admission is free and open to all. Civic leader Al Edwards also hosts a Juneteenth Festival at the George R. Brown Convention Center. The all-day extravaganza includes everything from music to a health fair. Eats are available, and the celebration ends with fireworks in front of the convention center. Call 525-5960 for details.

## EMMETT J. SCOTT

Emmett Scott, who was born in 1873, in a cottage in the backyard of a white family at the corner of Main and Bell streets near downtown Houston, went on to a distinguished career that included appointment as a special advisor to President William Howard Taft. Scott Street is named in his honor.

*(continued on next page)*

As a child, Scott had one real advantage. In an era when most African-Americans were illiterate, both of his parents could read and write. They encouraged him to get the best education possible. He graduated from Houston Academy, a private school for blacks, when he was only 16, and attended Wiley College in Marshall, Texas, the state's oldest black institution of higher learning.

Scott went to work for the *Houston Post* newspaper in the late 1800s. Although hired as a janitor, he quickly became a reporter and went on to found and edit the city's first black newspaper, which is now known as the *Houston Informer.* Married to Venora Baker of Galveston, and with her raising their five children in those segregated times, he saw the need for a public library open to black children. He used his powers of persuasion to convince the Carnegie Corporation to pay for the first library for Houston's African-American community.

Booker T. Washington of the world-famous Tuskegee Institute in Alabama became aware of the young Houstonian's talents and hired him as his personal secretary. In the 19th century, this was an extremely prestigious position. Young men employed as personal secretaries were actually serving a kind of apprenticeship under the mentorship of a powerful man.

Scott's intelligence and business expertise led to his becoming the first national secretary of the National Business League, which Booker T. Washington founded in 1900, and by 1909 he was a member of American Commission to the Republic of Liberia.

During World War I, he was a special assistant to the Secretary of War and wrote two books about the role of African-Americans in that conflict. He also authored the *Red Book of Houston: A Compendium of Social, Professional, Religious, Educational and Industrial Interests of Houston's Colored Population.* This is probably the most important work in existence detailing the bygone world of turn-of-the-century black Houston's wealthy professional class, thriving businesses, and rich community life.

He wrote many other books and articles as well as serving as a public relations advisor to four Republican presidential candidates. Emmett Scott ended his career as the first black vice president of the YMCA. He died in Washington, D. C., in 1958.

**Juneteenth Blues Festival.** Houston has produced some wonderful blues artists, and many of them, from the legendary to the up-and-coming, gather on the weekend nearest June 19th to celebrate freedom day in Texas. Houston performance sites include Miller Outdoor Theatre and Sam Houston Park (near City Hall). Many are free, a few are not. Call 525-6740 for dates and times.

---

### HOUSTON FACTOID:

*Although no longer in existence, the first major black-owned record label in the country, Duke-Peacock Records, was formed in Houston around 1948.*

---

**Bay Day.** This family-oriented festival held at La Porte's Sylvan Beach Park is designed to increase public awareness of Galveston Bay. Featured events include music, a carnival, a gumbo cook-off, and exhibits that introduce festgoers to the ecology of the area. The weekend-long shindig ends with fireworks above the bay. Admission is about $2–$4/less for kids and seniors. Call 868-3383 for details and directions.

**Galveston Caribbean Carnival Extravaganza.** From one island culture to another. The Galvestonians and their neighbors across the water know how to celebrate. There are colorful costumes and costume contests, steel bands, reggae and calypso music, as well as a parade and a marketplace for arts and crafts; drinks and island eats. Call (409) 942-9042 for further information.

**Alabama-Coushatta Reservation Pow-wow.** A real pow-wow is a weekend-long event that's nothing like the foolish junk you see in old western movies. The gathering of native people features traditional foods and crafts, as well as competitions for singers and the more-than-250 dancers who may be seen in their colorful, traditional regalia at the grand-entry ceremony each evening. Admission is about $5/less for kids. Parking is free, and please bring your own lawn chairs. Call (409) 563-4391 for dates, times, and tickets.

**Jewish Theater Festival.** The Jewish Community Center on South Braeswood hosts a monthlong series of works by Jewish playwrights and/or featuring Jewish themes. Past entries have included *The Wizards of Quiz*, a play about the TV game-show scandals of the 1950s that inspired Robert Redford's film *Quiz Show*, and several musicals featuring the works of Jerome Kern and Irving Berlin. Call 551-7255 for information.

---

### HOUSTON FACTOID:

*The University of Houston owes its Central Campus to philanthropists Ben Taub and Julius Settegast, who donated the land in 1939.*

---

**Ballet In The Park.** They've performed in China. They've performed in Europe. They wowed New York. Now you can take the whole family to see the world-class Houston Ballet absolutely free of charge. Each summer the ballet stages a series of free performances onstage at Miller Outdoor Theatre. All shows are full-out productions. Down-front seating at Miller Theatre is available by free ticket, but the best bet is a blanket, a picnic, and lots of bug spray. Call 523-6300 for dates and programs.

**Sounds Like Fun.** Throughout the month of June, and especially in the week leading up to the Fourth of July, the Symphony sponsors a special series of free programs for children at community centers and churches. The Miller Outdoor Theatre series, held at night, offers family entertainment, such as marches and television-show theme songs, in addition to popular classical works. Call 224-4240 for further information.

**Asian Performing Arts Gala.** Downtown at the Wortham Center you can enjoy the classical, folkloric, and contemporary arts of China, India, Indonesia, Japan, Korea, Pakistan, the Philippines, Polynesia, Thailand, and Vietnam. All are welcome at this happy addition to Houston's ethnic festival scene where there'll be

---

**HOUSTON FACTOID:**

*Houston's first Chinese residents (they numbered seven) were reported in the 1880 census. The first Chinese-American born in Houston was Lincoln Yuan.*

---

music, dance, and crafts as well as activities for kids. Sponsored by Asian Arts Houston. Call 995-8025 for ticket info and times.

## JULY

**Fourth of July.** Happy Birthday to the U.S. of A! In many other countries, the national holiday is a solemn occasion. Not here. Even the Founders wanted our Independence Day celebrated in a festive way, and Houston isn't about to let them down. There is some kind of fun happening in every corner of the city.

**Freedom Fest.** This is the big one. Stretching along the banks of Buffalo Bayou from downtown west to Taft Street and beyond, the Freedom Fest offers big name rock and country-music entertainment all day long and a fireworks display after dark. Please take note: Because the crowds are so enormous, security on the roped off grounds is tight. In what might seem like an oxymoronic set of rules for a Freedom Fest, the organizers forbid: alcoholic beverages, glass, hibachis or outdoor grills, fireworks or weapons, pets, and audio or video recorders, but they suggest you do bring sunscreen, lawn chairs, ice chests, food and drink, water, blankets, mosquito repellent, and hats. Streets nearby are closed. Parking is a nightmare. Take Metro. Call 227-3100.

**July Fourth at AstroWorld.** Festive doings all day and performances by ROTC units and bands throughout the park, ending with a band concert and fireworks spectacular at the Southern Star Ampitheater. Admission is included with regular Astroworld admission. Call 799-3295 for details.

**The Children's Museum.** Kids can make their own flags, listen to patriotic music, and hear stories of the country's birth. Admission $3–$5. Call 522-1138 for times.

**Houston Symphony Fourth of July Concert.** The city's most traditional celebration at Miller Outdoor Theatre attracts large crowds, many of whom come early and picnic. The evening concert features loved favorites such as John Phillip Sousa marches, the music of Leroy Anderson and Stephen Foster, and, as a rousing finale, Tchaikovsky's 1812 Overture complete with cannons. A spectacular fireworks display ends the evening. Free and open to all.

**Cynthia Woods Mitchell Pavilion.** The Houston Symphony repeats its Fourth of July program in The Woodlands. Admission is free. Call 363-3300 for day and time.

**"Tranquil Celebration."** As an antidote to Freedom Fest, the Houston Parks and Recreation Department and the Heritage Society sponsor a quiet, old-fashioned celebration in downtown's Sam Houston Park. There are kite-flying contests, face-painting, tours of the historic homes in the park, and patriotic music on the bandstand. Admission is free. Call 227-3300 for date and time.

**Galveston Celebrations.** Fourth of July events on the island range from a traditional band concert and a parade to the gorgeous beachfront fireworks display. There are free events in all the pub-

---

### IMAGES OF HOUSTON

*Up from the waters, a lush green*
*From the bayou from the landing*
*The urban the lush geology lapidiary layers peel*
*First banks then markets horizontal*
*Shops hotels then Banks*
*In constant replicate year by year . . .*

Lorenzo Thomas
Houston poet

lic parks, and a special patriotic concert and a children's parade in the plaza behind historic Ashton Villa. Moody Gardens hosts a party, at the Oleander Bowl on the grounds. Call (800) 582-4673 for info. The fireworks display over the water is best seen from Seawall Boulevard, and the annual Independence Day Parade is best seen on Broadway from 6th Street to 24th Street. Call (800) 351-4236 for parade and fireworks info.

**Clear Lake Fourth of July.** In the Clear Lake area, there's a parade in Crosby, and a carnival in Clear Lake Park, but the really big show is the fireworks shot off from the middle of the lake. As the bombs burst in air, a local radio station simulcasts patriotic music. It's a wonderful effect. Best viewing is from Clear Lake Park on NASA Road 1. Call 488-7676 for details.

**Lake Conroe Boat Parade.** Decorate your craft in red, white, and blue, then join the parade that route winds along the western shoreline to the FM 1097 bridge, crosses to the eastern side of the lake, and turns south, ending at Lake Conroe Park on Texas 105 for judging. Entry is free. All boaters welcome. Call (800) 283-6645 or (409) 756-6644 for information.

**Deer Park Fourth Fest.** This weekend-long celebration includes everything from a softball tournament to a sand castle contest. In Dow Park there's a carnival, games for the kids, arts-and-crafts, and lots of food, music celebrating and a fireworks grand finale. Call 478-2050 for information.

---

### HOUSTON FACTOID:

*Deer Park resident Chelsi Smith won the 1995 Miss Universe crown at the contest held in Namibia, southwest Africa.*

---

**Friendswood Fourth of July Celebration.** This is one of the longest-running fests in the area. There's a fun run, a parade, music, and a carnival at Stevenson Park during the day, and a military flyover, patriotic music, and a laser show and fireworks in the evening at Friendswood High School's football stadium. Call 482-3245 for details.

**Old Town Spring Fourth of July Parade.** Watching an old-fashioned Independence Day parade on the streets of this restored, turn-of-the-century village is a real treat. Afterward, there are musical performances, clowns, and rides for the kids and shopping for the grownups. Call 353-9310 for day and time.

**SplashTown July Fourth.** Throughout the day, there are live music performances at the Wild Wave pool. (We can only hope their instruments are acoustic.) At sunset, the water park will host a fireworks display. Admission to everything is about $16/less for kids. Call 355-3300 for details.

**George Ranch Historical Park Traditional July Fourth.** Here at the ranch, it's always the 19th century. Enjoy games and contests from the days when America was only 100 years old. Admission is about $5/less for kids and seniors. Call 545-9212 for information.

**Great Texas Mosquito Festival.** In Clute, they don't have mountains or other attractions, but they do have plenty of mosquitoes—and a great sense of humor. They also have what is probably the known universe's only Mosquito Festival. Willie-Man-Chew, the beloved 25-foot inflatable mosquito, presides over the event from his throne next to the outdoor dance floor and beer booth. Attractions include the world-famous Skeeter Beater Baby Crawling contest, concerts by the Ramsey III prison unit choir, the naming of Mr. and Mrs. Mosquito Legs, and the Mosquito Calling contest. Admission is about $5/less for kids and seniors. Call (409) 265-8392 for details.

---

**HOUSTON FACTOID:**

*According to mosquito control experts, in the marshy areas outside of town there is a "Googleplex of mosquitoes. A Googleplex being the largest number ever devised by humans. A zillion to the zillionth power."*

**Fulshear Follies.** People around here get pretty crazy in the summer heat. That must be how the folks in Fulshear came up with Cow Patty Bingo, one of the major attractions at the Follies. See, there's this official Bingo cow out there in the official Bingo field and if she . . . (ahem) relieves herself on your number, you win. Other events include the Texas Regional Lawn Mower Races and major chili and barbecue cook-offs with thousands of dollars in prizes. Of course there are also arts-and-crafts booths, carnival rides, live music, and a trail ride. Admission is free. Parking is about $2.

**Moon Day.** On July 20, 1969, human beings finally arrived on another world. And what was the first thing they said when they got there? "HOUSTON, the Eagle has landed." The date should be a holiday. Celebrate by going to NASA.

---

### IMAGES OF HOUSTON

*Remember a night in deep summer, nineteen hundred sixty-nine? The television bloomed blue in the dark and outside a light hung like a pale disc in the dark fold of sky. Our city was walking on the moon!*

Susan Wood
Houston Poet

---

**Market Square Walking Tour.** There isn't much left of historic Houston, a city with a bad case of amnesia, but most of the surviving structures such as the 1884 Cotton Exchange Building, are downtown in the vicinity of Market Square. The Greater Houston Preservation Alliance, which must feel like the Dutch boy with his finger in the dike, conducts guided walking tours. A number of these have a theme, like the life of Charlotte Baldwin Allen, an heiress who bankrolled her husband, Augustus, and his brother John's purchase of the land that became Houston. Tickets are about $7. Call 216-5000 for dates and details.

**Houston Summer Boat Show.** Even out on the water it's too darn hot. But inside the air conditioned George R. Brown Convention Center, there's everything you need to outfit your boat for those autumn afternoons. The exhibit includes watercraft of all types, hundreds of boating accessories, plus special seminars and clinics. Admission is about $5/less for kids. Call 526-6361.

**Slavic Heritage Festival.** Others might be bigger, louder, or better known, but this is Houston's oldest ongoing ethnic festival. There's music, dancing, cultural booths and displays, and of course food and drink galore at the University of St. Thomas. The fest celebrates the Houston area's many Bosnians, Croatians, Czechs, Poles, Serbs, Slovenes, and Ukrainians. Admission is about $2/kids free.

**Symphony Summer Festival.** This is your chance to hear the world-famous Houston Symphony Orchestra away from the concert hall. The programs are chosen with those sultry summer nights at Miller Outdoor Theatre in mind. Bring the brie and the picnic blanket. Admission free. Call 224-4240 for dates and times.

## AUGUST

**Eyesores Tour.** The Orange Show Foundation, which has an unerring sense of the bizarre, presents this guaranteed eyeful of ugly. Hunker down for a hallucinatory experience of Houston's most execrable taste as the "Show's" magic bus takes visitors on a tour of sites voted Houston's most aesthetically offensive. Food and drink are part of the deal. A good time is had by all, but bus space books up fast. Reserve your spot pronto. Call 926-6368 for date, time, and ticket information.

**Ballunar Liftoff Festival.** Perhaps the most beautiful festival of the summer takes place at Rocket Park, next door to Space Center Houston. Dozens of huge, gorgeously colored hot-air balloons lift off in various competitions. In early evening, when all of them take off at once, it is an absolutely spectacular sight. After dark comes the "Balloon Glow" event in which the pilots fire up the propane jets inside their balloons, which are still tethered to the ground, creating what looks like dozens of huge candles. There are also activities for kids, live entertainment, arts and crafts, lots of food, and aviation equipment displays. Admission is free. Parking at Space Center Houston is $2. Call 244-2105 for dates and details.

**Houston Shakespeare Festival.** It's hot. It's buggy. It's free. When Miller Outdoor Theatre hosts The Bard's plays, they are being performed in what must be close to the original conditions. The crowd is here to be entertained, not just edified, and much more often than not, it is. Best way to enjoy the fun and interesting festival productions is with a picnic on the hill in Hermann Park. Call 520-3291 for information.

**The Blessing of the Fleet.** Once upon a time, the blessing was little more than a prayer for a bountiful catch, the safety of the sailors and the boats, and that there might be enough fish left in the ocean to reproduce for the following catch. Now it's a festival as well. This Kemah/Seabrook extravaganza offers parades on both land and water, arts and crafts, lots of food, a street dance, and a carnival midway. The blessing itself takes place on Sunday afternoon as boats parade through the Clear Creek channel. Call 488-7676 for dates and details.

---

### HOUSTON FACTOID:

*The third-largest fleet of pleasure boats in the nation is moored in the Clear Lake area. Only the fleets at Los Angeles and the Chesapeake Bay are larger.*

---

**Houston International Jazz Festival.** Sponsored by the Jazz Heritage Society of Texas, this is one of the largest jazz festival in the Southwest and attracts many of the biggest names in the field. In a series of events scattered throughout town all month long, including the Mayor's Jazz Brunch at the Wyndham Warwick Hotel. Tickets are about $50. Call 227-8706. But there are plenty of other concerts and workshops offering something for everyone from kids to old-time cool cats. The main spot to watch is Sam Houston Park in downtown. Admission there is free. Call 520-3290 for information.

**Downtown Tunnel Hike.** Why broil your brains on the Memorial Park jogging trail when you can exercise in the air-conditioned comfort of The Park shopping center? This downtown mall is the starting point for an underground adventure. The hiking is non-competitive and kids are welcome. The extensive tunnel system under the dowtown skyscrapers is decorated with various themes. Admission varies. Call 654-HIKE for details.

**AstroWorld Series of Dog Shows.** Yes. The dog days of summer really are here. Thousands of pooches from all over the U.S., Mexico, and Canada have turned the Astrohall and Astroarena into a giant doghouse. There are contests, obedience competitions, and lots of doggie goods on sale. Tickets are about $7/less for kids and seniors. Call 791-9069 for dates and times.

**Happy Birthday Houston.** We live in a unique town. This is probably the only city on earth that began life as a newspaper ad. On August 30, 1836, J. K. and A. C. Allen, brothers from New York, took out an ad in a Texas newspaper announcing their wonderful new metropolis of Houston. Only trouble was, it didn't exist. The Allens were real estate speculators, and they were trying to drum up interest in their property. Obviously, they did. These days, the founda-

---

## IMAGES OF HOUSTON

*We are a city. And a city to any state is a thing apart, with its own definitions of self and style and what the good life means. We are closer in fact to Detroit than to Conroe. They are in many ways the same, cities. With few to call it their naturalborn home, a city is a refuge for hoboes and orphans, for magicians and hustlers and people doing various kinds of one-night stands. City dwellers dream of an earlier time when life was easier surely, warmer surely, better surely in some long-ago hoped-for way which they hope someday to return to, if things pan out. Restless people live in cities.*

Beverly Lowry
Southern Novelist

tion of the city is commemorated with a posh dinner at one of the city's major hotels and a presentation at Allen's Landing on Buffalo Bayou where Main Street crosses it on the north side of downtown. There are also birthday activities in historic Sam Houston Park at lunch time, when civil servants and office workers can sing the birthday song and share free cake. Call 523-5050 for details.

# SEPTEMBER

**Galveston Labor Day Weekend.** The end of summer means one last chance for that beach party, and the island is happy to play host. There are always special beach activities geared to the family crowd. Remember, except for designated areas, all the island beaches are alcohol-free. On the Bay side, The Strand hosts musical events throughout the weekend and Moody Gardens gets into the act with evening activities. Many activities are free, but Stewart beach parking is $5. Call (800) 351-4236 for info.

**Labor Day Ranch Reunion.** George Ranch Historical Park in Fort Bend County holds an annual end-of-summer shindig that features events such as a chuck wagon cook-off and old-time music. There's also a rodeo in the ranch's 65,000-square-foot covered arena. Admission is about $5/less for kids and seniors. Call 545-9212 or 343-0218 for details.

**The Mediterranean Festival.** A hugely popular ethnic fest that presents the cultures of a number of Mediterranean countries, all without leaving Southwest Houston. Music and dancing on the grounds of St. George Orthodox Church include performances by groups such as the Houston Balalaika Society, the Hellenic Folk Dancers of Houston, and local belly dancers. (Real belly dancing is an ethnic art, not a carnival act.) The petting zoo, featuring Monty the Python and Habebe the Camel, is a big hit with the kids, and of course there's mountains of authentic Mediterranean food. Admission is about $2/free if you bring two or more canned-food items. Call 665-5252 for dates and details.

**Caribbean Weekend.** Celebrate the cooler weather with the annual, downtown Caribbean Festival. There's a colorful parade and then everyone adjourns to Tranquility Park and Hermann Square for fun and food. If this fest's wonderful reggae and calypso music don't get you up and dancing, you must be dead. Admission is free. Call 227-3100 for dates and times.

**The Fort Bend County Fair and Rodeo.** If the big do in the Astrodome is too Hollywood for you, this might be more what you're looking for. Real cowboys and real local kids compete for prizes, and the fair is real down-home. Proceeds go to college scholarships for Fort Bend County students. Call 342-6171 for dates, times, and directions.

**The Garden Club of Houston's Bulb and Plant Mart.** This is the big deal for all those whose refrigerators are filled with bulbs instead of vegetables. Parking around the Metropolitan Multi-Service Center on West Gray can be horrific. Proceeds go to beautification and environmental projects. Call 871-8887, 621-2395, or 975-7147 for details.

**Party on the Plaza.** With the return of cooler weather, it's Party time downtown. Office workers and others can kick back every Thursday evening. The outdoor mixer is held just opposite Jones Hall and bands range from jazz and blues to all-out rock. Beer and wine are available, and the crowd is young professional. Admission is free. Call 227-3300 for dates and bands.

**Egyptian Festival.** Another wonderful, fall ethnic festival, the Egyptian introduces Houstonians to the wonders of this ancient civilization and to the food, music, and dance of present-day Egypt. Admission to the grounds of St. Marks Coptic Orthodox Church is free. Call 669-0311 for dates and times.

**Fiestas Patrias.** This is the Mexican version of Fourth of July. And whether your roots are south of the border or not, it's a big-time fun celebration. A colorful parade through downtown kicks things off, and a festival featuring hot-air balloon demonstrations and dance contests—to say nothing of fabulous food, music, a formal

---

## HOUSTON FACTOID:

*Unlike San Antonio and many other Texas towns, Houston never was a Spanish or Mexican settlement. The census of 1850 showed only six Mexican-born Houstonians. Today, this is our largest ethnic group.*

ball, and the presentation of a distinguished Mexican-American citizen award. Most events are free. For details in English, call 350-3907. Call 993-0596 for Spanish language info.

**Gatorfest.** In a manner of speaking, the folks in Anahuac, in Chambers County, had a lemon—so they made lemonade. The area is home to more alligators than people, so they created a festival to celebrate alligator hunting season. There are prizes for the biggest catches and for alligator tail cooked in a variety of ways. Fortunately, there are more-traditional eats as well as a beer garden overlooking Trinity Bay, and bands play everything from rock and country to zydeco and mariachi. Admission is about $5/less for kids and seniors. Call (409) 267-4190 for details.

**Pasadena Livestock Show and Rodeo.** Close to home, at the Pasadena Fair Grounds, is one of Texas' best real rodeos. While it lacks the glitz of Houston's big show, that's what makes it popular. The barbecue cook-off doesn't hurt either. Tickets for rodeo performances are about $5–$7. Call 487-0240 for dates and times.

---

## OCTOBER

---

*October is festival month in Houston. If something can be celebrated in this part of the world, this is the month we'll do it. There are literally dozens of fests each weekend. Here are some of the biggest and best.*

**Texas Renaissance Festival.** For decades now, Houstonians have been traveling back in time to a very Texas version of the late Middle Ages. Cheeky lads, bawdy lasses, and the ever-popular roasted turkey legs await at the festival grounds near Plantersville. Lords and ladies—including King Henry VIII and his court in full Renaissance regalia—stroll around the series of interconnected "villages" while jugglers, minstrels, and acrobats thread their way through the crowd. Visitors, too, are encouraged to come in costume. There are stages featuring early music and Shakespearean theatrical performances, but impromptu efforts by the singing executioners, the "mud show men," and other unusual acts attract their own crowds of onlookers. Simple games such as the centuries-old Jacob's Ladder prove every bit as entertaining for kids as Mortal Kombat, and of course there's more food than all of Europe consumed in the 15th century. The festival runs for at least six weekends on its own 237-acre site north of Houston. Admission is about $15/less for kids and seniors, but there are numerous promotional discounts available. Call (800) 458-3435 for days, times, ticket deals, and directions.

**Czech Fest.** Lots of folks are surprised to discover that Texas has one of the largest concentrations of Czechs in the country. This weekend-long festival has been going for more than half a century, and it celebrates the heritage of the Czech farmers who helped settle the Crosby area. There's always lots of music and dancing, to say nothing of barbecue. And, we trust, some Pivo. (The Czechs are, after all, the world's greatest beermakers.) There are also old-country games, arts-and-crafts booths, and a petting zoo for the kids. The fest takes place on the Crosby Fairgrounds, about a 25-minute drive north of downtown off U.S. 90. Admission to the dance is about $6/kids less. Other events free. Call the Crosby Chamber of Commerce, 328-6984, for dates and times.

**Galveston Octoberfest.** Galveston Island celebrates its diverse cultural heritage with food, dancing, and music one weekend at its fifth annual Octoberfest. Under a canopy of century-old oak trees at Kempner Park, ethnic dancers and German bands will entertain festival-goers while they sample a wide range of ethnic foods and browse through arts-and-crafts booths. Children's activities also have been planned. Admission $1. Call (409) 763-4311 for details.

**Greek Festival.** This huge event, the granddaddy of all Houston ethnic festivals, takes over the church grounds adjacent to the University of St. Thomas campus in Montrose for a celebration of Greek traditions. The crowds are enormous. Tens of thousands of people come to enjoy the Greek dances and foods, such as pastitsio (baked macaroni with beef filling), tiropita (feta cheese puffs), and baklava (thin pastry with nuts, honey, and spices). In addition to great food, there's folk dancing, tours of the splendid cathedral, films of Greece, and hand-crafted icons both on display and for sale. There are also craft booths and Greek take-home food for sale. Admission is about $2/kids free. Call 526-5377 for dates, times, and parking information.

**Westheimer Art Festival (Fall).** There are two of these, spring and fall, and they've been around forever. The location has changed a

---

**HOUSTON FACTOID:**

*The first Greeks believed to have settled in Houston arrived in the late 1880s. They were the Polemanakos brothers, who operated fruit stands.*

---

couple of times in recent years, but the shows still demonstrate that their roots are in the hippie days of the 1960s. The works range from wonderful to truly amazing junk. The paintings, ceramics, and jewelry are just the excuse. The real show is the crowd. Of course, the festival also offers musical entertainment plus food-and-beverage vendors of traditional festival fare. Admission is about $3/kids free. Call 521-0133 for dates and location.

**Asian-American Festival.** This is the only pan-Asian cultural arts festival in Texas, and it's designed to introduce Houstonians to the arts and foods of many Asian countries including Vietnam, China, Korea, India, Pakistan, the Philippines, Taiwan, Cambodia, Indonesia, Japan, and the Pacific Islands, as well as that of our neighbors in the Asian-American community. Call 861-8270 for further information.

**Texian Market Days.** This is billed as a Festival of Living History, and it does a fine job of presenting 19th-century life in this area. The George Ranch Historical Park in Richmond hosts the numerous hands-on activities as well as music, dancing, and costumed re-enactors. Admission is about $6/less for kids and seniors. Call 342-6478 for dates, times, and directions.

**Wings Over Houston.** This annual air show held at Ellington Field has been wowing Houstonians for more than a decade with everything from antique planes to the U.S. Air Force Thunderbirds. The show is wildly popluar so the crowds—and the traffic jams—are huge. Plan accordingly. Tickets cost about $10/less for kids, military, and seniors. Call 481-2828 for dates, rain dates, times and parking info.

---

**HOUSTON FACTOID:**

*The first wedding ceremony in an airplane took place over Houston on May 31, 1919, in a Handley-Paige bomber.*

---

**Conroe Cajun Catfish Festival.** Well, everybody else was celebrating something, so the folks up in Montgomery County adopted a "catfish" theme because of Conroe's proximity to the whiskered fish's favorite hangouts in the local rivers and lakes. They added "Cajun" because it's become a kind of synonym for good times—and this rollicking three-day event certainly is that. There's a parade through downtown, and stage shows feature everything from country and rock to bluegrass and zydeco. Call (409) 539-6009 for days, times, and admission fees.

**Galveston Island Jazz Festival.** This musical extravaganza on the waterfront boasts the best in jazz as well as arts and crafts, food, and general merriment. Admission runs $5 per day/less for kids and seniors. Call (800) 351-4236 for days and times.

**Fire-Fest.** To set the stage for Fire Prevention Week, the Houston Fire Museum hosts a celebration featuring demonstrations of modern and antique firefighting equipment, games, and food, as well as the annual introduction of the popular Houston Firefighters Calendar. Admission is free. Call 524-2526 for day and time.

**Katy Rice Harvest Festival.** This is still one of the world's major rice-growing areas, and once upon a time Katy boasted more paddies than subdivisions. Today they remember with a parade and a fair that includes arts and crafts booths, music, and more. Fest admission is about $2/kids free when accompanied by an adult. Call 391-2422 for dates and directions.

**Halloween.** This is fast becoming Houston's favorite holiday. There are horror houses all over town, as well as parades and parties for the kids. For adults, things can get really R-rated even in the suburbs, and Montrose is definitely NC-17. If you plan to go the commercial costume route, book early or you'll end up as Lamb-chop again this year.

**Scare on Market Square.** Mask-making, pumpkin-carving, and those incredible Art Cars from the Roadside Attractions parade at the Houston International Festival join musical entertainers in scaring up a good time. Eats are for sale as well. Call 868-3383 for date and time.

**Great Pumpkin Fun Run.** Featuring the Goblin Gallop, Great Pumpkin Dash, and a costume party and contest at Wortham Park following the race. Registration costs about $20/less for kids and seniors. Call 791-2540 for information.

**Zoo Boo.** The animals get to watch stupid human tricks as the zoo invites you to go trick-or-treating, and to visit a pumpkin patch and a haunted house. Designed for families with small children, the event ends early, but admission is free for kids in costume as long as they're accompanied by a paying adult. Call 525-3362 for date and time.

**Scaritage Park.** Materializing in Sam Houston Park downtown, this ghostly event features storytelling, fortune-telling, costume contests, and games. Admission, which benefits the Heritage Society is about $25/less for kids. Call 655-1912 for information.

**AstroWorld's FrightFest.** With three haunted houses and a haunted hayride through WaterWorld, this is frightful entertaining for teens. So are the hours. It's open until midnight. Admission is steep. It's almost $30/less for little kids, but there are promotional discounts available. Call 799-1234 for details.

**SplashTown's Nightmare Manor.** Another event designed for teens. This huge maze features dioramas of the dead and more than 20 scenes of terror. Besides, it's open from 7 until 11 p.m. Admission is about $7. In the afternoon, the park offers BoooTown: Designed for younger children, it features "Ghostly Goodies Scrambles" for more than 100,000 pieces of candy. Admission is free if you bring a can for the food banks of Interfaith and

Northwest Assistance Ministries. Call 355-3300 for dates, times, and directions.

**Halloween Monster Concerts.** The University of Houston and the American Guild of Organists, play the kind of music featured in Phantom of the Opera and in old Bela Lugosi movies. It's free and open to the public. Call 743-3009 for details and directions.

**Galveston's Great Pumpkin Party.** Moody Mansion is the ideal setting for Halloween ghost stories. There's also trick-or-treating and games for children. Admission is free. Call (409) 762-7668.

# NOVEMBER

**Arboretum Amble.** You've probably driven past the Houston Arboretum and Nature Center on Woodway near Memorial Park, but now's your big chance to see what it's like in there. Volunteers, corporate sponsors, and local celebrities invite you to learn more about your environment by "ambling" along the nature center's winding trails. At labeled stations along the woody paths there are nature talks, entertainment, and live animals to pet. Refreshments are available, and you are invited to join a two-mile Pledgewalk along the Arboretum's Outer Loop trail. Just collect contributions from your friends and neighbors. All proceeds go to the educational programs of the Houston Arboretum and Nature Center. Parking for the Arboretum Amble will be in the satellite parking lots at the south Memorial Park ball fields. Call 681-8433 for dates and times.

## IMAGES OF HOUSTON

*This far south November might just as well be summer some days,*
*it's that green and hot. Leaves don't turn here, or fall, drifting*
*down to be raked into bonfires of their own color.*

Susan Wood
Houston Poet

**Jewish Book Fair.** For several weeks at the beginning of November, Houston's Jewish Community Center on South Braeswood hosts some of the biggest names in contemporary literature. Well-known authors from around the world give guest lectures, readings, and autograph signings. All events are open to the public. Many are free of charge. Perhaps best of all, there are books on display and for sale guaranteed to delight every member of the family. Call 729-3200, ext. 3225, for dates, times, and admission charges for special events.

**Dinosaur Dash.** Houston's wackiest fun run attracts people who've always wanted to run from a Velociraptor. Participants in the 5 kilometer event are encouraged to dress as dinosaurs, and many individuals—and groups—do. The entry fee benefits the Museum of Natural Science. "Dino bash" afterward at the museum. Call 639-4600 for date, time, and fees.

**International Quilt Festival.** If you're a quilter, or just a fan of this traditional art form, the International is a really big deal. One of the largest shows in the nation, it attracts scores of entrants and features close to 1,000 new quilts, to say nothing of original cloth dolls, numerous art garments, and championship quilts from the past. There are also hundreds of exhibitor booths for early Christmas shopping. This is a big show and generally plays the George R. Brown Convention Center. Admission is by the day and runs about $8/seniors $4. Call 853-8220 for dates and times.

**Farm Fall Festival.** The Bay Area's Armand Bayou Nature Center sponsors this annual recreation of a bygone era. Return to the Houston area's bucolic roots at this old-time festival of traditional American and Native American farming skills. There's always music, crafts for both children and adults, lots of food to buy, and a chance to visit the animals at the Jimmy Martyn Farm, which is part of the Armand Bayou Nature Center. Admission is about $5 for adults/half that for seniors and kids. Parking is extremely limited. Call for dates, times, and parking info. 474-2551.

**Can Castle Competition.** Ever wanted to build a life-sized Taj Mahal out of beer cans? Well, this is your chance. Anheuser-Busch and Clean Houston will award prizes in various categories, both professional and amateur, for the most-elaborate, best-constructed

---

### HOUSTON FACTOID:

*American architectural genius Frank Lloyd Wright designed
a Houston private home, Thaxton House, located in
Bunker Hill Village.*

---

works of sculpture that use only clean, recycled beer cans. Past winners have included a race car, a cathedral and the Alamo. Admission is free for both spectators and participants, but architects, engineers, and sculptors should register in advance for either the professional or nonprofessional category. Call 871-2552, for dates, times and registration. As lagniappe—or inspiration—Anheuser-Busch, on whose grounds the contest is held, offers free brewery tours throughout the day.

**AutoRama.** This is the car show for people who don't like car shows. It's been playing the Astrodomain for decades, and by now the organizers have figured out something to appeal to the whole family. There are always Hollywood celebrities, as well as a gift fair, a swap meet, and various contests. But the biggest attraction is always the wheels. Classic cars, custom cars, funny cars, race cars, off-roaders, and trucks are on view. Often you can see rare private collections of classic and custom cars, too. Admission is about $10/less for kids. Call 799-9555 for dates and times.

**Thanksgiving Day Parade.** This is the official start of Houston's annual holiday season. From now on it's virtually non-stop celebrating all the way through to New Year's Day. Start the season off right by heading downtown for one of the nation's biggest and best

---

### HOUSTON FACTOID:

*Houston's first speeding ticket was given in 1903, when a driver
broke the six-mile-per-hour limit.*

---

holiday parades. While grandma cooks the turkey, enjoy the colorful procession of floats, marching bands, and such visiting digni-
taries as Santa Claus as they kick of the holidays, Bayou City style.

**"Home for the Holidays Celebration."** Old Town Spring, the ever-
quaint shopping village north of Houston, hosts this annual two-
weekend festive event. To put everyone in the mood for a down-
home Texas Christmas, there are strolling musicians singing and
playing carols, local choirs, handbell groups, colorful decorations.
Evenings, the twinkling lights and candlelight make it all the more
special. Bring the kids. Santa himself often rides through town not-
ing the presence of good little girls and boys. Old Town Spring is
about 19 miles north of downtown off Interstate 45. Admission is
free, but call 353-9310 for special holiday events, dates, and times.

**Trees of Hope Festival.** This elaborate display of designer-decorated
Christmas trees located in Memorial City Mall benefits the Star of
Hope Mission's homeless shelter. Kids love the gingerbread village
with the surrounding trees created by area radio and TV stations,
and by Houston's professional sports teams. There's also a feel-and-
touch tree for the visually impaired as well as the Tree of Hope decorated by the homeless children of the Star of Hope. Admission is
about $3/less for kids. Call 629-2707 for dates and times.

**Nutcracker Market.** It must be getting close to Christmas if it's time
for the Ballet Guild's annual Nutcracker mart. Hundreds of merchants help to put you in the holiday spirit—and give you a chance
to avoid next month's mall chaos by doing your shopping early.
Though the theme is balletic, the offerings include an incredible
variety of gift possibilities. You can buy everything from fruitcake
to furniture, all for the benefit of the Houston Ballet Foundation.
In recent years, the mart has gotten big enough to be held at the
Astrohall. Admission is about $7/kids under 12 free. Call the Bal-
let at 523-6300, ext. 271 for dates and times.

**Holiday in the Park Celebration.** There hasn't been a real "White
Christmas" in Houston since 1929, but every year AstroWorld
imports a mountain of snow so local kids can try sledding and
snowballing. More than a million twinkling Christmas lights turn
the theme park into a holiday fairyland. Carolers from local
schools add to the seasonal spirit, and there are special Christmas-

themed shows. While not terribly Christmassy, most of the rides stay open during Holiday in the Park. Fortunately for parents of young teens, screamers such as the Texas Cyclone, the Viper and the water attractions don't. Regular park admission charges apply, but during November, if you bring a canned food item for the Houston Food Bank, you can get in for half price. Call 799-1234 for details.

## DECEMBER

**Dickens Evening On The Strand.** The Strand is a street that was once the center of Galveston's business activity. Today it's the center of Galveston's tourist district. Each year at the beginning of December, the Strand shops turn back the clock to Victorian times in honor of Charles Dickens. Shopkeepers, visitors, and members of the Galveston Historical Foundation dress in Victorian garb and feast on vintage eats like roasted chestnuts, wassail, scones, and plum pudding. All the local attractions such as the 19th-century sailing ship *Elissa,* historic Ashton Villa, and the various museums get into the act. It's a wonderful way for families to kick off the holiday season. Adults in Victorian costume and kids under 12 get into the festival area free. Civilians pay about $9 each day. Call 280-3907 or (409) 765-7834 for dates, times, and directions. (Also see Galveston section.)

**The Silver Bells of Christmas.** The Houston Symphony's annual holiday program presents the orchestra, the Houston Symphony Chorus—and you. The famous audience sing-along invites one and all to join in the singing of holiday favorites from Silver Bells to the Hallelujah Chorus from Handel's Messiah. Evening performances are usually at 8 p.m. with a Saturday matinee at 2:30 and a 7:30 p.m. performance on Sunday, your best bet for the hard-to-get tickets. These are not cheap, generally running from about $12 up to $50. Call 227-ARTS or (800) 828-ARTS for tickets and information.

**Jingle Bell Run.** Maybe the fun-est fun run of the year. Some 10,000 folks, wearing jingle bells, Santa beards, antlers, elf caps, and who knows what else run, walk, and roll through the streets of downtown. Participants gather at the Downtown YMCA on Louisiana. Viewers line the streets. You'll never hear anything else

---

### HOUSTON FACTOID:

*Texas Avenue downtown is 100 feet wide. It was designed to allow 14 Longhorns to walk horn-to-horn during cattle drives.*

---

like all those bells echoing off the skyscrapers. Entry fees, which benefit a good cause, are about $20/less for kids. For date and time call 659-8501.

**Christmas in Old Montgomery Candlelight Home Tour.** The historic homes and buildings in the little town of Montgomery, about 15 miles west of Conroe, play host to a real down-home Christmas, the local historical society sells thousands of homemade cookies to visitors, and the Methodist Church serves an old-fashioned Christmas dinner. Bring the whole family. This isn't a re-enactment. This really is the way things used to be. There are separate admission charges for the tour and the dinner, but neither is very expensive. Call (409) 597-6304 for dates, times, and further information.

**Children's Parade.** A multi-cultural holiday event that children of all backgrounds can enjoy. All kids are welcome to participate. Marchers gather in front of Chelsea Market on Montrose, and parade about a quarter of a mile to Campanile Center. Refreshments and entertainment are available at the finish. Call 522-4505 for date and time.

**Lights in the Heights.** Traditional *luminarias* line Bayland and Omar streets from the Norhill Esplanade to Sparks Park at Travis School lighting the way for walkers, musicians, and carolers. Neighbors in costume add to the atmosphere and musical performers appear on a stage set up on the Norhill Esplanade. The "lights" also light the way to the traditional Heights Christmas pageant at St. Mark's United Methodist Church. Admission is free. Call 861-3104 for date and times.

**The Nutcracker.** For many Houstonians, it isn't really the Christmas season until the Houston Ballet begins performing Nutcracker. This family holiday favorite runs through much of the month of December, but tickets for prime-time performances sell out fast. Plan accordingly. With its Sugarplum fairies, Snow Queen, Mouse King, and of course the magical, growing Christmas tree, the lavish production uses more than 1,500 different costumes and props. Even kids who don't like dance, love Nutcracker. Tickets generally range from $10 to $50. Call 227-ARTS or (800) 828-2787 for dates and ticket information.

**Galveston's "Victorian Christmas" Home Tour.** As a warm-up for all the Dickens' Evening on the Strand festivities, the island's East End Historical District Association sponsors an early December visit to a number of appropriate-period private homes. Each is decorated in Victorian holiday style. You can even hire horse-drawn carriages to the trip from site to site. Along the route, Christmas carolers add to the holiday atmosphere, and Ebenezer Scrooge himself often puts in an appearance. The number of tickets (about $13) is severely limited. Get them in person at the Grand 1894 Opera House, 2020 Postoffice, or charge by calling (409) 765-1894 or (713) 480-1894. (Also see Galveston section.)

**Fantasy of Lights.** The town of Sealy's official Christmas celebration includes a holiday crafts show on Main Street that's enlivened by music and dance performances all day long. The major attraction, as always, is the magical Fantasy of Lights Night Parade. Call for dates, further information, and directions: (409) 885-3222.

**Great Hanukkah Adventure.** The exact dates of this festive Jewish celebration vary from year to year, but it's always part of the great American holiday season. You don't have to be Jewish to enjoy the Jewish Community Center/West Houston's celebration of Hanukkah traditions and history. Congregation members dress up in costume and families can travel through a "time tunnel" to see how Hanukkah originated. There's also storytelling, games, holiday crafts, and lots of food. Tickets at the door are only $1. Call the Jewish Community Center/West Houston for dates and directions: 556-5567.

**Victorian Open House in the Heights.** The Heights was largely a creation of the Victorian era, and this holiday celebration is a trip back through time. You can visit the elegantly decorated formal rooms at several private homes as well as at the Houston Heights Historical Museum. The Heights Women's Club offers period refreshments for sale. Tickets that admit visitors to all venues cost less than $10 and may be purchased on the day of the event at each of the tour's homes as well as at the Houston Heights Historical Museum. Call 868-0170 for dates and times.

**The Houston Christmas Bird Count.** For more than half a century, Houston birders have recorded the number of species seen in the area on a given day. It's one of the most important such events in North America, and joins with some 1,600 other count locations to create an accurate picture of which birds live where in North, South, and Central America. Call 855-2615 or 328-6236 for information, date, and time.

**Christmas Boat Parade.** Floating along Clear Lake, more than 100 boats of all sizes are decorated in the best holiday fashion. At dusk the moving lights reflected in the water create a spectacular effect. Spectators can just line the shore to watch the parade move from South Shore Harbour Marina in League City to the Clear Lake channel, where it passes beneath the Seabrook-Kemah bridge, then out into Galveston Bay before it circles back. The hotels, restaurants, and clubs along the lake, as well as those along Clear Creek channel in Kemah, offer special Christmas Parade package deals. Just watching from shore is free. Call 488-7676 for date and time. (Also see Clear Lake section.)

**Downtown Houston Holiday Celebration.** Join fellow Houstonians for this multicultural event downtown in front of City Hall. Live performances by musician and dancers help to further the holiday mood, vendors sell holiday eats, and the city's giant, official tree is lit. The Holly Trolley Holiday Tours take visitors around downtown free of charge, and the Heritage Society welcomes one and all to their Candlelight Tours of the historic homes in Sam Houston Park. The Candlelight Tours cost about $5/less for seniors and kids. The rest is free. Call 654-1912 for days and times.

**Other Christmas Celebrations.** There are numerous, religious-themed Christmas events such as Second Baptist Church's famous Singing Christmas Tree—a choir performing on a massive tree-shaped steel frame—and various Christmas pagents. The *Chronicle* carries listings in its religion section. Newer, secular traditions indude the Uptown Houston's light show on the streets near the Galleria, which is kicked off by a big ceremony and fireworks in late November.

**A Wild New Year's Eve.** The animals at the Houston Zoological Gardens invite you to celebrate the end of the year—free of charge. During regular hours, there is no admission fee on the last day of the year. Do the babysitter a favor, tire the kids out. Call 525-3300 for information.

# ARTS

Houston is one of the few cities in the nation that supports three major full-time cultural organizations on the scale of the Houston Ballet, Houston Grand Opera, and the Houston Symphony Orchestra. We also have a number of fine museums dedicated to the fine arts, to say nothing of numerous arts organizations.

The regional theater scene here is exceptionally lively and the film community is active. We also have public art in more places than most Houstonians realize. Explore!

## ART IN DOWNTOWN

Most big cities have some collection of public art in their central business districts. Houston is unusual in both the quantity and quality of the works placed among the glass canyons of downtown. There are dozens of them, ranging from huge pieces of sculpture by some of the biggest names in the world, to smaller works by local artists. The Cultural Arts Council of Houston, with the financial help of Business Artsfund and Business Volunteers for the Arts, has put together a Downtown Public Art Tour.

Those listed here are on the tour. You can get a well-marked map with the location of each work from the Houston Convention and Visitors Bureau's office on Market Square. (Call 523-5050.) Although all of the pieces are located in public places, some are accessible only during business hours.

One more caveat before you set off on foot. If it's summer, DON'T. Even in spring or fall, you might want to think twice. Downtown is much more spread out than it looks on a map. Still, if you're in good shape and have comfortable shoes, you might want to give it a try. Otherwise, there is public parking near most clusters of art. Unfortunately, the parking is not free. An interesting alternative is to skate by the sculpture at night. You'd be surprised at the number of people you'll see doing just that. Skates are for rent at several locations in nearby Montrose if you don't already have your own blades.

The list works like this:

**Artist's or Installation's name**
*Title of the work*
Year it was completed
Materials used
Where to find it

**DOWNTOWN ART**

**Jim Love**
*Area Code*
1962
Metal sculpture
Alley Theatre
615 Texas Avenue

**Market Square**
*Downtown Park*
bounded by Milam, Congress, Travis, and Preston
Sidewalks with fragments of historically significant objects; handpainted benches by Malou Flato; 80 photographs by Paul Hester.

**James Surls**
*Points of View*
1991
Treated pine sculpture
Market Square Park

**Emilio Greco**
*Grande Bagnate No. 2*
1957
Bronze
Drive-in bank
Preston and Louisiana

---

## HOUSTON FACTOID:

*By 1930, Miró, the Spanish surrealist painter born in 1893, had developed the lyrical, colorful style that made him famous. He loved the playful juxtaposition of delicate lines and amoebic shapes.*

**Albert Paley**
*Untitled*
1987
Multi-part forged and fabri-
cated painted steel with
ribbons
Wortham Centre
550 Prairie (interior)

**Team Hou: (Guy Hagstette,
John Lemr, Robert Liner,
Kerry Goelzer)**
*Sesquicentennial Park*
1989
Collection of structures,
fountains, ramps, walls
and landscaping
Buffalo Bayou
Next to Wortham Center

**John Alexander**
*Lilly Pads*
1977
Oil on canvas
Music Hall Lobby
Bagby at Walker

**John Biggers**
*The Quilting Bee*
1981
Acrylic on canvas

Music Hall (interior)
Bagby at Walker

**Carroll Simms**
*The Banjo*
1980
Bronze
Music Hall
Bagby at Walker

**Naomi Savage**
*One Step For Mankind*
1979
Photographic etching in
stainless steel
Tranquility Park, east wall
Bagby between Walker and
Rusk

**Daniel MacMorris**
*Untitled*
1939
Allegorical murals
City Hall (interior)
901 Bagby

**Louis Ameteis**
*Spirit of the Confederacy*
1907
Bronze
Sam Houston Park
1100 Bagby

---

### HOUSTON FACTOID:

*"Houston still can't seem to decide whether art collecting is some
kind of secret vice or a happy confluence of personal gratification
and civic benefit."*

New York art critic Peter Schjeldahl

## HOUSTON FACTOID:

*Dubuffet was a French painter and sculptor who died in 1985. His primitive, childlike, humorous paintings often have thick impastoes enriching the surface texture. He loved silly names. His* Cow with the Subtile Nose *is in the Museum of Modern Art in New York.*

**Claes Oldenburg**
*Geometrie Mouse X*
1971
Red painted steel
Library Plaza
501 McKinney

**A. Joseph Kinkel**
*Untitled*
1989
Bronze maquette
Julia Ideson Building
Public Library (interior)
500 McKinney

**Tim Bailey**
*Untitled*
1988
Forged steel
Allen Center I
500 Dallas

**Peter Reginato**
*High Plains Drifter*
1973
Corten steel
Allen Center II
120 Smith

**Louise Nevelson**
*Frozen Laces-One*
1979
Black painted steel
Allen Center IV
1400 Smith

**Charles Pebworth**
*Garden of the Mind*
1971/72
Metal sculptural relief
Hyatt Hotel (interior)
1200 Louisiana

**Jean Dubuffett**
*Monument au Phantome*
1977
Seven-part polycrome, poly-
    ester resin and fiberglass
    sculpture
100 Louisiana Building

**Robert Kushner**
*Architectural Arabesque*
1986
Four cast bronze figures
1201 Milam

---

## HOUSTON FACTOID:

*The name(s) of the artist or artists who created this magnificent space—the 712 Main bank interior—are one of the Houston art world's great mysteries. Periodically, new theories will emerge, but so far the artist remains unknown.*

---

**Ned Smyth**
*Palm Columns*
1986
Three mosaic and masonry
   sculptures
1201 Milam

**Tony Rosenthall**
*Bronco*
1980
Stainless steel
1010 Lamar Building
   (interior)

**Barbara Helpworth**
*The Family of Man*
1970
Nine figures in bronze
1001 Fannin

**Claes Oldenburg**
*Inverted "Q" Prototype*
Black epoxy-coated rigid
   foam
1001 Fannin (interior)

**Rufino Tamayo**
*America*
1955
Mural: acrylic on canvas
910 Travis (interior)

**Unknown**
*Untitled (Battle of San Jacinto)*
Stained glass window, art
   deco ceiling, and interior
   detailing
712 Main (bank interior)

**Joan Miró**
*Personage and Birds*
1970
Polychrome bronze
600 Travis

**Joan Miró**
*Personage and Birds*
1970
Model for sculpture;
   unpainted bronze
60th floor Observation Deck
Texas Commerce Tower
   (interior)
600 Travis

**Joan Miró**
*Disheveled Woman*
1969
Painted bronze
60th floor Observation Deck
Texas Commerce Tower
   (interior)
600 Travis

**Marcello Mascherini**
*Ballet Dancer*
1950
Bronze
Jones Hall
615 Louisiana

**Robert Fowler**
*Pair of Horses*
c. 1982
Steel
Jones Hall
615 Louisiana

**Carter Ernst/Paul Kittelson**
*1988*
1988
Ceramic art wall Multicultural Education and Counseling through the Arts (MECA)
1505 Kane Street

**Tim Glover**
*The Cactus*
1988
Sculpture. MECA
1505 Kane Street

**Pio Pulido/Sylvia Orozco**
*A United Community*
1985

Mural. MECA
1505 Kane Street

**Linnea Glatt and Frances Merritt Thompson**
*Passage Inacheve*
1990
Galvanized steel, concrete, and photographic images
Buffalo Bayou Park
Near downtown

**Henry Moore**
*Large Spindle Piece*
1968/74
Bronze
Allen Parkway
Near downtown

**Jesus Bautista Moroles**
*Ziggurat Playscape*
1992
Texas granite
Houston Police Officers' Memorial
Memorial Drive
Near downtown
Memorial Drive

---

## HOUSTON FACTOID:

*Rufino Tamayo, born in 1899, was one of Mexico's most important modern painters. Cubism, fauvism, and Mexican folklore echo in his work, which is both formal and decorative.*

## DANCE

Before the widespread use of air-conditioning in the 1940s, it was difficult to convince many people to turn out for anything as esoteric as a classical dance performance, but once climate could be controlled, folks were more willing to try new things. And they did. Although in the 1940s and 1950s, well-known companies such as the Ballet Russe de Monte Carlo and the precursor of the American Ballet Theater played Houston on a regular basis and drew respectable crowds. Eventually, a core of dance aficionados demanded the creation of a Houston Ballet, and they got it in 1955. The company became professional in 1969 and the arrival of artistic director Ben Stevenson, a world-famous teacher and choreographer, put the Houston Ballet on the map by the late 1970s. In the Ballet Academy, the school of the Houston Ballet, the company has one of the best training programs for young dancers outside of Moscow, St. Petersburg (Russia, not Florida), or New York. The Ballet tours widely and is well received around the world. Its success and the interest in dance that it generated helped to inspire a kind of dance renaissance in Houston, and we now boast a number of fine companies in various dance disciplines.

### ALLEGRO BALLET OF HOUSTON
**1507 Dairy Ashford, Suite 200 • Houston, TX 77077 • 496-4670**

Since its founding in 1951, Allegro has discovered young dancers though auditions and then presented them in concerts at home and abroad. The Allegro also awards need-based scholarships to promising kids to further their study of dance.

### CITY BALLET
**9902 Long Point • Houston, TX 77055 • 468-8708**

Once upon a time this company was known as the Greater Houston Civic Ballet, but it has moved on beyond its clubby, 1950s roots. Now the City Ballet is a private, nonprofit organization offering young dancers the opportunity to continue their education and to gain all-important company experience.

## DELIA STEWART DANCE COMPANY
**1202 Calumet • Houston, TX 77004 • 522-6375**

The Delia Stewart Dance Company presents jazz and musical theater dance concerts, workshops, and children's programs. It also works to establish and maintain a professional jazz dance company in Houston.

## HOUSTON BALLET
**1916 West Gray • Houston, TX 77019 • 523-6300**

The Houston Ballet is one of the city's shining stars. For the past quarter-century, it has grown in strength and prestige until by now it is one of America's best-known companies. The Ballet regularly performs in New York, Europe and even in China. The organization's school, the Houston Ballet Academy, has not only produced the majority of the company's featured dancers, it has also become the training ground for dancers from around the country. All this is a long way from 1955 when it was founded as an "educational undertaking." At the academy's top-of-the-line facility on West Gray, company instructors offer classes at all levels for children and adults as well as courses in dance fitness and body conditioning.

## RICE DANCE THEATRE
**P.O. Box 1892 • Department of Health**
**Houston, TX 77251 • 527-4808**

Rice Dance Theatre includes a performing company of Rice students and a professional touring company comprised of Houston-based artists.

## SOUTHWEST JAZZ BALLET COMPANY
**P.O. Box 38233 • Houston, TX 77238 • 694-6114**

Since it was founded in 1979, the Southwest Jazz Ballet has performed for millions of people. The group tours extensively both in Texas and in the rest of the country. On its foreign tours, Southwest uses both jazz and ballet to introduce people to American artists and America's dance heritage. The company also programs musical and dramatic performances.

## FILM

Film is *THE* art form of the 20th century—and will continue to dominate our culture in the 21st. Some of the earliest films ever made were cranked out in the Houston area (see Houston On Film section) and even during the 1928 Democratic Party Convention, which was held in downtown, the politicians insisted that the gathering be filmed for later showing in theater newsreels. Since then, Houston has developed quite a film industry and, perhaps more importantly, a solid group of film scholars and afficionados. You don't have to live on either of the other two coasts to have access to the best or the latest in film.

### RICE MEDIA CENTER

**Rice University • Entrance 8 • University Boulevard at Stockton**
**527-4882 • Admission**

The Media Center is Houston's premier showcase for foreign and independent cinema as well as classic films from the silent era. As part of its extensive program, The Media Center presents dozens of films each semester, with screenings on Friday, Saturday, and Sunday. The program publishes a free program guide that is available at the center or to subscribers. If you want to see the very best—and the very strangest—in moviemaking, this is the place.

### MUSEUM OF FINE ARTS FILM PROGRAM

**P.O. Box 6826 • Houston, TX 77265-6826**
**639-7515 (weekly info line)**

The Brown auditorium is a great place to watch film and the Museum's program presents many that are well worth watching. Curator Marian Luntz chooses several themes for each bimonthly series (write or call and leave your name and address to get on the mailing list). These have included everything from 1950s Hollywood Technicolor westerns to obscure Eastern European political dramas. They also showcase works, including shorts, by local filmmakers.

## SOUTHWEST ALTERNATE MEDIA PROJECT
**1519 West Main • Houston, TX 77006 • 522-8592**

SWAMP was founded in 1977 as a regional media arts center to promote creative activities and assist artists residing in Arizona, Arkansas, Kansas, Louisiana, Missouri, Nebraska, New Mexico, Oklahoma, Puerto Rico, Texas, and the U.S. Virgin Islands. But it is best known for the assistance it gives local artists in the production and exhibition of independent film and video. SWAMP co-coordinates experimental film and video presentations on KUHT, the local PBS member station, and offers a regional fellowship program. SWAMP also offers publications, workshops, project consultation, grant writing assistance, and information services, as well as the Southwest Film and Video Tour.

## WORLDFEST/HOUSTON INTERNATIONAL FILM FESTIVAL
**Various locations • Mid- to late April • P.O. Box 56566 • Houston, TX 77256 • 965-9955**

WorldFest, which has zapped through so many incarnations it probably should be known as the mighty morphin power festival, constantly confounds its critics by bringing some world-class films to town despite a lack of big-time community financial support. And no matter what their gripes with the fest, local movie fans should be ecstatic about its existence; it's an important ingredient in the cultural life of the city. While the film festival is a strange sort of hybrid event—part culture, part soul, part carnival, including everything from commercials and industrial films to some of Hollywood's latest, it also gives Houston film fans a chance to see some of the most important foreign and American independent films around. Most of these, unfortunately, never will get a commercial release. But more than a few, thanks in part to their reception at the festival, have gone on to some box-office success. Film buffs should be on the mailing list.

# HOUSTON ON FILM

Houston isn't Hollywood, but it has been in a surprising number of movies. Film critic Joe Leydon, a mainstay of the late lamented *Houston Post,* has seen them all. These are the ones he recommends. Most are available on home video, and in each of them the Houston area is one of the stars.

One of the very first films shot near Houston was an Edison Company production, a newsreel of the Galveston hurricane of 1900. Image-conscious city fathers were predictably unhappy about this intrusion, and initially tried to keep Edison's cameras from recording the damage. They failed, however, and the finished film eventually was released under such titles as *Panorama of East Galveston* and *Wreckage Along Shore.* (Clearly, title-choosing focus groups had not yet been invented.)

The history of cinema has always been a story of the struggle between art and commerce. In Galveston at least, art won the first round. In more recent years, filmmakers have been lured to Texas in general, and Houston in particular, by the sunny climate, the abundance of highly trained production personnel—and, yes, the economic advantages of filming in a right-to-work state. Of the many movies shot either partially and entirely in Houston since 1970, these five are of special note:

*ADAM* (1983)—Almost all of this fact-based made-for-TV movie was shot in Houston, even though none of the story takes place here. As often happens when filmmakers come to Space City, the producers of Adam chose to use Houston as a persuasive stand-in for a number of different locales. The city council chamber was transformed into a U.S. Senate hearing room, and the Mecom Fountain near the Warwick Hotel was used for exterior shots. The filmmakers also built a set inside an old convent at 4600 Bissonnet; it stood in for a Florida police station, and they used Westwood Mall because it resembled the Florida shopping mall where 6-year-old Adam Walsh was abducted by a deranged killer. (USA Home video)

*JASON' S LYRIC* (1994)—This underrated inner-city drama from the producers of *New Jack City* stars Allen Payne and Bokeem Woodbine as brothers who struggle to overcome the influence of their disturbed Vietnam vet father (Forrest Whitaker). The distinctive Houston skyline is used throughout *Jason's Lyric* for its symbolic value, looming in the background as a bright promise far beyond the reach of the movie's characters. Director Doug McHenry vividly depicts the city's poor but proud Third Ward neighborhoods, and also tosses in a couple of visits to the best soul-food restaurant in town, This Is It. (Since completion of the film, the restaurant has relocated a couple of blocks closer to downtown, though still on West Gray.) (Poly-Gram video)

*LOCAL HERO* (1983)—Scottish filmmaker Bill Forsyth wrote and directed this lyrical comedy of melancholy about a Houston oil company executive (the great Peter Riegert) who falls in love with the Scottish village he's supposed to turn into a refinery site. You can see a lot of Houston high-rises, and lots more Houston highways, in the scenes that bracket Riegert's extended stay in Scotland. And in the character of Felix Hopper, a flamboyant petroleum company president grandly played by Burt Lancaster, you can see one of the very few affectionate depictions of a Texas oil man featured in any movie of the past three decades. (Warner Home Video)

*SIDEKICKS* (1993)—Try to imagine a cross between *The Karate Kid* and *The Secret Life of Walter Mitty,* and you'll have some idea what to expect from this lively action comedy. Jonathan Brandis plays as asthmatic teenager who dreams of derring-do come true when he actually gets to meet his hero, movie star Chuck Norris. Sidekicks is an independent product, financed by Houston furniture-store mogul Jim "Mattress Mac" McIngvale, and it makes some imaginative use of local landmarks. The Transco Tower Water Wall is used to particularly good effect. On the other hand, the movie also depicts Lamar High School as a place where nerdy teenagers are routinely bullied by gym teachers. And the English teachers there appear to be *really* snotty. (Columbia/Tristar Home Video)

*TERMS OF ENDEARMENT* (1983)—Winner of the Academy Award for Best Picture, this hugely enjoyable comedy-drama (based on Texas author Larry McMurtry's novel) features Shirley MacLaine in an Oscar-winning performance as Aurora Greenway, a wealthy and feisty widow who refuses to age gracefully. Aurora lives in River Oaks. And, indeed, much of *Terms of Endearment* was filmed inside and outside the red-brick, Georgian facade home at 3060 Locke Lane. MacLaine and co-star Jack Nicholson (yet another Oscar winner) have their first date at Brennan's Restaurant, in the 3300 block of Smith Street near downtown, then take the long way home. They somehow manage to detour all the way to the beach in Galveston while making the 15-minute drive from Brennan's to River Oaks. (Paramount Home Video)

Other notable filmed-in-Houston movies include *Apollo 13* (1995, MCA Home Video). Tom Hanks stars in this super evocation of Space City's glory days, by local-boy-made-good Al Reinert. Also by Reinert, *For All Mankind* (1994, Columbia Tri-Star Home Video, Laserdisk) is one of the best documentaries ever made. A paean to the Apollo moon voyages, it was "filmed on location by the National Aeronautics and Space Administration." *Reality Bites* (1994, MCA Home video), Ben Stiller's witty comedy-drama starring Winona Ryder and Ethan Hawke as aimless Generation Xers; *Rush* (1993, MGM/UA Home Video), in which Houston doubles for various small-town Texas locales. In this one, a rookie narc (Jennifer Jason Leigh) and her veteran partner (Jason Patric) take their jobs much too seriously. Also look for *Brewster McCloud* (1970, MGM/UA Home video), Robert Altman's twisted fairy-tale about an eccentric bird fancier who lives—and wants to fly—inside the Houston Astrodome; *Urban Cowboy* (1979, Paramount Home video), the trend-setting musical drama that has John Travolta and Debra Winger doing the Texas two-step at Gilley's, the Pasadena nightspot that unfortunately no longer exists; and *The Man Who Loved Women* (1983), Blake Edwards' so-so remake of a French comedy by Francois Truffaut, which has Burt Reynolds (in the title role) meeting a Texas oil man's sex-crazed wife (Kim Basinger) at a party in the grassy area between the mirrored-glass buildings in Greenway Plaza.

## MUSEUMS AND NONPROFIT GALLERIES

### ART LEAGUE OF HOUSTON
**1953 Montrose • Central • 523-9530**
**Open Mon–Sat; Closed Sun • W • Free**

Since 1953, the Art League has supported Houston's art community through juried and invitational exhibitions and "survival" workshops designed to teach artists to succeed. The League's purpose is to promote all forms of visual art in Houston through classes, seminars, and art-related programs. Each year, it also sponsors a tribute to a Texas artist. And it maintains a gallery that's open to the public.

## SARAH CAMPBELL BLAFFER GALLERY

**University of Houston central campus • Entrance 16 (off 5500 block of Cullen) • 743-9530 • Open: 10–5 Tues–Fri; 1–5 Sat; Closed Sun and university holidays • W • Free**

Blaffer Gallery exhibitions might include anything from works by the Old Masters to decorative arts such as painted clothing and furniture. The gallery supports local artists, and included in the schedule of eight annual shows are two, end-of-term student exhibitions. The Blaffer also sponsors art lectures and seminars that are open to the public. Call for information.

## CONTEMPORARY ARTS MUSEUM

**5216 Montrose • Central • 526-3129 • Closed Monday • W • Free**

Once upon a time the CAM was Houston's most outrageous arts institution. Back in the 1970s, it kept "The Ant Farm," a resident hippie commune, and produced shows that ended in fistfights in the parking lot. One involved live cockroaches, and another, which included a lot of painted bread and the Kilgore Rangerettes, degenerated into a riot with chunks of bread flying and art mavens screaming. The visiting national art press went wild. Ever since then, some people would tell you, the museum has been trying to live down the fiasco years. Others would say that the museum hasn't done anything interesting since then. Actually, CAM has been around since 1948 and has introduced many now-major artists to Houston and the world. These days, exhibitions in the Upper Gallery and the Perspectives Gallery can take any form, representing diversity in style, media, and subject matter. The museum also offers art classes for both adults and children, and boasts one of the best gift shops in town.

## THE MENIL COLLECTION

**1515 Sul Ross • 525-9400 • W • Free**

Dominique de Menil (and to a lesser extent her husband, Jean) can be numbered among the greatest art collectors of the 20th century. With an unerring eye, Mrs. de Menil assembled one of the nation's most important collections of modern works, with a special emphasis on the surrealists. She also collected African art before it was popular to do so and gathered an extensive collection of works from the Byzantine period. All of this may be seen at the Menils' own museum in Montrose near the University of Saint Thomas. The collection is too extensive to be shown all at once, so rotating exhibits, often set around a theme, are displayed. Scholars have access to the entirety of one of the most important private accumulations of art in the world.

## MUSEUM OF FINE ARTS

**1001 Bissonnet • 639-7300 • Closed Mondays • W**
**Admission (Free to all Thurs 10 a.m.–9 p.m.)**

Founded in 1924, the Museum of Fine Arts has introduced Houstonians to artworks ranging from antiquity to the modern era. Highlights of the permanent collection are paintings by Western artist Frederic Remington and early European masters. There are also ancient and medieval art, 19th- and 20th-century decorative arts, as well as Asian, pre-Columbian, and Oceanic arts. The museum also hosts the art world's traveling "Monster Shows," which tour the nation like rock bands. Less glamourous but more useful to the community, it sponsors lectures, museum tours, a fine film series, and the Hirsch Library for art history. Nearby, at 5101 Montrose, the MFA's Alfred C. Glassell Jr. School of Art offers classes in visual arts and art history for adults and children, and exhibits contemporary art.

## RICE MEDIA CENTER

**Rice University • Entrance 8 • University Boulevard at Stockton**
**527-4594 • Closed Sat and Sun and during summer • W • Free**

Although best known for its film program, the Media Center also exhibits the work of one regionally or nationally known photographer each month.

## RICE UNIVERSITY ART GALLERY

**Rice University • Entrance 1 or 2 (off 6100 block of South Main)**
**527-5101, Ext. 5502 • Closed Sun and during summer • W • Free**

Many people remember this gallery under its old name, the Sewall Gallery. Whatever the name, the curators here organize five shows each academic year, and these run the gamut from painting to photography. The last exhibition before the summer hiatus is dedicated to student works. Group tours are available.

## ROTHKO CHAPEL
**3900 Yupon • 524-9839 • W • Free**

The walls of this octagonal brick structure near the University of Saint Thomas are hung with fourteen huge, dark, brooding works by the late abstract expressionist painter Mark Rothko, who it is said, came to Houston to oversee the design. According to one possibly apocryphal story, he showed the designers the inside of his wrist and requested that the walls be painted precisely that color. He then went back to New York and committed suicide. This tragedy notwithstanding, the chapel itself is a wonderful space, and the chapel foundation (another project of art patron Dominique de Menil, a deeply spiritual woman) sponsors multi-denominational events such as the visit of the Dalai Lama and the annual Carter-Menil awards for world peace, given in conjunction with the (President Jimmy) Carter Center of Atlanta.

# MUSIC

In 1910, the same year that the oil economy created at Spindletop changed Houston forever, the Metropolitan Opera of New York City arrived as well. The city's bigwigs, who were doubtless more accustomed to thinking of the works of Stephen Foster as high-brow stuff, were treated to a performance of Wagner's *Lohengrin*. Evidently, it took them five years to recover, because it took the Met that long to come back, this time to present *Parsifal*.

In the meantime, the ladies of Houston succeeded in raising the cultural tone considerably, and the Tuesday Musical Club, which was founded in 1911, paved the way for the Houston Symphony Orchestra. Miss Ima Hogg used all her powers of persuasion to convince the city fathers that we needed one—and her brothers to help pay for it.

The Symphony made its debut in a vaudeville house located where the *Houston Chronicle* now stands. The arts situation improved with the construction of the City Auditorium, which played host to numerous celebrity performers.

Ignace Jan Paderewski, the world-famous Polish pianist, composer, and statesman who headed his country's government between the World Wars and again from exile after the Nazi

## DOMINIQUE DE MENIL

Born to wealth in Paris, Dominique Schlumberger was the daughter and niece of the men who invented a crucial measuring device for the oil industry. She married another oil executive, Comte Jean de Menil, who gave up his title (count) when the couple fled to America one step ahead of the Nazis in World War II.

In France, Dominique de Menil had been a patron of controversial "new" artists such as Max Ernst, and once established in Houston after the war, she continued to encourage, support, and collect the works of people like Andy Warhol and others then outside the traditional artistic establishment. And that wasn't all. In the segregated and ultra-conservative world of 1950s and 1960s Houston, the de Menils were major supporters of civil rights and of liberal political causes. From early on, Jean de Menil was the mentor of civil rights activist Mickey Leland, who later became a U.S. Representative, and he donated extensively to liberal causes.

The Menils also became the center of a burgeoning Houston arts scene. Mrs. de Menil commissioned architect Philip Johnson to design her home on San Felipe, thus introducing him to the city where he would create Pennzoil, Transco, and some of his other most important works; she then virtually created the Rice Media Center, and brought in controversial Italian director Roberto Rossellini to launch it. Later she would support the arts program at the University of Saint Thomas and commission Johnson to design the main campus quadrangle, which is inspired by Thomas Jefferson's design for the University of Virginia.

*(continued on next page)*

After the death of her husband in 1973, Dominique de Menil became increasingly spiritual, and through the Rothko Chapel, another of her projects, she joined with former President Jimmy Carter to present an annual Human Rights award. This has brought such luminaries as the Dalai Lama and South African President Nelson Mandela to Houston.

When well into her 70s, Mrs. de Menil began to plan the museum that would showcase the works that she and her husband had accumulated together. The result is the Menil Collection and it is one of the world's most prestigious small museums.

takeover, was the first world-class performing artist to appear regularly in Houston, but others soon followed suit. Opera great Enrico Caruso, prima ballerina Anna Pavlova, and others all performed here. They appeared in the old City Auditorium and later at the Music Hall, but after 1966 when Jones Hall for the Performing Arts—universally recognized as one of the nation's great performing arts venues—opened, the city was able to attract the biggest names in the performing arts on a regular basis. This remians true today, thanks to the Jones Hall renovation and to the Wortham Center, which offers state-of-the-art facilities.

## HOUSTON GRAND OPERA ASSOCIATION
### 401 Louisiana, 8th Floor • Houston, TX 77002 • 546-0200

The Houston Grand Opera, which was founded in 1955, is one of the nation's premiere companies. Thanks in large part to long-time general director David Gockley, it enjoys a reputation for innovation and has sponsored the creation of such modern works as John Adams' *Nixon in China* and the controversial *Harvey Milk*, both of which had their world premiers in the Wortham Center amid much hoopla. The world press always turns out in droves for these events. HGO can be depended upon to keep Houston on the international opera map. Stop-the-presses events aside, the group's regular season is consistently entertaining. There are two series of repertory performances during its main season from October to

May with the works presented primarily in the original language, but there are "surtitles," translations projected onto a long, narrow screen above the stage. This sounds distracting, but unless you're an opera purist of the most absolute variety, it's not. HGO also offers a Light Opera series, which includes classic musical theater, and a Broadway series featuring the kinds of show tunes everyone knows. The company's Spring Opera Festival at Miller Outdoor Theatre is a great, cost-free introduction to opera. Quite a number of the singers come from the Houston Opera Studio at the University of Houston, one of the nation's best training programs, or from the Texas Opera Theatre, a division of HGO that is the largest touring opera company in the nation.

### THE HOUSTON SYMPHONY ORCHESTRA
**615 Louisiana • Houston, TX 77002 • 224-4240**

The oldest of Houston's performing arts organizations, the Symphony is much loved. Its concert season, which offers the standard classical repertory, runs from September to May, and the Pops series, offering lighter fare including favorites from the Broadway musical theater, runs from May to July. But this isn't all the Symphony does. The orchestra tours extensively both in the United States and abroad, even performing in China. All told, the Symphony puts on some 150 concerts a year. In addition to the 50 or so offered during the main season, and the Pops shows, there is Sounds like Fun, special, age-appropriate educational concerts for student groups from all over the area. Since 1939 the orchestra has performed free of charge in an annual summer series at Miller Outdoor Theatre. Also free of charge to neighborhood groups are some designated rehearsals in Jones Hall. Others are open to the public for a nominal fee. Call for information.

### KUHF RADIO
**University of Houston Campus • Houston, TX 77004**
**743-0887 • 743-KUHF (member services)**

Houston's Public Radio station is the best friend of classical music lovers, but this non-profit organization is always on the brink of financial disaster. Still, they somehow manage to keep putting on fine local programming and also to serve as the Houston outlet for National Public Radio, which broadcasts such music-lovers' faves as live concerts from the Metropolitan Opera in New York. The station runs the obligatory, public radio begging campaigns a couple of times a year. Please, pay attention. They need your support.

## THEATER

Back in March of 1837, a traveling actor from back east named G. L. Lyons arrived in town and announced that it was his intention to open a "dramatic temple" amid the collection of huts, tents, and log cabins that then constituted the city of Houston. Clearly, Lyons was a man ahead of his time.

Dreams of theatrical glory dancing in his head, this visionary slogged though the pestilential muck along Buffalo Bayou scouting locations for his proposed playhouse. (Evidentally, it would have stood somewhere in the vicinity of what is now the Old Spaghetti Warehouse restaurant at Allen's Landing.) Having found a site that looked promising, Lyons soon decamped for the United States and put together a troupe of actors.

After some months of fund-raising and preparation, the whole gang, together with trunkloads of costumes and props, boarded the schooner *Pennsylvania* for the return trip to the Republic of Texas. Bad Move. Their ship sank in a storm and the early hope of establishing Houston as a center for the theatrical arts went to the bottom.

It took many years, but Lyon's dream materialized—sort of. In theatrical terms, present-day Houston is not New York's major rival. Talk of "Third Coast" Hollywoods notwithstanding, it isn't even Los Angeles's nemesis, but our town does have the Alley, one of the nation's better regional theaters, and several good smaller playhouses. The university theaters often try new and/or adventurous material, and the community theater scene is lively. Even high schools, especially the High School for the Performing and Visual Arts, do some interesting work. All of these are worth a visit.

## A.D. PLAYERS

### 2710 West Alabama • Houston, TX 77098 • 526-2721

The A.D. Players present entertainment with a Christian world view through five productions a year at Grace Theatre and more than 35 plays in touring repertory. The group has a Christian Drama School with sessions throughout the year for adults and children, an Annual National Christian Drama Seminar, and a year-round recruitment and training program. If all this sounds very serious and pious, it isn't. A.D. puts on some of Houston's best kids shows and often does plays that are fun and/or thought-provoking.

## ACTORS THEATRE OF HOUSTON

### 2506 South Boulevard • Houston, TX 77098 • 529-6606

Some of the finest actors in Houston have trained or performed here. While the emphasis is on classical American works, they do offer some innovative plays, and the Houston premiers of works by some of America's best-known playwrights. The acting classes are top notch.

## ACTORS WORKSHOP OF HOUSTON

### 1009 Chartres • Houston, TX 77227-2366 • 236-1844

The Actors Workshop of Houston presents three or four classical plays per year and offers beginning and advanced acting classes. Its cabaret theater's repertoire includes mystery, comedy, classics, and musicals. Each fall the Actors Workshop presents a George S. Kaufman Classic, and some interesting experimental works.

## ALLEY THEATRE

### 615 Texas Avenue • Houston, TX 77002 • 228-9341 (info)
### 228-8421 (tickets)

Still *the* resident professional theater company in Houston, the Alley has a national reputation. Under the direction of Gregory Boyd, the theater is presenting some world-class works. With New York pricing itself out of the theatrical development market, the Alley and some of its regional theater counterparts have spent more time and effort developing what used to be called mainstream Broadway musicals. Some have been darn good. The organization has come a long way from its original, rat-infested digs down a narrow *alley* behind a fan factory. (Yes. That *is* the origin of the name). These days the theater presents some 12 plays a year on the Large and Arena stages. It also offers children's productions, performances by TREAT (Traveling Repertory Ensemble of Alley Theatre), new and innovative works in the Alley Ways series, and a statewide as well as a regional tour of one Large Stage production.

## CHANNING PLAYERS, INC.
### c/o 3917 Bute • Houston, TX 77006 • 785-9492

The all-volunteer Channing Players is the oldest, continually producing community theater in Houston, and it presents three shows each year to the public.

## CHILDREN'S THEATRE OF HOUSTON
### 1133-A West Clay • Houston, TX 77019 • 528-4881

The group doesn't perform in a regular theater, but it does offer innovative, multicultural theater programs for elementary schools and children's civic groups.

## THE COMPANY ONSTAGE
### 536 Westbury Square • Houston, TX 77035 • 726-1219

This long-lived community theater group does a good job of staging fun plays for the whole family, and its children's theater presentations are always well worth the trip to Westbury Square.

---

### HOUSTON FACTOID:

*Clark Gable, star of* Gone With The Wind, *learned his actor's diction in Houston. He studied elocution while living at the corner of Whitney and Hyde Park in the Montrose area.*

## COUNTRY PLAYHOUSE

**12802 Queensbury • Houston, TX 77024 • 467-4497**

This longtime community theater located in Town and Country Village presents dramas, comedies, and musicals. But the specialty of the company is fun mysteries, some by local playwrights.

## CURTAINS THEATER

**3722 Washington • Houston, TX 77008 • 862-4548**

A feisty up-and-comer on the Houston theatrical scene, Curtains covers the waterfront. The company has done everything from French farce to up-to-the-minute AIDS dramas, making good use of their old retail space.

## DIVERSEWORKS

**11171 East Freeway • Houston, TX 77002 • 223-8346**

This is the cutting edge of drama and performance art in Houston. DiverseWorks is, as the name suggests, diverse. You never know what you're going to find there. Like Kuumba House, it isn't strictly a theatrical venue, but often presents plays of one kind or another. When you're feeling adventurous, give it a try.

## ENSEMBLE THEATRE

**3535 Main Street • Houston, TX 77002 • 520-0055**

The Ensemble is the oldest black repertory theater group in the Southwest. The company has presented some of the finest works of African-American drama as well as new and experimental plays by local writers. There is also a children's program.

## GILBERT AND SULLIVAN SOCIETY OF HOUSTON

**P.O. Box 55456 • Houston, TX 77055 • 627-3570**

The society performs the comic operas of Gilbert and Sullivan. Open auditions attract singers and musicans from all walks of life for the annual opera in Jones Hall. A nonprofit organization founded in 1952, the society works to preserve the traditions established by the now-defunct D'Oyly Carte Opera Company in London. All the operas, in English, are suitable for all ages. The soci-

ety also provides entertainment for interested groups upon
request and availability.

## HISPANIC THEATER WORKSHOP

**University of St. Thomas • Houston, TX 77006**
**522-7911, Ext. 283, or 621-3245**

In Jones Theatre, 100 seats (upstairs) and 299 seats (downstairs),
HTW presents classical and modern works of the Spanish-language
theater.

## HOUSTON COMMUNITY COLLEGE-HEINEN THEATRE

**3517 Austin • Houston, TX 77004 • 265-5354**

The Heinen Theater houses two performing facilities that are
used by the college's fine arts department, which has been producing some cutting-edge works, especially those with minority
themes. Both of HCC's facilities are also available for community
rental. Theatre One, an 85-seat black-box theater, is best used for
recitals and small-cast productions. The 302-seat proscenium
Heinen Theatre is equipped with state-of-the-art rigging, lights,
and sound. It is a reconstruction of the former Temple Beth Israel.
Parking in college lots for the theaters is free. Both theaters have
full facilities for persons with disabilities, with 16 wheelchair seats
in the Heinen and ten in Theatre One.

## HOUSTON SKYLINE THEATER

**Houston House (ninth floor) • 1617 Fannin • Houston, TX 77002**
**523-1530**

Skyline, which boasts one of the most interesting theatrical
venues in the city—on an upper floor of a downtown highrise
apartment building—is commited to unique and daring productions. The theater has given world premiers of controversial
works and done fascinating stagings of more conventional plays.

## KUUMBA HOUSE

**811 Westheimer, Suite 110-B • Houston, TX 77006 • 524-1079**

Like DiverseWorks, Kuumba House houses a variety of creative
endeavors and it is not designed strictly as a theatrical venue, but

Goat Song productions, among others, often uses the space for works about the African and African-American experience.

## MAIN STREET THEATRE

**2540 Times Boulevard • Houston, TX 77005 • 524-3622**

Since 1975, Main Street Theatre has presented more than 100 productions ranging from Shakespeare and T. S. Eliot to Tom Stoppard and Studs Terkel. Variety is the theater's trademark, and its subscription series generally presents classics, but also offers comedy, serious drama, and an annual musical. Some of the best acting in Houston can be seen in MST's tiny space, and year-round children's theater productions are also some of the best in town.

## NO ENCONTRAMOS

**Performances at various theaters • Main office: 11770 Westheimer, Suite 2501 • Houston, TX 77077 • 589-7204**

The group offers works by Latin-American playwrights performed in both English and Spanish. They also bring works by Shakespeare, presented in Spanish, to area schools.

## PASADENA LITTLE THEATER

**4318 Allen Genoa • Mailing Address: P.O. Box 4193 Pasadena, TX 77502 • 941-4636**

A long-time pillar of the community theater scene, Pasadena Little Theater consistently produces fun versions of comedies and comic mysteries by big name playwrights, but more importantly, it gives local writers a showcase for their often considerable talents.

## PLAYHOUSE 1960

**6814 Grant Road • Houston, TX 77066 • 58-STAGE**

This is community theater that's fun and close to home for those in the burgeoning FM 1960 area. The repertoire runs toward long-time favorites such as Agatha Christie's *The Mousetrap* and new comedies and comic mysteries.

## RICE PLAYERS OF RICE UNIVERSITY
**Hamman Hall, Rice University • 527-4040**

Although the players are students, the productions are often of surprisingly high quality. The troupe performs theatrical classics, innovative works, and some by student and local playwrights.

## SHAKESPEARE GLOBE CENTRE OF THE SOUTHWEST
**c/o University of Houston • 4800 Calhoun**
**Houston, TX 77004 • 743-2916**

Rutherford Cravens, a longtime pillar of the Houston theater community, directs "Shakespeare Outreach," a program of the Shakespeare Globe Centre, which offices at the University of Houston. The group performs scenes from Shakespeare for Houston's schools, libraries, and nonprofit institutions. The scenes are intended as tools for English teachers in breaking down "Shakes-fear," high school students' belief that the Bard's plays are boring, incomprehensible, and irrelevant. While remaining true to the text, Shakespeare Outreach tries to involve the audience in an exciting and fun contemporary theatrical experience.

## SOCIETY FOR THE PERFORMING ARTS
**615 Louisiana • Houston, TX 77002 • 227-5134**

When Houston got Jesse H. Jones Hall back in 1966, we needed some nifty performances to put in it. That's where SPA came in. The society presents internationally famous violinists, pianists, guitarists, and other solo artists, but it also brings some of the best in theater performances to town. It is one of the few independent, nonprofit, presenting organizations in the United States.

## STAGES REPERTORY THEATRE
**3201 Allen Parkway, Suite 101 • Houston, TX 77019 • 527-0240**

Stages, like Main Street, is a professional regional theater. While its scale doesn't match the Alley's, it does offer some really good productions of theater classics and Southwest and world premiers of new and experimental works. The theater also produces occasional cabaret shows and offers "Early Stages," a daytime repertory of quality performances for young audiences and families. One of

Stages most important contributions to theater is the annual Texas Playwrights Festival, which is already nationally known for discovering and developing Texas theater artists.

### THEATER LAB HOUSTON

**1706 Alamo • Houston, TX 77270-0755 • 868-7516**

Theater LAB has presented the Houston premiers of some fine and controversial works by top playwrights such as Larry Kramer (*The Normal Heart*) and offers interesting stagings of nominally large plays in an intimate setting.

### THEATRE SOUTHWEST

**3767 Harper • Houston, TX 77005 • 977-6028**

Theatre Southwest's season includes farces, drama, and original productions, but the theater's strength is comic mysteries, which they do exceptionally well. Monthly meetings and regular auditions are open to the public. Theatre Southwest also sponsors workshop scenes to assist new directors, playwrights, and actors to develop their crafts.

### THEATRE SUBURBIA

**1410 West 43rd Street • Houston, TX 77018 • 682-3525**

Theatre Suburbia has been an active community playhouse since 1961. Its schedule includes traditional favorites—mostly comedies—but Suburbia also offers works not frequently performed in Houston, including quite a few by local playwrights.

### THEATRE UNDER THE STARS

**4235 San Felipe • Houston, TX 77027 • 622-1626**

This nonprofit musical theater organization is Houston's version of Broadway. TUTS brings some of the nation's most popular touring shows to town and stages its own lavish versions of musical theater classics. In the beginning, more than a generation ago, TUTS was as the name implies: Theater Under the Stars with productions in Miller Outdoor Theatre in Hermann Park. Gradually the organization expanded, offering indoor winter entertainment at the downtown Music Hall. Still one of Houston's most popular summer outdoor entertainments, TUTS' major productions at Miller Outdoor Theatre are free to the public every summer. The Humphreys School of Musical Theatre, which is a wing of the organization, offers classes for ages 4 through adult.

## UNIVERSITY OF HOUSTON DRAMA DEPARTMENT
### 4800 Calhoun • Houston, TX 77004 • 743-3003

The University of Houston Drama Department sponsors three professional projects: the Houston Shakespeare Festival, the Children's Theatre Festival, and the Festival Mime Company. Each year between September and May, the drama department produces five plays at Wortham Center on campus.

# SPORTS AND FITNESS

Houston is a sports-crazy town. Since the earliest settlers, who staged regular races, shooting contests, and even swimming races in the bayou (where the known presence of 12-foot alligators and equally huge, nasty buffalo gar, no doubt inspired speed records), Houstonians have enjoyed athletic competition.

We have professional entries in all of the major sports as well as college teams of all descriptions playing regular schedules. There are race tracks for both dogs and horses, though their futures aren't necessarily assured. There are also some of the best high school sports in the nation. (Contact your local school district for schedule information.)

Because the weather almost never gets below freezing, sports played seasonally elsewhere are year-round possibilities in Houston. So, whether you prefer spectator sports, or the do-it-yourself variety, there's something here to enjoy.

---

**HOUSTON FACTOID:**

*Before the advent of the Astros, or even the Colt.45's, there was the Texas League team, the Houston Buffs. Home plate from old Buffs Stadium is now located inside the Finger Furniture store—home of the Houston Sports Museum—on the Gulf Freeway.*

---

# PROFESSIONAL TEAMS

## BASEBALL

### HOUSTON ASTROS

**Astrodome • Kirby at South Loop • 799-9555**
**799-9567 (group and season tickets)**

Is there a black cloud over the Astrodome? For a generation, the Astros broke fans' hearts by coming . . . *this close* to the National League Championship. Just when it was about to happen for real back in 1994, Major League Baseball went out on strike. End of dream. The next season, the 'stros owner announced that he was losing so much money he, like Bud Adams, would have to move the team out of town. The city was not amused. The Greater Houston Partnership said this would be bad for Houston's image, and launched a season-ticket drive. So, until the next crisis at least, it's still possible to spend 81 home games pondering the mysteries of baseball in the Dome. Stay tuned.

## BASKETBALL

### HOUSTON ROCKETS

**The Summit • Southwest Freeway at Edloe • 627-3865**

The professional basketball championship of the known universe took up residence in Houston in 1994 and stayed on through 1995. There are two Rocket banners hanging from the ceiling of the Summit to prove it. In recent years, basketball has become *the* spectator sport for upwardly mobile types. If you want to impress business associates or clients, tix to some of the Rockets' 41 home games would not come amiss. That is, of course, if you can find any. Even at ticket agency prices, fans find it a good investment and a great opportunity to see the visiting greats of the NBA. Hot teams sell out quickly, so plan accordingly. The tickets are expensive. Think twice about taking very small children.

## FOOTBALL

### HOUSTON OILERS
**Astrodome • Kirby at South Loop • 797-1000**

Emotionally—if not physically—the Bud Adams franchise (once known as the Houston Oilers) is gone. The owner took his pros to Nashville, so why not transfer football loyalties to some people who'd appreciate it, the local college teams? The Cougars (University of Houston), Owls (Rice University), and Tigers (Texas Southern Universtiy) each play a fun brand of football, and there's nothing like a crowd of college students cheering on their school's team when it comes to enthusiasm. Each school plays at least one game against a long-time rival. That's when the pageantry is at its most colorful. There are *real* cheerleaders, there are college kids in animal suits impersonating school mascots, and there are the bands. The UH Cougar Band is in the classic college tradition, if TSU's Ocean of Soul doesn't get you clapping and dancing you've got to be dead, and the Rice MOB's cynical, goofy takeoffs of half-time shows is like nothing else. Best of all, the ticket prices won't bankrupt you.

## HOCKEY

### HOUSTON AEROS
**The Summit • 10 Greenway Plaza • 621-2812 for tickets and info**

This is an improbable town in which to start up a hockey franchise, especially when most people here have never even *seen* natural ice, but it seems to be working out just fine. The Aeros, heirs to the name of the old World Hockey Association team that featured Hall of Famer Bobby Hull and his two sons, have a rabid following. The team plays in an NHL league of the triple-A variety, and yes, it is true. Some people go for the fights and discover that a hockey game has broken out. But, fights and all, the team is always entertaining. So is the fan-friendly hoopla that accompanies every contest. Tickets are much less expensive than ducats for the Rockets and Oilers, and kids enjoy the non-stop action.

## INDOOR SOCCER

### HOUSTON HOTSHOTS
**The Summit • 10 Greenway Plaza • (713) HOT-5100**

The Continental Indoor Soccer League has teams all over the U.S., but also in several Mexican cities, which adds real international flavor to this indoor variation of the world's most popular sport. For those who've never seen it, indoor soccer is kind of like hockey without the skates. The action is fast and furious—especially in the Hotshots' "Black & Blue" division. The games are all played on weekends (Friday night, Saturday afternoon or evening, or Sunday afternoons) so they're easy to plan for. They're also a lot of fun. The franchise works hard to make these family affairs, with lots of kid-oriented hoopla. It doesn't hurt that the tickets are reasonably priced.

# COLLEGE SPORTS

### RICE UNIVERSITY (OWLS)
**6100 Main • 527-4068 for tickets and information**

The Owls are at a decided disadvantage in big-time sports such as football and basketball. Unfortunately for their fans, stiff academic requirements mean that the Owls often play on an Ivy League level while their competition plays like the NBA or the NFL. Still, football in Rice Stadium, with the school's hilarious Marching Owl Band, the MOB, entertaining at halftime, is a wonderful fall experience. Tennis, swimming, and women's sports, all played on campus, are often strong.

### TEXAS SOUTHERN UNIVERSITY (TIGERS)
**3100 Cleburne • 313-7271 for tickets and information**

For SWAC football games against traditional rivals Jackson State and Prairie View, the Tigers draw big crowds. Some football games are played at the Dome, others at nearby Robertson Stadium on the UH campus. TSU basketball teams are always worth watching and have been invited to play in the big national tournaments.

## UNIVERSITY OF HOUSTON (COUGARS)
**4800 Calhoun • 743-9444 for tickets and information**

When they're hot, the Cougar football team could probably beat the weaker entries in the NFL. Football is taken *very* seriously in Cougarland. So is the basketball program, which has turned out NBA stars such as Hakeem Olajuwan and Clyde Drexler. Track is the coming thing since Olympic multi-medalist Carl Lewis put the program on the map, and women's volleyball is also very strong. Football games are played in the Dome as well as Robertson Stadium, and other sports are played on campus.

---

### HOUSTON FACTOID:

*On January 20, 1968, the largest crowd ever to see a regular-season college basketball game (52,893) saw UH end UCLA's 47-game winning streak, 71-69, in the Astrodome. UCLA's captain that night was Michael Warren, later the star of TV's* Hill Street Blues.

---

## DO-IT-YOURSELF SPORTS

### GOLF

There are lots of private country clubs in the Houston area, and there are some that allow non-members to play. These are true public courses, open to all. And "all" means kids, duffers the likes of which you usually see only at Putt-Putt, and some truly great golfers. Take your chances. The fees are low, but the lines can be long.

**Brock Park,** 5201 John Ralston Road, 455-1550

**Glenbrook Park,** 5205 N. Bayou, 644-4051

**Gus Wortham Park,** 7000 Capitol, 921-5227

**Hermann Park,** 6201 Golf Course Drive, 529-9755

**Memorial Park,** 6001 Memorial Loop Drive East, 562-4055

**Sharpstown Park,** 5200 Bellaire Boulevard, 955-2099

## TENNIS

Ever since grand slammers Zina Garrison and Lori McNeil came out of Houston's public courts to play at Wimbledon and the U. S. Open, thousands of kids have decided to follow in their footsteps. Adults, too, some with Walter Mitty-esque fantasies, turn out on the public courts, but most who play here just want the tennis experience without the expense of a private club. The fees are reasonable, but you really need to book well in advance.

**MacGregor,** 5225 Calhoun Road, 747-5466

**Memorial Park,** 1500 Memorial Loop, 561-5765

**Southwest,** 9506 S. Gessner, 772-0296

# GYMNASIUMS AND SWIMMING POOLS

The city's parks and recreation department operates nearly 60 gymnasiums and swimming pools throughout the city and offers low-cost classes in a variety of sports. For information, call 845-1000.

# JOGGING TRAILS

Parks and Rec also maintains a city-wide system of hike-and-bike trails that covers more than 30 miles. The sections that get the most use are in Memorial Park, along Buffalo Bayou leading into downtown, and along Braes Bayou in the southwest part of the city. During prime after-work time, they can be as crowded as the freeways at rush hour. Plan accordingly.

# YMCA

The Y isn't exactly a public facility, but it isn't just a health club either. With more than 120,000 members, the Y performs a variety of volunteer charity functions, aids inner-city youth, and offers some of the best fitness facilities around. Almost thirty branch Ys are scattered around Houston, offering everything from weight lifting to child care. Call the Metro Area Office for an information brochure, 659-5566.

## FITNESS

There are an infinity of fitness clubs in the Houston area. They open and close every day. If there was a club near you that is no longer, your best bet is to watch the location. Many spots have housed several different incarnations, and even those who've been around for quite some time change their offerings and/or their prices. For the latest trends and prices, check in Houston *Health & Fitness*, a free publication that's been covering the local fitness scene for years. Meanwhile, the following are some of the longtime establishments.

### BAYOU PARK CLUB
**4400 Memorial Drive • 880-9330**

Ages 25 to 35. 1/1 male/female. Open seven days. $50 per month, with $150–$300 initiation fee. Stairmasters, lap pool, rowing machines, and aerobics.

### CHANCELLORS RACQUET AND FITNESS CLUB
**6535 Dumfries • 772-9955**

Ages 30 to 70. 1/1 male/female. Open seven days. $35-$84 per month, with $100-$150 initiation fee. Stationary bikes, pool, racquetball and tennis courts, circuit-training equipment, treadmills, and child care.

### DOWNTOWN YMCA
**1600 Louisiana • 659-8501**

Ages 16 to 80. 3/2 male/female. Open seven days. regular members: $200 initiation fee (or if you join in January or when they're running another special, $100) There is also a $47.55 monthly charge for full membership. This includes access to all Houston-area Ys for only $12 extra per month. Off-peak memberships (limited access): $100 initiation fee ($40 in January) plus $34.20 per month thereafter. Call for information on student and senior citizen discounts.Weight-training equipment, free weights, 60 exercise classes, individualized fitness programs, 20 racquetball/handball courts, three squash courts, indoor-outdoor track, three gyms, stationary bikes, pool, aerobics classes, fitness evaluations, and body-fat percentage testing.

## FITNESS CENTER AT SOUTH SHORE HARBOUR

### 3000 Invincible Drive, League City • 334-2560

Ages 14 to 78. 1/1 male/female, general fitness and recreation enthusiasts. Open seven days. Individual $50 per month, with $360 initiation fee; family $65 per month, with $350 initiation fee. Tennis courts, track, pool, stationary bikes, racquetball courts, free weights, volleyball court, aerobics classes, and circuit-training equipment.

## FITNESS EXCHANGE

### 3930 Kirby at Southwest Freeway • 524-9932

Ages 18 to 78. 3/1 male/female. Open seven days. $15 per month, depending on access to facilities. Stationary bikes, free weights, aerobics, circuit-training equipment, and aerobics.

## HANK'S GYM

### 5320 Elm • 668-6219

Ages 14 to 70. 3/1 male/female. $25-$43 per month, with no initiation fee. Personal trainers and huge selection of weight-training equipment.

## THE HOUSTON CENTER CLUB

### 1100 Caroline • 654-0877

Ages 35 to 50. 3/1 male/female. Open seven days. $57–$114 per month, with $1,000–$5,100 one-time initiation fee. Aerobic conditioning, basketball court, free weights.

## THE HOUSTONIAN

### 111 N. Post Oak Lane • 680-2626

Ages children to 80, many professionals, families, young people, singles. 1/1 male/female. Open seven days. Resident membership: $125 per month single/couple, $150 per month family, with $12,500 initiation fee; associate membership: $90 per month single, $110 per month couple, $125 per month family, with $3,500 initiation fee (10 percent discount corporate rate for three or more). Stationary bikes, pool, five tennis courts, eight racquetball courts, full-court basketball, weight-training equipment, volleyball court, personal trainers, **aerobics, free** weights, running track, child care, seven restaurants, **and the** Phoenix Fitness Resort.

### INSTITUTE FOR PREVENTIVE MEDICINE
**Methodist Hospital, Scurlock Tower • 6560 Fannin • 790-6450**

Ages 30 to 60. $650 per year, **includes** parking and exercise facilities. Junior Olympic pool, indoor track, free-weight room, racquetball court, aerobics, aquatics, Nautilus equipment, stationary bikes, treadmills, rowing machines, dry sauna, individual and large whirlpools, and professional personal trainers.

### MASTERSON YWCA
**3615 Willia • 868-6075**

Aerobics, heated indoor pool, yoga, Dancercise, water exercise, chair exercises, prenatal water exercise, and body sculpting.

### METROPOLITAN RACQUET CLUB
**One Allen Center • 340 W. Dallas • 652-0700**

Ages 18 to 75. Call for fees. Thirteen indoor tennis courts, eight racquetball courts, four squash courts, basketball, full weight room, and aerobics.

### NORTHWEST YMCA
**1234 W. 34th • 869-3378**

Ages 17 to 45. $13 per month, with $39 initiation fee. Weight room, exercise room (treadmill, bicycles, waist twister), nine-station hydrafitness center, basketball gym, outdoor pool, three baseball fields, shower-locker room, aerobics.

### POST OAK FAMILY YMCA
**1331 Augusta • 781-1061**

Ages newborn to seniors. 3/2 male/female. $35 per month first year, $24.50 thereafter, with $50 initiation fee. Circuit-training equipment, Stairmasters, rowing machines, stationary bikes, free weights, aerobics, and child care.

## THE TEXAS CLUB
### 601 Travis • 227-7000

Ages 25 to 45. 3/2 male/female. Open seven days. Family and individual memberships; call for fees. Free weights, exercise equipment, aerobics, basketball, scuba training, stationary bikes, track, pool, five racquetball courts, squash, wallyball, and volleyball.

## THE UNIVERSITY CLUB
### 5051 Westheimer • Post Oak Towers • 621-4811

Ages 25 to 65. Call for fees. Ten tennis courts, three racquetball courts, two squash courts, Nautilus, cardiovascular equipment, free weights, outdoor heated pool, indoor track, basketball, and massage.

## WESTSIDE YMCA
### 1006 Voss Road • 467-5911

Ages 18 to 55. 1/1 male/female. Open seven days. $27–$50. Three pools, two racquetball courts, sauna-whirlpool, weight equipment, and tennis courts.

# GREEN HOUSTON

In recent years, Houston—the place where plastic grass was invented—has become much more garden conscious. While there are still those who prefer flowers to be made of silk and their ficus trees out of PVC, there are also more and more people for whom gardening is serious fun.

Perhaps as an offshoot of all this planting, farmers markets and home-grown vegetables are no longer considered the exclusive domain of aged hippies or health-freak sprout eaters. Nowadays perfectly reasonable people are turning green, and there is lots of advice out there on how to do it.

Folks with a professional interest in gardening range from the local discount mart to radio hosts across the spectrum from "nuke it first and ask questions later" to "all creatures have a right to live." There's also some good objective advice out there at the plant societies and in the Gardening Newsletter. Happy plantings.

## GARDEN CENTERS

Houstonians just love to get their hands dirty. Gardening is one of our favorite hobbies, and business has taken note. Big discount stores have tacked "nurseries" onto the sides of their buildings, sometimes making plants a loss leader. Competing with that is tough, but many Houston nurseries combine unusual plants, specialized knowledge, and quality stock that makes them stand out.

Some of the most interesting can be found in the Heights, where pocket nurseries have long proliferated. Most prominent is **Buchanan's Native Plants,** 611 E. 11th St., 861-5702, where hardy plants suitable for Gulf Coast growing conditions abound: trees, shrubs, flowers, and herbs. Just down the street at **Another Place in Time,** 1102 Tulane, 864-9717, you'll find plants your grandmother grew. Heirloom-variety vegetables fill a front section, while black-eyed Susan vine showers the chain-link fence behind with tiny orange flowers. The owners have a penchant for succulents and prehistoric ferns, too. At **Joshua's Native Plants and Garden Antiques,** 111 Heights, 862-7444, looks like a hobby has taken over the property. The resulting bazaar of plants and garden art is not haphazard, but shoppers do have a sense of exploration and discovery. Plants are moderately priced, but the antiques are more serious business, ranging from froglike white gargoyles (about $45) to a pair of Italian marble angels suitable for your 17th-century cathedral (about $4,500). Nonantique garden sculpture includes secular birdbaths and a Catholic collection of religious figures, from the Infant of Prague to Our Lady of Guadelupe to the ubiquitous St. Francis of Assisi.

**Lucia's Garden,** 2942 Virginia, 523-6494, offers the Houston area's broadest collection of herb plants. Owners Lucia and Michael Bettler share their expertise through classes, a customer newsletter, and casual chat. They also sell dried herbs, crafts, potpouris and candles as well as plants; Lucia is also a certified aromatherapist.

**Briarpatch Organic Farm,** 2020 State St., 868-3919, opens to the public on weekends only . Classes here focus on growing and cooking, and new owner Deborah Beeman plans to produce vegetables as well as herbs. The site and growing conditions are certified organic by the Texas Department of Agriculture.

**Anderson Nursery in Spring Branch,** 2222 Pech, 984-1342, carries the best selection of native trees and shrubs. A bonus is owner Mike Anderson's father-in-law, Lynn Lowrey, "sort of" retired but usually on the premises at Anderson's. Proprietor of Lowrey's Nursery in Conroe for many years, he's intimately familiar with hundreds of species that are native but oddly exotic—since they're not in commercial cultivation, most of us never see them. Both men are a treasure trove of Texana and expert advice, and are very accessible.

**Bill Bownds Nursery,** 2815 Campbell (Spring Branch), 462-6447, specializes in trees of all kinds: hundreds are cultivated on the storefront's "back 40" and at the company's Sugar Land nursery. Other tree specialists: **RCW Nursery,** 15809 Tomball Parkway, 440-5161, which also carries a fine selection of roses and other ornamentals (including peacocks, but they're not for sale) and the **Houston Palm Tree Co.,** 20420 Gulf Freeway, 943-7466.

**Condon Gardens,** 1214 Augusta, 782-3992, is probably the loveliest nursery in town. Beautiful plants are mingled with garden art, benches, and copper water sculptures throughout the grounds, effectively showing customers how to use plants in a livable environment.

**The Color Yard,** 4513 Brittmoore, 896-0717, beckons passing drivers in the Beltway 8 area with an outdoor display of blooming plants in season. Plants that aren't blooming are bargains here, they go to the mark-down bins to move quickly.

**Covington Nursery on Airline,** 8620 Airline, 447-1690, boasts the best selection of vegetable plants within seed-spitting distance of Houston. Never does spring arrive without 80 or more different tomatoes, which owner Dan Loep chronicles in a how-to-grow-'em fact sheet for his customers. This is a nursery in the sense Webster originally intended: Loep grows most of his vegetables, plus some hardy hibiscus and other ornamentals, from seed in the greenhouses behind the store. Lots of pepper varieties here, too, plus fruit trees and other edibles.

**Cornelius Nurseries** (four locations) was the first local nursery to install lavish landscapes beyond its property lines, including the medians on Voss Road and Dairy Ashford. The color show lured plenty of passing motorists while making the neighborhoods pretty; they also helped make hibiscus, a Cornelius favorite, a staple in Houston gardens. In the fall, Cornelius has the best bulb selection this side of the Bulb Mart (see below).

**Teas Nursery,** 4400 Bellaire Blvd., 664-4400, is a family-owned and-operated business that ranks among Houston's oldest. The landscape staff has few peers in Houston, and high quality plants and garden art ensure Teas' place as the nursery of choice for Bellaire, West U and points beyond. Roses are a specialty here, with hybrid teas the breed of choice.

**Natural Gardens** (formerly Garden-Ville), 2919 Main St. in Stafford, 261-7645, is a beacon for organic gardeners, especially in

Houston's southwest quadrant. But owner Mark Bowen is an evangelist who knows no bounds; he's active in community garden programs all over town, especially Urban Harvest. His retail store specializes in organic soils, products and processes, generally an information exchange for low-toxic-minded horticulture.

To the west, two specialty dealers offer Houston-area gardeners both special expertise and a great day trip in the bargain.

**Lilypons Water Gardens,** 839 FM 1960 in Brookshire, 391-0076, is the lily and lotus capital of the South. Owners Rolf and Anita Nelson recently hosted an International Water Lily Festival, and they've not stopped running since. Open-house or seminar events are held in March, April, June, September and November.

**Antique Rose Emporium,** FM 50 in Independence (near Brenham), (409) 836-5548. Old roses are among Houston's most reliable plants: beautiful, long-blooming, and largely free of the pest and fungus attacks that plague florist's roses like hybrid teas. The ARE is a showplace that will inspire you to plan landscapes around these gorgeous, heritage-rich plants. Visit during the April open house and savor the wildflowers all the way.

## GARDENING RESOURCES

There are dozens of gardening books and guides that are helpful to Houston-area gardeners. Many are available at the River Oaks Bookstore, 3270 Westheimer, which specializes in home- and garden-oriented works. Also see the Saturday garden pages of the *Houston Chronicle*.

### ESSENTIAL BOOKS:

*Houston Garden Book*, Shearer Publishing, $19.95 softcover. Lavishly photographed and rich with charts and tips for growing in Houston, this guide was written by John Kriegel, longtime garden editor of *Houston Home & Garden*. The most comprehensive garden book for the area.

*A Garden Book for Houston,* Gulf Publishing, $24.95 hardcover. Another indispensable book by the River Oaks Garden Club. While sections on native plants and other subjects were expanded in the recent edition, homeowners with Memorial-style landscapes will find this book most useful. The last word on azaleas.

---

### HOUSTON FACTOID:

*It seems a lot brighter here in Houston, but the odds of seeing the
sun shine at least half the daylight hours are 57 percent, the same
as Baltimore, Chicago, and Cincinnati.*

---

## RADIO SHOWS:

**KTRH** (740) *Gardenline,* with Bill Zak and John Burrow, broadcasts six
days a week, three times as often as its competitors. Mon–Fri 10–noon,
Sat 8–11 a.m. Call-in line: 526-4740. These good ol' boys can make you
think it's 1950 (they address female callers as "hon," "darlin'," or
"missy" and it goes over big). Too often they'll refer questions to adver-
tisers instead of answering themselves, but these longtime hosts are
engaging and full of information, affectionately shared.

**KPRC** (950) *Garden Report,* with Ben Oldag, Saturdays 10–noon,
Sun 9–noon. Call-in line: 777-5772. A former ag agent, Oldag
seems more comfortable talking about vegetables than his rivals.
He addresses callers of the opposite sex as "dear."

**KSEV** (700) *Your Livable Garden,* Shawn and David Kelly, Saturdays
9–11 a.m. Call-in line: 558-5738. Landscape pros (Shawn has a horticulture degree as well), the Kellys are younger, hipper, and less eager
to use pesticides than other hosts. They're big-picture, beautiful-yard
guys; if you've got a problem with a peach tree or a tomato plant, call
KSEV's sister station KPRC and chat up Ben Oldag instead.

## NEWSLETTER:

*Gardening Newsletter for the Texas Gulf Coast,* nine times per year, P.O.
Box 7946, Houston, Texas 77270; 468-8580. Covers ornamental
plants, vegetables, organic and chemical pest management and
landscaping. Includes a timely section on what to plant, fertilize,
and prune now. Formerly *Bob Flagg's Gardening Newsletter.*

---

**HOUSTON FACTOID:**

*In the summer of 1980, Houston had 14 straight days of more than 100 degrees. Nonessential water was rationed.*

---

## ANNUAL GARDENING EVENTS & SALES

The gardening year, too, has its own calendar. Some of these events special to gardeners are also of interest to those who rarely venture into the world of living things. If members of your family would prefer to AstroTurf the lawn or to install plastic shrubs, why not treat them to some of these events?

**Azalea Trail.** Recently celebrating its 60th year, the trail is an annual rite of spring in Houston. Usually the first two weekends in March, this home-and-garden tour features several River Oaks-area homes, the late Ima Hogg's Bayou Bend estate, and the Forum of Civics building at 2503 Westheimer; sponsored by the River Oaks Garden Club, 523-2483.

**March Mart.** The annual plant sale supporting Mercer Arboretum features many unusual and native plants that the mainstream nurseries rarely stock. Organizers take pride in carrying new oddities each year, but such goodies are usually snatched up by the earliest shoppers. Usually the fourth weekend in March; 22306 Aldine-Westfield Road in Humble, 443-8731.

**Bulb Mart & Plant Sale.** The Garden Club of Houston, determined to excite Houston gardeners about daffodils, tulips, and other bulb flowers, launched this annual event on the steps of City Hall more than 50 years ago. Now the mart takes over the Metropolitan Multi-Service Center, 1475 W. Gray, for a weekend in late September. The event has grown far beyond bulbs, too—there's no better source for gingers, for example, and Houston gardeners find colorful vines, unusual trees and shrubs, and a wide selection of perennials. Pre-order information: 871-8887.

## PLANT SOCIETIES

Garden clubs proliferate in Houston. In some, membership is by invitation, which may require some social standing and, shall we say, the "right demographics"; others are neighborhood groups that promote home gardening and civic beautification.

Listed below are groups that cross garden-club lines: societies dedicated to specific plants.

**African Violets.** NASA Area African Violet Society, meets 1st Wednesday, 7:30 p.m., Clear Lake Park Building, NASA Road 1; info: 473-1490.

Spring Branch African Violet Club, meets last Thursday, 7:30 p.m.; info: 468-0844. Show/sale: March.

**Amaryllis.** Greater Houston Amaryllis Club, meets 1st Monday, Sept.–May, 10 a.m., Houston Garden Center. Show/sale: December.

Houston Amaryllis Society, meets 4th Tuesday, Sept.–April, 10 a.m., Houston Garden Center. Show/sale: April.

**Begonias.** American Begonia Society, Astro Branch, meets 1st Sunday, 2 p.m., various sites. Write: 4407 Joyce Blvd., Houston, TX 77084, 463-1101.

Houston Satellite Branch, 946-4237; meets 4th Tuesday, 9:30 a.m. League City National Bank.

**Bromeliads.** Bromeliad Society of Houston, meets 3rd Tuesday, 7:30 p.m., Houston Garden Center. Sale: May. Call 529-5371.

**Cactus.** Houston Cactus & Succulent Society, call 436-1629 for meeting schedule. Show/sale: September. Write 3214 N. Peach Hollow Ct., Pearland, TX 77584-2021.

**Camellias.** Houston Camellia Society, meets 3rd Thursday, 7:30 p.m., River Oaks Recreation Building, 3600 Locke Lane. Show: December. Contacts: Bob Ackerly, 461-7522, and B. L. Ross, 468-4675.

## FARMER'S MARKETS

Despite a nearly year-round growing season, Houston has never developed a local produce industry such as, say, Austin's. But if you have a yen for fresh veggies—and want more than the considerable bounty of such grocers as Fiesta—here's where to go:

---

### HOUSTON FACTOID:

*Texas' Whole Foods Market, with several Houston outlets, is the nation's largest retailer of natural foods.*

---

**Airline Farmer's Market,** on Airline Drive just inside Loop 610 (near I-45), is the biggie: 15 acres of open-air shopping. Canino Produce dominates the entry, reeking of fresh melons or strawberries in season. Beyond Canino's, four long rows of merchants include a yard-egg dealer and sellers of every fruit and vegetable remotely in season. Mexican produce abound: chiles, *tunas* (prickly pear fruit), and *guaces* (the long, flat beans used in salsa-making). At Ray's Produce, owner Ray Self caters to co-op shoppers with lots of attention, good variety, and quality produce. Flores Spice & Produce is an olfactory delight, with Salvador Flores' heady mix of odd and common spices. John and Karen Randle sell vine-ripened tomatoes amid other specialty vendors. Farmers Marketing Association, 2520 Airline, 862-8866.

**The Fannin Street Flower Markets** are an informal collection of stands just south of downtown. They line both sides of the road and compete in selling the cheapest bouquets of cut flowers. A few of them also offer potted plants and even balloons. Most of the blooms are close to their "expiration dates," but if you're looking for an inexpensive armload of pretty, this is the place.

### OTHER FARMERS' MARKETS.

**Cy-Creek Farmer's Market,** 9814 Grant Road, 469-5200

**Montalvo Produce of Mexico,** 5009 Fulton, 694-6197

**Nature's Market,** 10924 FM 1960 West, 469-7665

**Pasadena Produce Market,** 2905 Spencer Highway, 947-0760

**J. Theiss & Sons,** 17045 Stuebner Airline Road, 370-3276

## Market Information

KNUZ radio (1170 AM) broadcasts a daily market update at 8:45 a.m.

### Locally grown vegetables in season

**May–June:** New potatoes, string beans, Kentucky Wonder beans, fresh pinto beans.

**May–October:** Anaheim, banana, cayenne, and jalapeño peppers; large and Oriental eggplant.

**Late May–July:** Tomatoes, some peaches.

**May–September:** Cantaloupe, cucumbers, zucchini and yellow crookneck squashes.

**Mid-June–September:** Watermelon, okra.

**June–July:** Sweet corn; purple-hull, black-eyed, and Dixie butter peas.

**Late July/September through first frost:** Sweet potatoes (previous season's harvest available winter through April).

**October–March:** Except in years of severe frost, butternut, acorn and other winter squashes, yellow crookneck squash (October), collard greens, kale, spinach, turnips and turnip greens, bok choy, cabbages, daikon, lettuces.

**Year-round:** Mustard greens.

### Market gardens by subscription

An outgrowth of the city's largest community garden program, local growers offer homeowners the chance to buy fresh, seasonal produce from organic-method gardens around town. These are not pick-your-own operations: you can visit some (and even point at the produce you want to be picked); others are far enough from downtown that they use drop-off points to get the week's harvest to their subscribers. Most participate through Urban Harvest, a community garden and orchard program of The Park People, 4710 Bellaire Blvd., Suite 360, Bellaire, TX 77401; 668-2094.

# THE RESTAURANT GUIDE

*Q: Who created the modern food service industry?*
*A: French revolutionaries.*

When all those angry folks started yelling "off with their heads" back in 1789, they certainly weren't talking about crawfish.

As discontent simmered in the streets, politicians pandered to the mobs. Next thing you know, the Committees of Public Safety in Paris and the provinces had created a terrible shortage of aristocrats—leaving the late upper crust's unemployed chefs to invent the modern restaurant business.

Quite a few of those chefs ended up here in the new world where previous notions of haute cuisine had consisted largely of roast varmint with whatever vegetables the bugs hadn't got to first.

Fortunately for us, the culinary situation has improved a lot in the past 200 years. In Houston, it has improved a whole lot in the last 20.

For most of its history, this was a steak-and-potatoes town. Period. For a change of pace, people frequented a few Mexican restaurants and a few "Continental" establishments. And then, pretty suddenly, everything changed. The mid-1970s brought a booming oil economy, which brought in people from all over the world—who brought their diverse tastes in food with them.

Now Houstonians can do Ethiopian for lunch and Argentine for dinner with a stopoff for Vietnamese snack food in between. In one generation, Houston's restaurant scene has gone from small-town conservatism to spectacular international eclecticism. And the number of choices just keeps on growing.

There are already at least 8,100 restaurants in town, and they serve more than 750 million meals a year. That's as if Houston restaurants served three meals a year to every man, woman, and child in the United States of America with an Amarillo's worth of people handing them the plates.

So . . . .

Where shall we eat?

I have eaten in hundreds of Houston restaurants since beginning these guidebooks, and I've enjoyed almost every minute of it. There are some really wonderful restaurants in this town. There are also some with big problems. The two are not mutually exclusive. Even the best of establishments can have an off night. The ones you won't see here are the chronic offenders.

Not every place on the list offers a gourmet dining experience—in fact, most don't. What they do offer is dependability. You can count on a certain level of quality in both the food and the service. Enjoy.

### KEY TO SYMBOLS

|     |     |
| --- | --- |
| AE  | American Express |
| CB  | Carte Blanche |
| DC  | Diners Club |
| MC  | Mastercard |
| V   | Visa |
| Dis | Discover |
| Cr. | All of the above |
| W   | Wheelchair access |

**Dinner for one, exclusive of drinks and tips**

|       |     |
| ----- | --- |
| $     | Inexpensive Under $7 |
| $$    | Moderate $7–$15 |
| $$$   | Expensive $16–$29 |
| $$$$  | Very Expensive $30 and up |

All prices, of course, are subject to change. They reflect dinner for one, exclusive of liquor, tax, and tip.

## ALFRED'S

**9123 Stella Link • Southwest • 667-6541 • Open Sun–Tues 8–3;**
**Wed lunch only; Thurs–Sat 8–8 • No reservations • $–$$; Cr. • W**

One of Houston's restaurant institutions, Alfred's serves the kind of deli food New Yorkers die for. Traditional kosher sandwiches, such as corned beef piled high on rye, can be accompanied by the essential coleslaw and potato salad for a real ethnic fix. The chicken-liver omelets are out of this world, and the cheesecake will remind displaced Manhattanites of home.

## ABDULLAH'S

**3939 Hillcroft • Southwest • 952-4747 • Mon–Sun lunch and**
**dinner • No reservations • $; Cr.**

It isn't fancy, and the location isn't trendy, but the Middle Eastern food, especially the vegetable dishes like spinach with black-eyed peas and the fabulous chile and garlic tomato salad, are worth the trip. The baba ghanouj is worth *walking* to Hillcroft for.

## AMÉRICAS

**1800 Post Oak Boulevard (Saks Pavilion) • Galleria Area**
**961-1492 • Mon–Fri lunch and dinner, Sat dinner only**
**Reservations recommended • $$$; Cr. • W**

Notice the last four digits of the phone number. These people think of everything. The literally fantastic decor probably would qualify as an installation at the Contemporary Arts Museum. The food is a fascinating melange of dishes from all over the Western Hemisphere—some bizarre, some surprising, just about all wonderful. The charcoal-grilled vegetables are a special treat. When they recommend reservations, believe them.

## ANDRE'S CONFISERIE SUISSE

**2515 River Oaks Boulevard • Near Southwest • 524-3863**
**Tues–Sat breakfast, lunch, tea; Mon lunch only; closed Sun**
**Reservations for large parties only • $$; V, MC, Dis • W**

Andre's is a Houston tradition. Its small blond-wood-paneled dining area with heart-shaped Heidi chairs and friendly waitresses hasn't changed much in the past quarter-century. The prix fixe luncheon menu includes a choice of three main dishes or the house special, quiche Lorraine. Each plate lunch comes with a green salad in vinaigrette, carrot salad, and sometimes fresh fruit. There are no substitutions. Andre's justly famous Linzer torte or Napoleons are included in the price. While the atmosphere is colorful with the flags of Swiss cantons, the food is generally bland in the 1950s fashion. It is well prepared and presented, just not piquant. The pastries, however, are another matter. Andre's is, as it claims to be, a confiserie, and the European-style desserts and candies are wonderful.

## ANTHONY'S

**4007 Westheimer • Near Southwest • 961-0552 • Mon–Fri lunch; Sat dinner only, closed Sun • Reservations recommended $$$–$$$$; Cr. • W**

For years Tony Vallone has been the maestro of Houston restaurateurs, and with good reason. Anthony's, formerly a lovely but less-than-haute Italian presence on Montrose Boulevard, has been transmogrified, becoming an elegant French-accented addition to Highland Village, where it now occupies the old Confederate House location. From serving some of the city's best Italian food, Anthony's has gone to serving some of the city's best French—and none of that minimalist, nouvelle stuff either. The imaginative menu features dishes such as a rich, satisfying bouillabaisse, New Zealand deer steak, a massive prime rib, and a fabulous, vestigial Montrose risotto. Save room for dessert. Bar.

## ANTONE'S

**807 Taft • Central • 526-1046**

**8111 South Main at Kirby southbound • Near South • 791-9800**

**1639 South Voss • West • 781-1788**

**4522 FM 1960 West • West • 580-244**

**Additional Antone's locations in Houston are franchises No reservations • $; MC, V • W**

Antone's po' boys are legendary. Though the restaurants only serve five kinds of sandwiches—tuna, turkey, "piggie," meat, and extra meat—the place offers an astounding array of imported edibles. Need saffron by the gram? Tea biscuits? If it comes from abroad, Antone's probably has it somewhere. As a lunch spot, the near-town location attracts everyone from surgeons to street people. Everyone sits on upended olive barrels at a long, banged-up table in the back room surrounded by wines from everywhere but Mars. This is for the adventurous and, at lunchtime, those who don't mind long lines. Beer and wine.

## ARMANDO'S

**2300 Westheimer • Central • 521-9757 • Open daily, lunch and dinner only • Reservations recommended • $$–$$$, Cr. • W**

Having fled its funky, much-added-to bungalow on Shepherd for new, tres-L.A. digs on Westheimer, Armando's has kept its many River Oaks fans' loyalty with Mexican and pasta dishes, some heart-healthy recipes with actual taste, and carefully prepared meats. The crowd is still studiously casual-chic and the reservations caveat is still serious. Bar.

## ASHLAND HOUSE

**1801 Ashland • Heights • 863-7613 • Lunch, Mon–Sat $$; MC,V, AE, Dis**

The two-story Victorian house location is a major part of the Ashland's unpretentious appeal. The food is a nice version of Sunday dinner at Grandma's. While fresh fish is often featured, the best bets are the old-time pot roast and chicken. Each entrée comes with a salad, three vegetables, rolls, and cornbread. The delicately flavored ice teas are terrific. Alas, the Ashland is no longer open for dinner, but will entertain private parties in the evening; catering is also available.

## ATHENS BAR AND GRILL

**8037 Clinton • Southeast • 675-1644 Open daily, lunch and dinner only • $$; Cr.**

There's no way to explain the appeal of the Athens to anyone with common sense. The place is hard to find, the neighborhood is terrible, the menu—fried seafood and bland Greek dishes —is nothing to write home about; still, the restaurant remains a Houston institution. On the Ship Channel and frequented by genuine ethnic sailors, it perhaps gives patrons that *frisson* of danger so often missing from modern existence: belly-dancing (sometimes on the tables) on weekends. Freelance plate destruction at irregular intervals. Bar.

## BABA YEGA

**2607 Grant • Central • 522-0042 • Open daily, lunch and dinner only; Sat and Sun, breakfast also • $; Cr.**

Baba Yega, named for the good witch in Russian fairy tales, has been in Montrose forever. An eccentric converted house with a tree-shaded patio, this funky neighborhood establishment has been quietly offering some of Houston's better burgers for the better part of two decades. Nowadays, BY also features steak and some grilled seafood dishes. The new house specialty is a rich, flavorful chili. Also special is the time trip back to the good old bohemian days of Montrose. Bar.

## BACKSTREET CAFE

**1103 South Shepherd • Central • 521-2239 • Open Tues–Sun, lunch and dinner only • Reservations for large parties • $$; Cr.**

In spring and fall the back patio, under huge old trees, provides a restful place to enjoy the fine blackboard menu in this nicely restored house on the edge of River Oaks. In winter, the fireplace is cozy. Younger professional clientele enjoys the happy hour. Bar.

## BARRY'S PIZZA

**6003 Richmond • Southwest • 266-8692 • Open daily, lunch and dinner only • No reservations • $–$$; AE, MC, V**

Barry's is something of a cult favorite. The ingredients are fresh, the pies piping hot, and the beer flowing. There are those who swear that's all a pizza purist needs. Beer and wine.

## BECK'S PRIME

**2902 Kirby Drive and other locations • Central • 524-7085**

**2615 Augusta • Southwest • 266-9901**

**Open daily, lunch and dinner only • $; AE, V, MC • W**

Beck's burgers are repeatedly voted among Houston's best. Try them, you'll see why. Beck's is so committed to burger purism that it insists its creations need no condiments. The freshly ground lean chuck, grilled to perfection over mesquite logs, makes a good argument for the case. Old-fashioned malts, thick with rich ice cream, genuine Hershey's chocolate syrup, or fresh strawberries and cream, prove that simple fare can be taken to the level of high art. Beer and wine.

## BELLAIRE BROILER BURGER

**5216 Bellaire Boulevard • Southwest • 668-8171 • Mon–Sat, lunch and dinner only • $, No cr. • W**

If James Dean and Natalie Wood didn't hang out here, Richie Cunningham and the Fonz probably did. Great greasy burgers and other basic stuff. This isn't the Disney version. It's not a '50s theme restaurant. It's just the real thing.

## BENIHANA OF TOKYO

**1318 Louisiana • Downtown • 659-8231**

**19707 Westheimer • West • 789-4962**

**Open daily, lunch and dinner only • Reservations suggested • $$$; Cr. • W variable**

You've seen the commercials, now see the performance live and in person. The chef performs acrobatic wonders with those lethal-looking knives. The grilled steak and shrimp are surprisingly wonderful in their own right. Downtown is popular with the business crowd, and Westheimer is a good place to bring Mom and Dad for a safely exotic treat. Bar.

## BERRYHILL'S HOT TAMALES

**2639 Revere • Central • 526-8080 • Open daily, breakfast, lunch and dinner • $, V, MC, AE, Dis • W**

Berryhill's is named for the creator of the tamale recipe, an old vendor. The place maintains that kind of simplicity throughout. Order at the counter and sit outside on the deck. Don't be put off by the idea of fish tacos, the lightly fried catfish and remoulade-like sauce are really spectacular. Because the space is so small—room for 30, max.—it can get *really* crowded on weekends. Beer & wine.

## BIRRAPORETTI'S

**500 Louisiana • Downtown • 224-9494**

**1997 West Gray • Central • 529-9191**

**Open daily, lunch and dinner only**
**Reservations necessary for large groups • $$; Cr. • W**

Once upon a time this was a reliable, if somewhat less-than-imaginative Italian restaurant crossed with a semi-rowdy Irish bar. Then it went all L.A. on us. The minimalist decor is light and airy. And while the menu is still Italianate, the food now has a heavy California accent. The desserts remain ridiculously rich. Bar.

## BISTRO LANCASTER

**701 Texas • Downtown • 228-9502 • Open daily • Reservations recommended • $$$$ Cr. • W**

The splendid little restaurant in the Lancaster Hotel is a favorite of Houston's power breakfast elite, but its strong suit is special-occasion or pre-theater dinners. Be warned: It is very expensive, but the cuisine, which features imaginative versions of Gulf Coast specialties from oysters to venison, is elegantly prepared and served. The salads, including a wonderful Caesar and the house special, have been named the best in town. Because it is located in the heart of the theater district, Bistro Lancaster knows how to get you to the show on time. Further, it offers free valet parking, and while you are welcome to pick up your car after the show, it's much more fun to end the evening in the Bistro with coffee and a light-but-rich white chocolate mousse. Bar.

## BLACK-EYED PEA

**Various locations • Open daily, lunch and dinner only**
**No reservations • $; AE, MC, V • W**

It isn't fancy. It isn't even the city's best down-home, Grandma's-Sunday-dinner-type fare, but the Black-Eyed Pea serves its consistent, dependable all-American meals with admirable dispatch. This undoubtedly explains lunchtime crowds so huge that the wait for a table can run 20 minutes. Meat loaf, chicken fried steak, and the Sunday turkey and dressing all are winners. Some of the veggies are fine, especially the tree-sized serving of nicely blanched broccoli. Others exhibit a '50s sensibility—they tend to be bland and overcooked. The wheat rolls, cornbread, and various fruit cobblers, though, are worth writing home about. Bar.

## BLACK LABRADOR

**4100 Montrose • Central • 529-1199**
**Open daily, lunch and dinner • $$; Cr. • W**

A tonier version of the standard British public house, the Black Lab is located in the cozy little Campanile Center near the University of St. Thomas. It also shares a parking lot with the wonderfully restored church that has become the Montrose Public Library, thereby attracting a tweedy intellectual crowd. Rice University types and grad students from all over join their artier colleagues in enjoying the pub's top-notch sandwiches and burgers. The soups and desserts, too, are first rate. Live music (usually some version of folk) adds to the ambiance on weekends. Outdoor tables and a garden chess set complete the pleasant picture. Bar.

## BLUE OYSTER BAR

**8105 Gulf Freeway • South • 640-1117**
**Open daily, lunch and dinner • $–$$; V, MC, AE, DC**

Before Tony Mandola opened the spiffy and pricey Gulf Coast Kitchen in the River Oaks area, the marvelous Mandolas started serving their wonderful oysters, shrimp, gumbo, and cole slaw here. They still offer some of the best seafood in town at unpretentious prices in this unpretentious location. Beer, wine, and margaritas only.

## BONNIE'S BEEF & SEAFOOD

**6867 Gulf Freeway • South • 641-2397**
**Open Mon–Sat, lunch and dinner only • $$–$$$; Cr. • W**

Admit it. You've wondered about that place with the waterwheel on the Gulf Freeway near Woodridge. It's had many incarnations, but the present is an unpretentious winner. The food isn't innovative, but there's lots of it. The soup and salad bar comes with every dinner, and the entrees, steaks, and prime rib as well as chicken and several Cajun-influenced seafood dishes are well prepared. The smoking section in the bar is especially warm and cozy, especially for single diners. Bar.

## BRENNAN'S

**3300 Smith • Central • 522-9711 • Weekdays, lunch and dinner only; Sat and Sun, brunch and dinner**
**Reservations necessary • $$$–$$$$; Cr. • W variable**

This isn't just eating out. It's *dining*. Brennan's remains true to its New Orleans roots, and New Orleans is a city that appreciates fine dining. Located on the southern edge of downtown in a 1929 French Quarter-style building designed by John Staub, Brennan's provides the thoughtful decor and flattering lighting—to say nothing of the splendid patio—that gives real meaning to the term ambiance. The French-Creole-Southwestern dinner menu admirably showcases Cajun and Creole cookery with just a touch of nouvelle Southwest. The desserts are spectacular and the Sunday Brunch is so festive it makes you feel like dancing. For a dressy, pricey-but-worth-the-price dining experience, it's hard to go wrong here. Bar.

## BRENNER'S

**10911 Katy Freeway (I-10) • West • 465-2901**
**Sun–Fri lunch and dinner; Sat dinner only • $$$–$$$$; Cr. • W**

*Steak!* Sirloin Strips! Ribeyes! *Steak!* This is as good as it gets. Brenner's, which has been around forever, is the way Houston dining used to be back in the "awl" days. The wait staff knows many patrons by name—and their drinks by heart. Business types will drive miles to chow down on melt-in-your mouth meat and gorgeously greasy German fried potatoes. Bar.

## BUTERA'S

**621 Montrose (at Chelsea Market) • Central • 520-8426**
**Open daily, breakfast, lunch and early dinner • No reservations**
**$–$$; Cr. • W**

If the food weren't so darn good, the fruits and veggies so fresh, the quiche so rich with flavor, the desserts so down-home delicious, and the deli-style sandwiches so special, right-thinking people wouldn't put up with lunchtime lines that stretch from here to Alpha Centauri. Every yuppie within 500 miles seems to breakfast here on weekends—witness the latest fitness fad togs at every table. Kids feel welcome. Beer and wine.

## CADILLAC BAR

**1802 Shepherd • Central • 862-2020**
**Open daily, lunch and dinner only • $–$$; AE, DC, V • W**

Friends in from out of town? Want some local color? You could do a lot worse than the Cadillac. It's loud, it's crowded, it's fun, it's fashionable. And the Tex-Mex menu's not bad either. Lethal margaritas, great enchiladas, and you-never-know-who popping up in the crowd all serve to make the Cadillac a dining must. Bar.

## CAFE ANNIE

**5860 Westheimer • West • 780-1522 • Open Tues–Fri, lunch and dinner only; Sat, dinner only • Reservations suggested**
**$$$–$$$$; Cr. • W variable**

This is the Valhalla of Southwestern cuisine—and the owners know it. Still, many Houstonians would tell you that celebrity chef Robert del Grande has created the best restaurant in town. The atmosphere is elegant without being too stuffy, the service is impeccable, and the food is never less than intriguing. Fine wines, also served by the glass, complement the meals, and the desserts are worth dying for. Bar.

## CAFE ADOBE

**2111 Westheimer • Central • 528-1468 • Open daily, lunch and dinner only • No reservations • $$; AE, MC, V • W variable**

The patios, front and back, are the draw here. The Tex-Mex menu—with some regional Mexican specialties—offers good, solid choices. The after-work crowd can be huge and rowdy, especially on Fridays, but on a beautiful evening, with the Spanish colonial facade of St. Anne's church across the street adding to the illusion, you can imagine yourself at a Mexican outdoor cafe. Bar.

## CAFE EXPRESS

**1800 South Post Oak in the Pavilion • Southwest • 963-9222**

**210 Meyerland Plaza • 349-9222**

**3200 Kirby • Central • 522-3994**

**1422 West Gray • Central • 522-3100 • Open daily, lunch and dinner only • No reservations • $–$$; Cr. • W**

Order at the counter and wait for your number to be called. The salads, pastas of the first order, turkey burgers, and chicken dishes all are just fine. The soups are great and the homestyle desserts are yummy, but the atmosphere is post-modern and a bit loud and cold. Carry your own tray to the outdoor seating and enjoy the early evening; the lunchtime lines are endless. Bar.

## CAFE NOCHE

**2409 Montrose • Central • 529-2409**
**Open daily for lunch and dinner; Sun brunch • $$–$$$; Cr. • W**

Wildly popular with the media and art crowds as well as with those who appreciate imaginative cuisine, this stark, art-filled restaurant is only minimally Mexican. The food is as beautiful as anything you see on the walls. The Red Chile Spinach, a kind of vegetable-only omelet, should be framed. Beware of unexpectedly extra-piquante dishes such as chicken enchiladas *mole*. Ask the personable wait staff for advice. Bar. (Open 'til 2 a.m.)

## CAPTAIN BENNY'S HALF SHELL

**8018 Katy Freeway (I-10) • West • 483-1042**

**11777 Wilcrest • Southwest • 498-3909**

**Lunch and dinner only; closed Sun**
**No reservations • $–$$; No cr. • W variable**

Oysters the old-fashioned way are fresh on the just-opened shell or dipped in cornmeal and fried. There isn't much more to it, but Captain Benny's does it better than anyone else in town. Longtime patrons consider the demise of the ancestral shrimp-boat location on South Main to be a tragedy on a par with the loss of the Astrodome's exploding scoreboard. Has Houston no respect for its monuments? Beer only.

## CARRABBA'S

**3115 Kirby • Central • 522-3131**

**1399 South Voss (at Woodway) • Southwest • 468-0868**

**11339 Katy Freeway • West • 464-6595**

**Mon–Sat, dinner and lunch only; Closed Sun • No reservations $$–$$$; Cr. • W**

Homemade pasta and wonderfully seasoned specialties keep the Carrabba's locations crowded and exuberantly noisy. (For aural relief, try the smaller back room at the Kirby location.) The pastas are wonderful; these folks sure know how to use garlic. The pizzas, salads, and sausages are mouth-watering. Join the rest of Houston in the lunchtime line. Evenings are slightly less crowded. Bar.

## CASABLANCA MOROCCAN RESTAURANT

**2514 Suffolk at Westheimer • Southwest • 621-0863 • Mon–Fri, lunch and dinner only; Sat, dinner only; closed Sun • Weekend reservations required • $$–$$$; Cr. • W**

Casablanca has atmosphere to spare—this is elegance with a difference. Done up like an opulent sultan's tent, with cushions and divans replacing Western tables, the restaurant carries over the Moroccan-North African theme to the food itself. Offering traditional five-course dinners that feature a wide selection of wonderfully savory lamb, veal, chicken, beef, seafood, and even hare, as well as exotic dips, vegetable dishes, and honey-rich desserts, Casablanca invites diners to eat Middle-Eastern style: with the fingers of their right hands. (For the less adventurous, flatware is also provided.) Lunch is much less elaborate. Weekend nights, when belly dancers entertain, can be quite dressy. Bar.

## CENT'ANNI

**2128 Portsmouth • Central • 529-4199 • Open daily, lunch and dinner only • $$–$$$; • Cr. • W variable**

Located one block south of Richmond, between Shepherd and Greenbriar in the ultra-trendy lower Richmond area, Cent'anni (which comes from the Italian wish, "may you live Cent'anni—100 years") offers well-prepared northern Italian cuisine with and emphasis on veal dishes and grilled seafood. This isn't checkered-tablecloth and candle-in-a-Chianti-bottle Italian: The ambiance here favors light, restful decor and a festive, crowded bar scene. Bar.

## CHARLEY'S 517

**517 Louisiana • Downtown • 224-4438 • Lunch and dinner only; closed Sun • Reservations necessary • $$$$; AE, DC, MC, V**

In the heart of the downtown business district and most convenient to the Wortham Center, the Alley Theatre, and Jones Hall, Charley's 517 is the perfect location for dressy dining. The menu, which emphasizes American dishes with French sauces, often highlights excellent grilled seafood specials. The regular fare includes meltingly tender veal chops, quail stuffed with venison sausage, and a range of fine steaks. Charley's boasts one of the most extensive wine lists in the state of Texas, and the staff is always willing to recommend an interesting or exceptional vintage. Bar.

## CHEZ NOUS

**217 South Avenue G, Humble • Far north • 446-6717 • Dinner only, closed Sun • Reservations recommended • $$–$$$; Cr. • W**

Pass the word. Humble is hiding one of Houston's best French restaurants. Chez Nous, located in a converted church, offers true classic French cuisine, elegantly prepared and finely sauced. This is not for fans of the nouvelle, this is for purists. Magnificent wine list. Bar.

## CHILI'S

**Various locations • Open daily, lunch and dinner only No reservations • $–$$; AE, DC, MC, V**

This is a chain that gives chains a good name. The food is always dependable, and there are even a few standouts, such as the tuna steak sandwich. The "Guiltless Grill" menu offers low-fat items ranging from pasta to fajitas. The ambiance is consistent—loud and fun with lots of singles after work—and it's a good place to bring the kids. Bar.

## CHURRASCOS

**9788 Bissonnet • Southwest • 541-2100**

**2055 Westheimer at Shepherd • Central • 527-8300**

**Open Mon–Sat, lunch and dinner only; Sun, dinner only**
**Reservations recommended • $$$; Cr.**

In no time at all, this Pan-American establishment became Houston's hottest restaurant, and with good reason. This is a stunning northern adaptation of the traditional South American grill, with inspired Central American touches. The food is deliciously different—where else are you going to find featured such dishes as charcoal-grilled pork tenderloin basted in tropical fruit juices, rum, and herbs? When they say reservations are recommended, they mean it. Bar.

## CONFEDERATE HOUSE

**2925 Weslayan • 622-1936 • Lunch and dinner only; closed Sun**
**Reservations necessary • $$–$$$; Cr.**

Although the portraits of the Confederate generals didn't make the move to the main dining room of the former Black Angus location, the spirit of the Confederate House did. The luxe, wood heavy main dining room is graced with flattering baby pink lighting. The pace is leisurely—no rushed table turnover here. This is one of Houston's longest-established restaurants and it shows. Since 1948, it has hosted generations of ladies (some in hats) and gentlemen attired in impeccable suits as they dine on country-club fare. This is the land where time stood still; it maintains the illusion that Houston is still a small town in which everyone who counts knows everyone else who does. The food is also true to the '50s—well prepared but bland. The pecan ball dessert is a tradition. Fine wine cellar. First class Bar.

## DACAPO'S

**1141 E. 11th Street • Heights • 869-9141**
**Tue–Sat 8–5; Sun 9–2 • $; No cr.**

Basically a neighborhood bakery serving some of the very best cookies and pastery you will find anywhere, DaCapo's has branched out into breakfasts, sandwiches and soup. All of them are world class. The only dilemma is how many friends to let in on the secret of this lovely little Heights establishment.

## DAILY REVIEW CAFE

**3412 W. Lamar (at Dunlavy) • Central • 520-9217 • Tue–Sat lunch and dinner; Sat continental breakfast also; Sun brunch only; Closed Mon • $$-$$$; Cr. • W**

In an odd location between West Gray and Allen Parkway, this small, trendy cafe on the former premises of *The Daily Court Review* newspaper serves imaginative Mediterranean bistro-inspired food with unusual combinations of greens, cheeses, fruits, and nuts along with meats and seafood. The menu changes constantly and the hip crowd keeps growing. The tiny deck is wonderful in good weather, and the weekend brunch is wonderful, period. Beer and wine.

## DAMIAN'S CUCINA ITALIANA

**3011 Smith • Central • 522-0439 • Lunch and dinner only; closed Sun • Reservations necessary • $$-$$$; AE, MC, V, DC • W**

Before wonderfully prepared Italian food became a trend, Damian's was serving some of the best cooking this side of the Seven Hills. The calamari is enough to convert even those traumatized by an early encounter with Jules Verne. Other favorites include the taglierini in butter sauce with perfectly grilled veggies, and trout dusted with parmesan. All the pasta tastes like it was made by a loving Italian grannie. After a disasterous fire in 1994, the lunchtime waits are once more excruciating, and evenings fill the place with a fashionable and diverse clientele. The reservations caveat is serious. Bar.

## DE VILLE

**1300 Lamar (in the Four Seasons Hotel) • Downtown • 650-1300 Mon–Sat breakfast, lunch and dinner; Sun brunch, no dinner Reservations suggested • $$$; Cr. • W**

This is luxe, downtown hotel dining at its best. The space is elegant—and so is the service. The menu offers a wide selection of heart-healthy items (such as the safely sauteed Gulf snapper in a sauce of roasted chiles and pesto) that are so rich in taste that there's no need to tempt fate. Should you choose to, however, the desserts are wonderful. The Sunday brunch is as well. Bar.

## DOZIER'S MARKET

**8222 FM 359, Fulshear • Far west • 346-1411**
**Tue–Sun lunch and dinner; closed Monday • $; V, MC**

Take a trip back in time. Drive on out to the little town of Fulshear and chow down on some of Texas' best barbecue. The ambiance is pure country—plastic red-and-white checkered tablecloths—and the service is country friendly. Sit out under the trees sipping ice tea and take home some of the Market's terrific peppered bacon for tomorrow's breakfast.

## DIRTY'S

**1710 Durham • Northwest • 861-7046 • 3230 Chimney Rock**
**Southwest • 781-1655 • Open daily, lunch and dinner only**
**No reservations • $; Cr.**

This is your basic burger joint, with old-license-plate-style kitsch on the walls, sports on the big-screen TV, and beer by the pitcher. If that's what you're in the mood for, you could do a lot worse. It's loud, and kids are welcome. Beer and wine.

## DONG TING

**611 Stuart • Central • 527-0005 • Mon–Fri lunch and dinner, Sat**
**dinner only; closed Sun • Reservations suggested on weekends**
**$$$; Cr. • W**

Dong Ting occupies a very special position in the pantheon of fine Chinese restaurants. Instead of offering scores of menu items, this artfully French-Chinois-appointed establishment concentrates on a handful of exceptionally well-prepared dishes, ranging from light, savory dumplings and hot and sour soup—arguably the best in town—to wonderfully seasoned meats and seafoods. Crisp, flavorful veggies provide the perfect complement. The quietly elegant atmosphere, unobtrusively attentive service, and near-downtown location make Dong Ting a lunchtime favorite of high-powered business types. Evenings tend toward dressy. Private banquets in the intimate wine room are a real treat. Reservations suggested. Bar.

## 8.0
**3745 Greenbriar • Central • 523-0880 • $$; Cr. • W**

8.0 is one of the anchors of the current capital of hip Houston, the Lower Richmond area, but don't hold that against it. It's true that a great deal of preening goes on, and much seeing and being seen, but the space is fascinating with edgy, up-to-the-minute murals and old-fashioned booths. The food isn't bad either. Blackboard menu items change daily. Brunch attracts the ne plus ultra crowd, and a lot of others, too. Plan accordingly. Bar.

## ELEVENTH STREET CAFE
**748 East 11th • Heights • 862-0089 • Tue–Fri 7–3 and 5–10; Sat, Sun 8–3; closed Mon • $; No cr.**

Back when the Heights was a separate town, this was undoubtedly the kind of place where the neighbors gathered for good, basic food and hearty Sunday breakfasts. Nowadays the crowd is a bit more ecclectic, including writers and artists as well as firefighters and oil company workers, but the food is every bit as downhome good.

## EMPIRE CAFE
**1732 Westheimer • 528-5282 • Mon–Fri 7–11:30 p.m.; Sat, Sun 7–1 a.m. • $–$$; Cr. • W**

The location has had a checkered history. It was a gas station and a leather bar among other incarnations. But the Empire has made it both an outpost of Montrose-arty chic and a darn good place to breakfast. The numerous imaginative egg variations are all worth a try. Lunchtime attracts adventuresome downtown types. The space is spare, the decor bizarre and the the style is order at the counter. Beer and wine.

## FELIX
**904 Westheimer • Central • 529-3949 • Open daily, lunch and dinner only • No reservations • $–$$ Cr. • W**

There is just no explaining the appeal of Felix to anyone who hasn't lived in Houston for at least 25 years. Back in the days before this became a major international city, when chicken-fried steak and boiled-to-death veggies were the order of the day, Felix provided the alternative. The Tex-Mex menu today is nothing special, but for many in this town, the memories it conjures up are. Bar.

## 59 DINER

**3801 Farnham • Central • 523-2333**
**8125 Katy Freeway West • 681-5559**
**Open daily, breakfast, lunch and dinner • $; Cr • W**

The 59's motto is "EAT BIG," and they serve the portions to prove it. This is a wry twist on the traditional diner. The owners actually have it both ways. The decor is a photo-realism version the real thing, and the food is basic: burgers and club sandwiches, pancakes and eggs for breakfast plus the traditional blue plate specials for lunch. But the crowd of young professionals, writers and artists is in on the joke. Also serves the "world's smallest sundae."

## FOUNTAIN VIEW CAFE

**1824 Fountain View • Southwest • Open daily, breakfast and lunch only • No reservations • $; No cr. • W**

Even folks in trendy southwest Houston need the ambience of a small-town cafe from time to time. The Fountain View fulfills that function admirably. Serving substantial plate breakfasts from open 'til close, the Fountain View also features deli-style sandwiches, such as pastrami and corned-beef melts, as well as old-fashioned two-fisted burgers.

## GOLDEN BO RESTAURANT

**8655 Southwest Freeway at Gessner • 988-1301**
**Open daily, breakfast, lunch, and dinner**
**Reservations suggested for Sat brunch • $–$$, AE, MC, V**

Golden Bo, which has become something of an institution, serves traditional Cantonese-style meals at lunch and dinner, but that's not the real attraction. The main interest is the Chinese tea brunch, dim sum, which is served every day from 9 to 3. On weekends everything changes, as hordes of families, most of them Asian but with a goodly sprinkling of western regulars, arrive for the pull-out-the-stops version of dim sum. From 11 a.m. to 1 p.m. pandemonium reigns, as waiters push carts loaded with everything from sweet-bean-paste-filled rolls to roasted ducks' feet up and down the aisles while diners point to whatever catches their fancy. Children are welcome and much in evidence. Beer and wine.

### GOLDEN ROOM

**1209 Montrose • 524-9614 • Open Mon-Fri, lunch and dinner; Sat, dinner only; closed Sun • No reservations • $–$$; Cr.**

In its lovely, newish digs this longtime Montrose favorite continues to offer some of the best Thai food in Houston. The Golden Room's converted house provides quiet tables for conversation and convivial corners for groups. Just about everything on the menu is a winner, but the chicken curry, simultaneously incendiary with peppers and cool with coconut milk, is a masterwork. Beer and wine.

### GOODE COMPANY BARBECUE

**5109 Kirby • 522-2530 • 8911 Katy Frwy • 464-1901**
**Open daily, lunch and dinner only • No reservations • $–$$; Cr.**

By now, Goode Company Barbecue and its eponymous owner are such Houston institutions that Jim Goode has gone clean-shaven. If you're entertaining Yankees who're just dying for some gen-u-ine Texas barbecue, this is the place to take them. There's the rich smell of the mesquite-wood smoke, a clutter of farm implements, historic beer signs and vintage license plates decorate the walls, and Bob Wills sings on the jukebox. Add that to the mouth-watering meats and just-sweet-enough sauce and you have a primo barbecue experience. Beer and wine.

### GOODE COMPANY HAMBURGER AND TAQUERIA

**4902 Kirby • Central • 520-9153**
**Open daily, lunch and dinner only • $; Cr.**

Across the street from Goode Company Barbecue are some of the best burgers and fajitas in town. The place is perpetually crowded, and on weekends it can look like a yuppie convention. Don't be put off. The food is worth it. Kids feel welcome. Beer and wine.

## GOODE COMPANY SEAFOOD

**2621 Westpark • Central • 523-7154**
**Open daily, lunch and dinner only • $; Cr.**

Houston just can't seem to get enough of a Goode thing. Growing out of a silver railroad dining car, the seafood version keeps to the tradition of well-prepared, traditional recipes and hospitable service. If Jim Goode built it, they will come. Casual, loud, kids feel welcome. Bar.

## GREAT CARUSO

**10001 Westheimer • West • 780-4900 • Tue–Sun, dinner only;**
**closed Mon • Reservations necessary • $$$; Cr. • W variable**

What to do when Mom and Pop visit from out of town? You could do a lot worse than take them here. Hard to categorize—is it a restaurant with singing waiters, or is it a music hall with food? It doesn't really matter. The Great Caruso succeeds in doing both quite well. The entertainers are of at least off-Broadway caliber, and the food can be very well done in a middle-of-the-road kind of way. The atmosphere is festive with lots of Victorian kitsch. Leave your jaded sophistication behind and just have fun. Bar.

## GROTTO

**3920 Westheimer • Southwest • 622-3663**
**Open daily, lunch and dinner only • $$$–$$$$, Cr. • W**

Tony Vallone strikes again. Chummier and noisier than Anthony's across the way, Grotto serves up clever variations of Italian food, and the best dishes are very good indeed with calimari always a winner. Nothing here is wispy or wimpy. Even the salads are hearty. Save room for dessert if you dare. The crowds are huge and the service is brisk. Take that into account. Bar.

## HARD ROCK CAFE

**2801 Kirby • Central • 520-1134**
**Open daily, lunch and dinner only • $–$$; AE, MC, V • W variable**

The success of the Hard Rock chain is hard to explain. The food isn't great, though the burgers, steaks, salads, and other basics are perfectly acceptable; the crowd alternates between younger business types at lunch and tourists. Suburban kids who would be trendies are much in evidence in the evening. All that said, there's something clever about any place that explicitly bans both drugs and nuclear weapons. The relentlessly upbeat atmosphere and the wonderful collection of rock memorabilia make it a good place for divorced dads to bring the kids on Saturday. Bar.

## HARRY'S RESTAURANT

**318 Tuam • Central • 528-0198 • Open Mon–Sat, breakfast, lunch, and dinner • No reservations • $; No cr.**

Harry was George's father. George is the intense, funny, argumentative guy behind the steam table. He serves up arcane soccer statistics and political opinions with the liver and onions, meat loaf, baked chicken, fried fish, and the other components of the restaurant's basic plate-filling fare. Breakfast, which begins before dawn, draws an amazing mix of downtown business types and street people. Lunch is crowded, and dinner is for those who want to argue sports with George. A Houston institution.

## HOBBITT HOLE

**1715 South Shepherd • Central • 528-3418 • Open daily, lunch and dinner only • Reservations necessary for groups of six or more • $–$$; AE, MC, V**

Once upon a time this was the realm of Bilbo Baggins and Thorin Oakenshield. When the hippie era ended, the Hobbit Hole clung longer than most to its identity as an oasis of peace, love, and natural food. Today the atavistic all-natural sandwiches are about all that's left of the '60s. The menu now includes excellent burgers, fish, and stir fries, in addition to the vegetarian fare and smoothies. Enjoy the shady backyard patio. Beer and wine.

## HOFBRAU

**1803 Shepherd • Central • 869-7074 • Open daily, lunch and dinner only • No reservations • $$; AE, MC, V**

This is the Houston incarnation of the Austin institution. Aging Longhorns can get all misty and nostalgic. The place is noisy and still has something of that late-night-on-the-Drag air about it, but the great sizzling steaks and drippy, perfect burgers are just right. Bar.

## HOUSE OF PIES

**3112 Kirby • Central • 528-3816**

**6142 Westheimer • West • 782-1290**

**Open daily, 24 hours • No reservations • $–$$; AE, MC, V**

Desperate for a sugar fix? Dreaming of chocolate cream? Dutch apple? No matter how improbable your desire for a delicious diet-buster, you can probably find it here. Breakfasts, served at all hours, are pretty good. The burgers and other fare are okay. At the Kirby location, (a.k.a. House of Guys) the middle-of-the-night floorshow, when the drag queens come in for an after-work coffee, is interesting lagniappe.

## HOUSTON'S

**5888 Westheimer • Southwest • 975-1947**

**4848 Kirby • Central • 529-2385**

**11103 Westheimer • West • 780-4699**

**Open daily, lunch and dinner only • No reservations**
**$–$$; Cr. • W**

The space is cozy with booths, brass, and dark wood. The crowd is large and basically young professional. Even the wait staff wears heavily stanched button-down white shirts and khakis (they get no laundry allowance, so tip accordingly). If this is the atmosphere for you, you're in luck. Houston's serves the city's biggest and probably best salads with the Original—paper-thin grilled chicken, shoestring taco strips on greens dressed with honey lime and Thai peanut sauce—the star of the lot. Tasty iron-skillet beans are a welcome change from french fries. Bar.

## HUNAN PALACE

**801 Chartres at Rusk • Downtown • 225-5661 • Mon–Sat, lunch**
**and dinner • Reservations accepted • $; Cr.**

One of the better basic downtown Chinese eateries, the Hunan Palace is fast and convenient at lunchtime. It offers a more leisurely pace in the evening when many Asian families dine. Bar.

## HUNAN RIVER

**2015 West Gray • Central • 527-0200 • Open daily, lunch and dinner only • No reservations • $$; Cr. • W**

Small and quiet, this edge-of-River Oaks establishment offers a reliable menu of Hunan country-style cooking. The lunchtime crowd, including shoppers from the palmy R.O. Center, can fill the place quickly. Evenings are less hectic with the outdoor patio a restorative. Daytimes, Hunan River does a large delivery business to offices and homes in the vicinity. Bar.

## HUNGRY INTERNATIONAL

**14075 Memorial • West • 493-1520**

**2365 Rice Boulevard • Central • 523-8652**

**Open daily, lunch and dinner • $; MC, V, AE, Dis • W variable**

Want a quick sandwich and can't bear the thought of Mickey D's? Try Hungry's. The Rice Boulevard location is much favored by students late at night. The food is nothing special, but generally reliable and more varied than that found at the big chains. Beer and wine.

## INDIA'S

**5704 Richmond • Southwest • 266-0131 • Open daily, lunch and dinner only • Reservations necessary on weekends • $$–$$$; Cr.**

India's keeps the decor simple and the food complex, offering a wonderful array of specialties from the subcontinent. The tandoori chicken, the curries, and my fave the saag paneer (creamy spinach with chunks of mild cheese) are arguably the best in town. On weekends, India's attracts large numbers of Indian families as well as discriminating Yanks. Bar.

## IRMA'S

**22 North Chenevert • Downtown • 222-0767 • Mon–Fri, breakfast and lunch only • $$; Cr.**

*Waaaaay* downtown amid the warehouses is the funky old-timey building that houses one of Houston's best restaurants. Irma's doesn't offer anything fancy, just Mexican-style plate lunches, but every item on the unwritten menu is a standout. The servers, most of whom are Irma's kids, recite whatever's been prepared for the day. It might be spinach enchiladas; rich, spicy chicken molé, or any one of a half-dozen or so others. Each is made of top-quality ingredients with a minimum of fat, and each tastes wonderful. The lemonade, chock-a-block with grapes and melon, is special, too. The explosion-of-kitsch decor defies description, and the immense crowd includes Federal judges and Astros ballplayers. Margaritas on the rocks, beer, and wine.

## JAGS

**5120 Woodway at Sage • Southwest • 621-4766 • Open Mon–Fri, lunch only • $$; AE, MC, V • W**

Society's favorite caterer, Jackson Hicks, has turned this high-chic space in the Decorative Center into one of Houston's hottest lunch spots. Fresh fish is the featured attraction, with an array of pastas to suit every taste. The service is casually elegant. Lots of top-notch people and fashion-watching. Dressy. Bar.

## JAMES CONEY ISLAND

**Various locations • Open daily, lunch and dinner only
No reservations • $; No cr.**

That all-American institution, the hot dog, is raised to new heights at this Houston establishment. Fancy or plain, with chili or cheese, James Coney Island dogs are hard to beat. Beer.

## KAHN'S DELI

**2429 Rice Boulevard • Central • 529-2891
Open daily for lunch only • No reservations • $; No cr.**

New York deli food is sadly underrepresented on Houston's restaurant roster. Fortunately for Villagers, and others willing to make the drive, Kahn's serves up the real thing. They even know the difference between Thousand Island and real Russian dressing. The space is as tiny and crowded as a Manhattan establishment would be. New Yorkers would feel right at home but for the service, which is too polite.

## KAM'S

**4500 Montrose • Central • 529-5057 • Mon–Sat lunch and dinner, Sun dinner only • Reservations • $$–$$$; Cr.**

In the shadow of the 59 Bridge, this sleek, nouveau Chinese establishment serves inventive versions of staples such as Asian vermicelli and pungent, spicy meats and seafoods. A see-and-be-seen place for the museum crowd. Beer and wine.

## KHYBER NORTH INDIAN GRILL

**2510 Richmond • Central • 942-9424 • Mon–Fri lunch and dinner, Sat dinner only, Sun lunch only • No reservations • $$–$$$; Cr.**

Indian food scares quite a few people who imagine it's all incendiary. That's where Khyber comes in. Owner Mickey Kapoor knows how to play to his audience. Traditional dishes of the northern sub-continent are prepared with all the flavor, but little of the fat or fire found at home. The sauces are uniformly wonderful. Be sure to notice the silly sign war Kapoor is waging with next-door Pappadeaux. Beer & wine.

## KIM SON

**1801 St. Emanuel • Downtown • 222-2461**

**8200 Wilcrest at Beechnut • West • 498-7841**

**Open daily, lunch and dinner only • $-$$; Cr. • W**

The glamorous, two-story downtown location is every bit as huge as the old, funky one. The crowds are just as big, if slightly more upscale, so's the spiffy fish pond. Other additions include an upstairs banquet hall that's booked through something like 2525 and a "catering hotline." Thankfully, the traditionally enormous menu, with nearly 250 offerings, includes everything from ducks' feet to glorious veggies, remains intact. Be adventurous and take a chance on an unknown dish. Bar.

## LA COLOMBE D'OR

**3410 Montrose • Central • 524-7999 • Open daily; • Reservations recommended • $$$$; Cr.**

In a converted mansion on once-elegant, always-interesting Montrose Boulevard, is a tiny (six-suite) hotel known around the world for its ultra service. The restaurant only adds luster. Such dishes as lobster-stuffed raviolis and smoked squab with grilled wild mushrooms join French classics in one of Houston's hautest kitchens. Extensive wine list. Bar.

## LA GRIGLIA

**2002 West Gray • Central • 526-4700 • Mon–Fri, lunch and dinner, Sat–Sun dinner only • Reservations recommended • $$$–$$$$; Cr. • W**

Pronounce it La-GREE-yah, and you'll be just about right. It means grill in Italian, and that's what they do— but it's not *all* they do. They entertain Houston's haute crowd, and visiting celebs, with hearty, clever Italianate receipes that include everything from grilled tuna steaks to portobello mushroom torta. Weekend crowds are huge. The tiny patio is lovely. Desserts are to die for. Bar.

## LA MADELEINE

**4002 Westheimer • Southwest • 623-0644 • Several other locations Open daily, breakfast, lunch, and dinner • $$; No cr. • W**

Salad is the thing 'ere in zeese French café. From a modified cafeteria line, the French-accented staff serves wonderfully crusty breads and a rotating group of salads, including the house special Caesar—which is excellent, though for the price the portion is small. Other menu items, including soup and quiche, are fine as well. The French pastries are top-of-the-class. These artfully coun-trified establishments can get very crowded especially at lunchtime and on Saturday afternoons when they become a favorite hangout for tennis-togged sportifs. Beer and wine.

## LA RESERVE

**4 Riverway (Omni Hotel) • West • 871-8177 • Lunch and dinner only; closed Sun • Reservations necessary • $$$$; Cr.**

In the quietly elegant confines of La Reserve, Super-Chef Tim Keating showcases regional variations of French-influenced dishes. Gulf ingredients such as shrimp, crab, and mussels are used to advantage and favorites such as roast lamb are superb, as is the unobtrusive service. For a truly sophisticated evening on the town, conside La Reserve. Dressy. Bar.

## LA TOUR D'ARGENT

**2011 Ella Boulevard • Northwest • 864-9864 • Lunch and dinner only; closed Sun • Reservations necessary • $$$$; Cr.**

An unusual establishment in an unusual location, La Tour D'Argent is one of Houston's most interesting restaurants. In an early log cabin, a bit overdecorated in a hunting motif, La Tour serves the kind of top-shelf French food that usually comes in a mirrors-and-gilt setting. The menu includes several excellent veal dishes, quail, duck, and—off the menu—herbed lamb chops for which you will find no peer. The wine list, too, is exceptional. Bar.

## LANGIAPPE

**3009 Post Oak Boulevard • Galleria • 621-5900 • Lunch and dinner daily • Reservations recommended • $$$; Cr. • W**

Neo-Cajun?? Yes, it is strange. Strangely wonderful. Most dishes are hard to imagine. Don't ask, just eat. For the more middle-of-the-road, the Redfish Baton Rouge is a winner. For the more adventurous, there are Asiatic crawfish dumplings. No matter what, this is a major addition to the Galleria-area restaurant scene, offering something for business visitors and Houstonians alike. Over-the-top decor, and a menu that's a bit too self-conscious don't detract from the wonders emanating from the kitchen. Bar.

## LANDRY'S/WILLIE G'S

**22215 Katy Freeway (I-10) • West • 392-0452**

**1605 South Post Oak • Galleria • 840-7190**

**6159 Westheimer • Southwest • 952-1010**

**Open daily, lunch, dinner, Sun brunch • Reservations suggested for large parties • $$–$$$; Cr.**

This clannish bunch of New Orleans-flavored restaurants features first-class seafood. Though the menu varies somewhat from location to location, the stellar shrimp, oyster, and snapper dishes are worth a visit. Willie G's, in the Galleria area, also emphasizes steaks served to the business crowd, which predominates. The other locations are less expense-account heavy. All, however, boast a French Quarter feel and the kind of Creole-inspired cooking that keeps Houstonians coming back for more. Desserts, such as the Louisiana-style bread pudding and pecan pie, all are homemade. Bar.

## LAST CONCERT

**1403 Nance • Downtown • 226-8563 • Open Mon-Fri, lunch and dinner only; Sat, dinner only • $–$$; AE, MC, V**

For about four decades, this former bordello has been serving down-home Tex-Mex food in a bizarre location. Hidden away among the warehouses just north of University of Houston Downtown, the Last Concert takes some doing to find. Once found, it takes a knock on the unmarked and locked red door to gain admission. This routine is supposed to be a holdover from the days of Prohibition. These days, the food takes second place to the wealth of longnecks and the live music that comes free with the meal. Some of Houston's best bands play on the patio, and at lunch local guitarists strum for your listening pleasure. The menu of Tex-Mex is perfectly okay. Faux-margaritas (don't ask), beer, and wine.

## LE PEEP RESTAURANT

**6128 Village Parkway • Central • 523-7337**

**4702 Westheimer • Southwest • 629-7337**

**5505-A FM 1960 West • Northwest • 586-7337**

**Open daily, breakfast and lunch only • $; Cr.**

Le Peep may serve the best breakfasts in town, including fantastic egg dishes and more heart-smart variations of flapjacks than you could imagine. It's bright and breezy, with a yupscale crowd that doesn't mind the weekend wait. Kids feel welcome.

## LULING CITY MARKET

**4726 Richmond • Central • 871-1903 • Open daily, lunch and dinner • $–$$; Cr.**

Once upon a time, this near-Galleria establishment was a singles hotspot. The trendy crowd has moved on, probably much to the relief of true barbecue aficionados. The Luling still serves really satisfying renditions of links and ribs in a down-home atmosphere.

## LUTHER'S

**Various locations • Open daily, lunch and dinner only $; No cr. • W**

For a chain, Luther's serves up some pretty darn good barbecue. But the best of the lot is probably the chicken salad. In a flour tortilla "bowl," the greens and tomatoes are topped by a generous serving of barbecued white-meat chicken. The sandwiches, burgers, and plates are all dependable. The heart-smart turkey, while dryish, isn't bad. Lunchtime crowds at the downtown and southwest locations can be huge. Even the call-ahead take-out line can be long. When you're in the mood for Luther's, planning a later lunch hour will prevent frustration. Beer and wine.

## MA MAISON

**1515 South Post Oak Lane • West • 840-0303 • Lunch and dinner only; closed Sun • Reservations suggested • $$$–$$$$; AE, MC, V**

Romance amid the skyscrapers. Small, flatteringly lighted, flower bedecked, and elegantly appointed, Ma Maison is one of Houston's wonderful surprises. A fine French establishment where there is salmon in champagne sauce, grilled swordfish, and other first-rate seafoods. The rack of lamb is pretty special, too. Save room for dessert. Bar.

## MASSA'S

**1160 Smith • Downtown • 650-0837 • Mon–Fri lunch and dinner; Sat dinner only; Closed Sun. • $$$–$$$$; Cr. • W variable**

The Massa family has been serving Creole-style seafood and business lunches in downtown Houston since the 1940s. The latest location, in the old Harry's Kenya spot near the Hyatt Regency hotel, is the best yet. It's classy without being stuffy, and the festive, Louisiana-influenced murals painted by a family friend add just the right touch of fun. There's nothing shocking on the menu, so if you're looking for "furbelow" food, look elsewhere. If you want old-fashioned Gulf Coast cooking from a reliable kitchen, Massa's is the best in downtown. Lagniappe: For a quiet drink in a cozy atmosphere, check out the tiny bar. Frequented by professionals from the nearby office towers, it's a good after-work spot for grown-ups.

## MAXIM'S

**3755 Richmond • Near Southwest • 877-8899 • Mon–Fri lunch and dinner; Sat dinner only; closed Sun • $$$$; Cr. • W**

Maxim's is a Houston institution. It's been around forever, first downtown, and in later years here near Greenway Plaza. Essentially, it was designed for the expense-account crowd, when the expense-account crowd was exclusively male. Perhaps this accounts for the neo-bordello decor. The menu emphasizes steaks and Continental style dishes, and, for its intentions, is quite well done. Bar.

## MEDINA'S SPANISH VILLAGE

**4811 Lillian • Central • 802-2921 • Open daily, lunch and dinner
No reservations • $$; Cr. • W**

Yes, the Christmas lights are still there! Rescued from the demise
of the late, lamented Almeda location, the festive lighting and the
world's best margaritas join the archetypal 1950s-style Tex-Mex
plates to make this latest incarnation of Spanish Village feel like
home to longtime Houstonians. Bar.

## MERIDA

**2509 Navigation • Central • 227-7067**

**515 East NASA Road One • Southeast (Seabrook) • 486-1434**

**Open daily, breakfast, lunch, and dinner • No reservations •
$–$$; AE, MC, V**

In the beginning, Merida was known as "that place down the
street from Ninfa's Navigation." Then people began to appreciate
Merida for its own merits, which are considerable. Reliable Tex-
Mex dishes that satisfy purists join with Yucatecan black bean and
pork combinations. Lagniappe: the magic-realism mural trans-
ports diners to another dimension. Kids feel welcome. Bar.

## MIYAKO

**3910 Kirby • Central • 520-9797**

**6345 Westheimer • West • 781-6300**

**910 Travis • Downtown • 752-2888**

**201 W. Bay Area Boulevard • Southeast (Clear Lake) • 332-3328**

**Mon–Sat lunch and dinner only; closed Sun • $$–$$$; Cr. • W**

Outside of California, Japanese food hasn't found a really big
audience. Most folks don't care for the notion of raw fish. Miyako
understands that, and has tailored its menu to American tastes.
There is, of course, uncooked tuna, salmon, and yellowtail. All of
it is startlingly fresh. For those less adventurous, there is an extensive menu of crisp, lightly fried tempura dishes. On Sundays, some
locations offer a sushi buffet that's worth the trip. Bar.

## A MOVEABLE FEAST

**2202 West Alabama • Central • 528-3585 • delivery 952-8200**
**Breakfast, lunch and dinner daily • $$; Cr. • W**

If you think vegetarian cuisine consists largely of tofu and bean sprouts, the Feast will help you to reconsider. The changing daily menu includes pancakes, faux bacon that's tastier than the real thing, and vegetarian lunch and dinner dishes that encompass everything from chili to rich pastas. In addition to the cafe, which can get crowded on weekends, the Feast is also a natural foods shop.

## MRS. ME'S CAFE

**100 Waugh • Central • 522-5343 • Open Mon–Sat**
**$; No cr. • W variable**

If Mrs. Me (now deceased) and her daughters didn't actually introduce Houston to the joys of Vietnamese cooking in their tiny storefront location in Montrose, they were among the first to popularize it. Though now ensconced in sterile digs that share a strip center with Domino's Pizza, the Cafe continues to serve the best Vietnamese eggrolls and won-ton soup in town. The lunchtime buffet attracts everyone from starving artists to millionaires. Save room for the sweet, rich Vietnamese coffee and the excellent flan. Beer.

## MUCHO MEXICO

**1310 North Wayside • East • 673-4598**
**Open daily, lunch and dinner • $–$$; No cr.**

A long time ago, adventuresome Houstonians enjoyed the odd delights of Las Cazuelas (of lamented memory). Now we have Mucho Mexico to fill the need for gen-u-ine Mexican food, none of it dumbed down for the gringos. And from the white-cheese chiles rellenos to the frijoles a la charra, everything, both on the menu and off, is worth having. The Eastside location helps when it comes to the freelance entertainment. Patrons who feel like singing do so—and some of them are darn good. There's also scheduled entertainment on weekends. Bar.

## NASHVILLE ROOM

**(At Allen Park Inn) • 2121 Allen Parkway • Near downtown
521-9321 • Open daily 24 hours • $$; Cr • W**

The Nashville Room is a godsend for night people. Other than
burger joints, IHOPs, and the One's A Meals, the Houston restau-
rant scene rolls up the sidewalks early. This is just about the only
place in town where it's possible to get a real meal such as steak or
shrimp at 3 o'clock in the morning. The atmosphere is more
restaurant than coffee shop; the patrons include everything from
cops to visiting movie stars, and the food is perfectly OK.

## NINFA'S

**Various locations • Open daily, lunch and dinner only
Reservations necessary for groups of six or more • $$; Cr. • W**

By now the story has become as familiar as the name Horatio
Alger. Young widow Ninfa Laurenzo decides to support her family
through the one thing she knows well. She opens a small restaurant, and the rest is history. Well, not quite . . . but close enough
for government work. The original restaurant, still the core of the
Navigation Street location, helped to create the Tex-Mex and faji-
ta craze that later swept the nation. The fajitas are still world-class
and so are the lethal margaritas. There tends to be an early
evening wait at several locations. Kids feel welcome. Bar.

## NINO'S

**2817 West Dallas • Central • 522-5120 • Mon–Fri lunch and dinner
only; Sat dinner only; closed Sun • Reservations early and for
large parties • $$–$$$; Cr. • W, but call ahead**

From a small family-operated hole-in-the-wall, Nino's has grown
into one of Houston's favorite restaurants. Just because it's wildly
popular doesn't mean that the food is lowest common denomina-
tor, though. Delicious eggplant and succulent veal, to say nothing
of some really fine pastas and extravagant desserts, keep the
crowds coming to this less-than-fashionable location just west of
Montrose Boulevard. Bar.

## ONE'S A MEAL

**2019 West Gray • Central • 523-8432**

**5525 Memorial • Central • 861-8300**

**Open daily, 24 hours • $; No cr.**

The Memorial location, in a former IHOP near the park, attracts a yupscale clientele including lots of joggers. Weekend breakfast is incredibly crowded. But the real Onesie's, on West Gray, is like nothing else in Houston. A small-town cafe that could as easily be in Fort Stockton, Port Mansfield, or Jasper, this is the gathering place for an amazing collection of characters. At five in the morning, be-earringed musicians winding down from late-night gigs meet city counselors slugging down the first coffee of the day and trying to focus on the *New York Times*. The regulars all know each other and often talk. Differences fade as business types, truck drivers, cops, artists, River Oaks matrons in aerobic sweats, and retired people from all walks of life talk politics, sports, TV, or the weather. The waitresses, many of whom have been here for decades, know most customers by name and their regular orders by heart. The food is basic, and the homemade Greek chicken soup added by the Bibas brothers, who own the place, is the standout.

## OTTO'S

**5502 Memorial • West • 864-2573 • Mon–Sat, lunch and dinner only; closed Sun**

**500 Dallas (in Allen Center) • Downtown • Mon–Fri, breakfast, lunch, and dinner • No reservations • $; Cr. • W**

The Memorial location is reputedly former President George Bush's favorite barbecue joint. If so, that comes as no surprise to the generations of Houstonians who've enjoyed this unpretentious Memorial Park-area institution. The after-softball crowd gives the place a festive air, and the downtown lunch bunch stands in long lunchtime lines for succulent ribs, burgers, and some of the best sliced beef in town. Beer.

## OUISIE'S TABLE

**3939 San Felipe • Southwest • 528-2264 • Open Tues–Fri, lunch
and dinner; Sat–Sun breakfast and dinner; • Closed Mon
$$$–$$$$; Cr. • W**

After a six-year hiatus and a move from the Rice U area to the
tonier precincts of River Oaks, the legendary Ouisie's Table—and
its famous blackboard menu—is back among us. The large, spare
dining room and the outdoor veranda offer a casually upscale set-
ting, with the garden where Eloise Cooper and her kitchen wizards
pick their own fresh herbs nearby. The culinary offerings—such as
the superb grilled redfish and the to-die-for polenta—are pricey,
but worth the trip. Save room for the killer desserts. Reservations
highly recommended.

## PAPPADEAUX

**Several locations • Open daily, lunch and dinner
$$–$$$; Cr. • No reservations • W**

Papadeaux offers great seafood value. Good food, the usual Pap-
pas' large portions, and consistent execution. Charbroiled catfish
fillets are a standout. Oysters Fondeaux is an other-worldly appe-
tizer; surely not good for you, but doctors be damned. Specials are
fine, but tend to be fish of the day with a Yuppified pile of sauced
shrimp, crabmeat, and artichokes. The fries are ok, but it's worth
paying the difference to substitute the huge, loaded-to-the-max
baked potatoes. This Cajun version of Pappas Seafood Houses has
outstripped the popularity of the originals. Bar.

## PAPPAS SEAFOOD HOUSE AND OYSTER BAR

**6894 Southwest Freeway (U.S. 59) • Southwest • 784-4729;
call for other locations • Open daily, lunch and dinner only
No reservations • $$; AE, MC, V • W**

Fish of all descriptions, fresh and lots of it, seems to be Pappas
recipe for success. The daily specials offer everything from trout to
the latest blackened craze. Crab salad is especially good. Lunch
can be crowded. Kids feel welcome. Bar.

## PAPPAS BAR-B-Q

**Four locations • Open daily, lunch and dinner only**
**No reservations • $–$$; Cr.**

Those who remember the funky old downtown Brisket House, will be happy to discover it's been acquired and spruced up to Pappas standards. The 'cue sandwiches have lost their classic fattiness, but you won't miss it. The other locations have less character, but equally good barbeque. Beer.

## PAPPASITO'S CANTINA

**6445 Richmond (near Hillcroft) • South • 784-5253; call for other locations • Open daily, lunch and dinner only • No reservations $$; AE, MC, V**

Why is Pappasito's so popular? Why are there lines around the block on weekend nights and huge crowds of lunchtime regulars? Simple. It's because the Pappas family, of Pappas Seafood House fame, knows how to serve good food and plenty of it in a relaxed and festive atmosphere. Here the food is mostly Tex-Mex, with the emphasis on such standards as enchiladas and fajitas al carbon, but for those who prefer lighter fare, fine grilled seafood is also on the menu. Bar.

## PAT AND PETE'S BLUES BURGERS

**311 Travis • Downtown • Tues–Sun lunch and dinner; Mon lunch only • 222-7337 • $; Cr.**

The regular beef burgers are great, and the turkey burger may be best in town. Gadzillion bottled beers, try something exotic. Sweet potato fries with a jalapeño chile dip is killer stuff. Hip juke box and memorabilia; late-night hours except Sun and Mon. Beer and wine.

## PICO'S

**5941 Bellaire • Southwest • 662-8383**

**4527 Lomitas (at Kirby) • Central • 942-9955**

**Open daily; closed Mon • $$; Cr.**

An interesting change from the Tex-Mex norm. Pico's authentic, interior Mexican cuisine includes everything from rich moles to Yucatecan redfish steamed in banana leaves. Great liquados (rather like Mexican smoothies) and stellar soups. Kids feel welcome. Mariachis on weekends. Bar.

## RAINBOW LODGE

**1 Birdsall Street (off Memorial) • Central • 861-8666**
**Mon–Fri lunch and dinner; Sat dinner only; closed Sun**
**Reservations strongly suggested • $$$; AE, MC, V, DC, Dis**

You don't really go to the Rainbow Lodge to eat. You go for the dining experience, which is romantic beyond the dreams of Harlequin. The restaurant is on the lush green banks of Buffalo Bayou, only a few miles west of downtown. Its rustic charm and the spectacular setting, to say nothing of the well-prepared meats, make it well worth the trip. Can be crowded, especially on Valentines Day. Bar.

## RIO RANCH

**9999 Westheimer • West • 952-5000 • Open daily for breakfast,**
**lunch and dinner • $$–$$$; Cr. • Reservations for large or private**
**parties • W (call ahead)**

Star Chef Robert del Grande was commissioned to create a fun restaurant that could be "chained" with some Hilton hotels, and Rio Rancho is the prototype. The down-home-style food is well done, with standouts such as the classy grilled salmon salad and fine chicken enchiladas. Sunday brunch is bountiful. Bar.

## RITZ-CARLTON HOTEL

**1919 Briar Oaks Lane • Central • 840-7600**
**Dining room open daily for lunch and dinner • $$$$; Cr.**
**Reservations accepted • W**

The Grill Room is considered one of the best places in town for would-be trophy wives to spot (and snag?) wealthy bachelors. For those not on the Marriage Mart, the food is the attraction, and it can be spectacular. The chile-roasted beef filet is superb. Very dressy. Bar.

## RIVER OAKS GRILL

**2630 Westheimer • Central • 520-1738 • Lunch Mon–Fri; Mon–Sat dinner only; closed Sun • Reservations recommended $$$$; Cr. • W**

In blue-collar neighborhoods, regulars meet at the local diner; in River Oaks, they meet here. The intimate, dark-green and brass space improbably shares a strip center with Buffalo Hardware. The Grill's soups and pastas are first rate, and the lamb chops are world class. Go to see and be seen. The tiny bar is often crowded.

## RIVER CAFE

**3615 Montrose • Central • 529-0088 Open daily for lunch and dinner; brunch on Sat and Sun Reservations suggested • $$$–$$$$; Cr.**

This is the most "Los Angeles" of Houston's restaurants. The sensibility is very Left Coast, what with local artists exhibiting on the walls and jazz musicians playing the bar. But don't be fooled. The River Cafe serves some of the more interesting fare in town. The pasta dishes are top-notch, and the daily specials, often seafood, are a treat. The crowd alone is worth the trip, the bar stays open late and, in fine weather, the sidewalk tables make for a wonderful evening. As lagniappe, there's a big band in the back room every couple of weeks and a jazz brunch every Sunday. Bar.

## RIVOLI

**5636 Richmond • West • 789-1900 • Mon–Fri, lunch and dinner; Sat, dinner only; closed Sun • Reservations necessary • $$$–$$$$; AE, MC, DC**

One of the handful of places in town where celebrities, socialites, and power brokers all feel equally at home. The several luxuriously appointed dining areas are matched by fine service and an award-winning French-continental menu. Despite a much-noted change in ownership, favorites such as the stuffed Dover sole and the 14-ounce veal chop with wild mushroom sauce remain on the menu. The tableside flambés still make a dramatic impression, as does the extensive wine list. Bar.

## ROMANO'S MACARONI GRILL

**Four locations • Open daily, lunch and dinner**
**Call ahead for large parties • $$; Cr. • W**

The "Maccaroni's" gives real value in basic country Italian. Wonderful soups (warning: "bowl" is huge) and entrées of roasted chicken and pasta are excellent. Desserts are good, too, but dinner servings are so large you'll be lucky to have room.

## ROTISSERIE FOR BEEF AND BIRD

**2200 Wilcrest • West • 977-9524**
**Mon–Fri, lunch and dinner; Sat dinner only; closed Sun**
**Reservations necessary • $$$–$$$$; Cr. • W**

Warm and inviting, this Houston favorite gives equal attention to beef, seafood, and fowl, all grilled to perfection. In addition to the stellar steaks and chicken dishes, the Rotisserie offers a marvelous grilled duck, venison, a roast goose straight out of Dickensian feasts, and lobster aplenty. The dessert menu rivals visions of sugarplums with its patented cobblers, pies, and puddings. Bar.

## RUGGLE'S GRILL

**903 Westheimer • Central • 524-3839**
**Lunch and dinner only; closed Mon and for lunch on Sat**
**Reservations recommended • $$$; Cr.**

Ruggle's is the latest incarnation of one of Houston's longest-surviving restaurants, and its popularity has never really waned. Always true to its time, from the hippie funk to neo-homestyle, the grill these days is fun, upbeat, and culinarily cutting edge. The grilled lamb and grilled tuna are wonderful, and the veal liver is the best in town. The dessert tray takes second place to none. Everything is homemade. Bar.

## RUTH'S CHRIS STEAK HOUSE

**6213 Richmond • Central • 789-2333**
**Open daily, dinner only • $$$$; Cr. • W**

If you're a business *GUY* with a really big expense account, this is the place for you. The mammoth, choice steaks are the best there is. They come sizzling on a platter, drenched in New Orleans-style herbed butter. Everything else is considered a side dish, and these tend toward 1950s country club style. Bar.

## SAM BO JUNG

**7665 De Moss • Southwest • 776-9108**
**Open daily • Reservations accepted • $$; Cr.**

Southwest Houston neighbors love this unpretentious place. The omelets are the standout, especially the green-onion version and an oyster omelet that is unexpectedly yummy. Beer and wine.

## SAMMY'S LEBANESE

**5825 Richmond • Southwest • 780-0065 • Open daily**
**Reservations necessary for large parties • $–$$; Cr.**

The Beirut of happy memory is gone, but in this little corner of Lebanon the wonderful food of the Levant still is served up seven days a week. There are other good Middle Eastern restaurants in Houston now, but Sammy's is still special. The mezza, an assortment of dips and appetizers, including my fave, baba ghanouj (eggplant, lemon, and garlic dip), is the best bet for the convivial. The unusual tastes continue with such entrées as beef sawerma in sesame sauce and a particularly fine baked kibbe, with pine nuts and cinnamon. Beer and wine.

## SAUSALITO

**3215 Westheimer • Central • 529-6959 • Mon–Fri, lunch and**
**dinner; Sat, dinner only; Sun, brunch and dinner • Weekend**
**reservations suggested • $$; AE, MC, V • W variable**

In a pleasant garden-style setting, Sausalito serves a great collection of pasta and seafood dishes. The Bammel Garden salad with goat cheese is a fresh and piquant winner, as is the tomato with fresh basil. The linguini with salmon and garlic pesto is pungent without being overpowering. Grilled chicken breast with peppercorn sauce is another favorite. Ask for daily off-the-menu specials; at Sausalito, they are often worth writing home about. Bar.

## SFUZZI

**1800 Post Oak • (in Pavilion Center) • Central • 622-9600**
**Open daily • Reservations recommended • $$–$$$; Cr. • W**

All done up in neo-Pompeiian wall murals and constantly crowded with fashionables (many wearing the latest from nearby Saks and assorted designer boutiques), this is a place to see and be seen. The passing parade is of more-than-passing interest with frequent appearances by local and national glitterati. Take the reservations injunction seriously. The food is what you might call nouvelle Italian and is often wonderful, especially the featured entrées. Bar.

### SHANGHAI EAST

**Galleria I (third level) • Central • 627-3682**
**Open daily • $$; AE, V, MC, DC • W variable**

Since the earliest days of the Galleria, Shanghai East has served a combination of popular standbys—such as mu shu pork, shrimp with lobster sauce, and sweet-and-sour dishes—as well as vegetarian items—like the Buddhist favorite (mixed veggies and tofu in clear sauce)—and some exceptional hot-and-spicy dishes. The lichee beef with orange peel is a winner. So is the lobster with pine nuts. A great break from shopping. Beware of the MSG! Ask to have it left out if necessary. Bar.

### SHANGHAI RED'S

**8501 Cypress East • 926-6666 • Open daily, lunch and dinner only**
**Reservations suggested • $$–$$$; Cr. • W variable**

The location is so weird, especially on foggy nights, that Hollywood couldn't have invented it. On a branch of the Ship Channel near a dockyard, it offers diners in the multilevel space a chance to watch freighters cruising by. Best to call for directions if you're coming from anywhere but the immediate neighborhood. . . . Oh, yeah, the food. It's basic steak and seafood, and it's okay. Bar.

### STRACK FARMS RESTAURANT

**5707 Louetta • North • 376-0901 • Open daily, breakfast, lunch,**
**and dinner • No reservations except for very large groups • $$;**
**AE, MC, V • W variable**

Although the eponymous farm is no more, the Farms restaurant prospers up in the woods north of Houston. It is a fine, family-style place that gives lie to the belief of Inside-the-Loopers that only airline food is served beyond the confines of Loop 610. In the large, comfortable series of dining rooms, the friendly wait staff serves up humongous portions of steak, chicken, ribs, and other home-style entres. The baked potatoes are a meal in themselves, and the onion rings are well worth a try. Bar.

## SWEET MESQUITE

**Seven locations • Open daily, lunch and dinner • Reservations suggested for large parties • $–$$; Cr. • W**

Don't let the name fool you. This is not a barbecue joint. Sweet Mesquite serves a fine selection of steaks, fish, and chicken grilled over mesquite wood. The chuck for the burgers is ground fresh, the fajitas are made with top cuts of meat, and the salads are fresh, fresh, fresh. Not only are kids welcome, there is a special kids' menu that offers more than the ankle-biters can eat—topped off with ice cream—for a mere $1.50. Such a deal. Beer and wine.

## SWINGING DOOR

**FM 359 at Hwy 90 • Richmond • 342-4758 • Wed–Sun open for lunch and dinner; closed Mon–Tue • $$; Cr.**

Do it! Drive to Richmond. It's worth it. This is old-style Texas Church picnic barbeque with the kind of cole slaw and potato salad your grandma and great aunts made. On weekends there's a country band and two-steppin' in the back. Beer and wine.

## TAJ MAHAL

**8328 Gulf Freeway (I-45) • Southwest • 649-2818**
**Lunch and dinner only; closed Mon**
**Reservations suggested on weekends • $$; Cr. • W**

Taj Mahal is one of Houston's favorite Indian restaurants. The decor may be plain, but the food is not. An extensive menu of sub-continental specialties attracts families of all ethnic backgrounds. Bar.

## THAI HOUSE

**5704 Fondren • 789-2666 • Reservations accepted • Open Tues–Fri, lunch and dinner; Sat–Sun, dinner only • $–$$; Cr.**

Thai House offers a pleasant range of standard dishes, many with the spices adjusted for less-than-flameproof American palates. The service is exceptionally friendly, and families with well-behaved children are welcome. Beer and wine.

## THIS IS IT

**207 West Gray • Central • 659-1608 • Open daily, breakfast, lunch, and dinner • No reservations • $; No cr. • W variable**

Tired of fern bars and the latest food fads? This Is It, once hidden away deep in Fourth Ward, is still serving simple, down-home fare with genuine soul-food taste. The menu is not for the diet-minded. The meats—smothered chicken and pork chops leading the list—are enough to give fat gram counters a fit. But they taste so *good* that rationalization comes easy. The steam table full of vegetables, everything from sweet potatoes to greens, offers something to please every chow hound. If you're trying to drop ten pounds, go somewhere else. If you're hungry, *THIS IS IT.*

## TOKYO GARDENS

**4701 Westheimer • Southwest • 622-7886 • Mon–Fri, lunch and dinner; Sat–Sun dinner only • $$–$$$; Cr. • W**

For almost three decades, this Japanese inn just east of the Galleria has been offering fine, fresh sushi at the bar in addition to full meals served in the old country manner, with shoeless diners seated on tatami mats around low tables. Classical Japanese dancing nightly. A lovely change of pace. Bar.

## TONY MANDOLA'S GULF COAST KITCHEN

**1962 West Gray • Central • 528-3474 • Open daily; Sun, dinner only • Reservations recommended • $$; Cr.**

The marvelous Mandola brothers (see also Damian's and Nino's) can be counted on to come up with crowd-pleasing versions of favorite foods. The Kitchen serves fresh seafood with just enough of an Italian-Cajun twist to make it interesting. The shrimp and oyster dishes are especially good, and there's always Mama Mandola's cole slaw. Because it's located in the busy River Oaks Shopping Center, the place can be crowded. Call for reservations. Bar.

## TONY'S

**1801 Post Oak Boulevard • West • 622-6778**
**Mon–Fri, lunch and dinner; Sat, dinner only; closed Sun**
**Reservations suggested • $$$$; Cr.**

For years Tony's was the ne plus ultra of Houston dining; then, supposedly in a spat with the building's owner, Tony Vallone closed

the restaurant. Social Houston was thrown into a total tizzy. Fortunately for both the social X-rays and for those who appreciate fine
dining, it reopened. This is a true 4-star restaurant, with elegant
cuisine and an encyclopediac wine collection. Very dressy.
Extremely expensive. Bar.

**TREEBEARD'S**

**315 Travis • Other downtown locations • 225-2160 • Lunch only;
closed Sat and Sun • $; AE**

A good case can be made for Treebeard's being downtown's
favorite lunch spot. From the courthouses nearby come prosecu-
tors and defense attorneys, and from the bank towers come the
gray suits and power ties. The rest of the crowd is a mixture of
shoppers and visitors all bent on enjoying first-class Cajun-style specialties. The lines are long, but the food is worth the wait. Favorites
shrimp etouffé and chicken-and-sausage gumbo are piquant and
satisfying without being incendiary. The shrimp and fruit salads
are summer favorites as is the annex, located in the cool and restful cloister of Christ Church Cathedral, around the corner at 1117
Texas Avenue. Beer and wine.

---

### HOUSTON FACTOID:

*The seal of the Episcopal Diocese of Texas is decorated with two
longhorns in memory of the cows that stampeded through the
dedication of Christ Church Cathedral downtown.*

---

**VARGO'S**

**2401 Fondren • West • 782-3888 • Mon-Fri lunch and dinner; Sat
dinner only; Sun brunch only; Dinner and brunch reservations
highly suggested • $$$–$$$$; Cr. • W variable**

Older relatives visiting from out of town? Planning a pre-wed-
ding dinner or a romantic evening for two? Vargo's is just the
place. Boasting one of the most romantic settings in Houston,
Vargo's has a glassed dining area that overlooks an exquisite small
lake complete with swans and lush gardens stalked by improbably
beautiful peacocks. The food, while secondary to the setting, is

quite good. The menu leans toward continental dishes and seafood with French-style sauces, and the prime rib and various other steaks are first-rate. Bar.

## WONDERFUL VEGETARIAN RESTAURANT

**7549 Westheimer (at Hillcroft) • Southwest • 977-3137**
**Lunch and dinner only; closed Mon • $$; Cr. • W variable**

Although the title is the strip-center establishment's name, it can also be taken as a value judgment. This is like no other vegetarian restaurant in town. The dishes range from the expected—seaweed rolls and salad—to imitation everything. They offer honey-roast vegetarian ham, imitation squid, and even fake duck. The strangest part is that all of it is delicious, and although it is perhaps not exactly indistinguishable from the original, it is certainly close enough to give pause. Most dishes have a spicy Hunan-Szechuan slant, and the veggies are crisply stir-fried. The menu even gives the protein and calorie count for each dish. It's certified Kosher, too. Beer and wine.

## WUNSCHE BROS.

**103 Midway • Spring • Far north • 350-1902 • Tue–Sun lunch and dinner; Mon lunch only • $; AE, MC, V • W variable**

The last four digits of the phone number are the year Wunsche's was built. The rambling turn-of-the-century building, now added to, houses a fine burger joint that also serves a few other specialties, such as chicken-fried steak and several kinds of sandwiches. The side orders, especially the house specialty sausage-sauerkraut balls, are first-rate, as are the sinful desserts. Down-home atmosphere, loud and fun; kids are welcome. Call for live-music information. Beer and wine.

## YILDIZLAR

**3419 Kirby • Central • 524-7735**
**Mon-Sat, lunch and dinner only; closed Sun • $–$$; Cr.**

In a bland shopping center at the corner of Richmond and Kirby is one of Houston's happy surprises. Yildizlar serves up stellar versions of Middle Eastern specialties. The dips, both chickpea and eggplant, are first-rate, and the kabobs are tender and tasty. Exotic fruit drinks and some of the ultra-sweet desserts are wonderfully redolent of rosewater.

# CLUBS & PUBS

Workin' on your night moves? Well, Houston's a great place to do it because, with a relatively young population, our town supports a thriving nightlife. In the parallel universe of the evening, where no one ever has to go to the office, there are hundreds of bars, clubs, and even late-night restaurants catering to those who can't face the thought of going home before dawn.

The biggest problem for would-be party animals is keeping up with the comings and goings of night spots. Those listed here are hardy perennials, but there are lots of others. The best way to find them is to check the entertainment sections of the weekly papers, the *Houston Press* and *Public News.*

Because it can cost millions of dollars to build nightclub infrastructure, few buildings that house clubs ever become anything else. A night spot may close for a while, retool to suit the latest trend, and then reopen under another name, but you can bet your Lotto bucks it won't become a Burger King. So, once you find a likely location, the best bet is just to watch the space. Sooner or later, a new club will appear. Meanwhile, if you're temporarily clubless, try some of these.

## SERIOUSLY HIP

Hip central moves around with the times. In the 1950s it was at the Cork Club and the Shamrock Hotel; in the '60s and '70s, Montrose and lower Westheimer; in the '80s, it was near the Galleria. At this juncture in the '90s, it's the Shepherd Plaza area bounded by

Richmond and the Southwest Freeway between Shepherd and Greenbriar. While the "hippest location" changes often—as does the terminology—the attitude that fuels it never does. It's the need for an area where the young, clever, and fashionable can congregate to see and be seen. Locations are in a constant state of flux, but one thing stays constant: There will always be one part of town that's considered the cutting edge of chic. For now, the Shepherd Plaza area is it. Some of the hot spots:

## 8.0

**3745 Greenbriar • Central • 523-0880 • Open daily; Cr.**

Occasional music. Occasional movies. Occasional guest chefs. A track record of being hipper than thou. Plastic outdoor chairs indoors. Changing art. Exposed concrete ceilings. Good, interesting food. Lava lamp drinks. Martinis. Small outside patio. None of this sounds like much, but in the business of being hip, the crowd is the show. Fortunately for 8.0, all the right players show up. Artists, models, would-be models, lawyers, doctors, and *et ceteras*. Develop an attitude. Show up late. Live fast. Wear a little black something. Admission free.

## Q CAFE

**2205 Richmond • Central • 524-9696 • Live music on Wed. Open daily; Cr.**

A single pool table. Is that hip or what? The right crowd seeing and being seen—and all just 100 yards from 8.0! How convenient. From the same people who brought you the '80s EXCESS, with an X. Wear more than a little black here, please. Like 8.0, admission to Q Cafe is free.

## THE BALL ROOM

**2170 Portsmouth • Central • 942-0010 • Live blues band on Wed. Open daily; Cr.**

Just a sashay away from 8.0 and Q Cafe, this blatant knock off of Gotham in Santa Monica, California, is supposed to be a pool hall. Remember Paul Newman in the Hustler? Sorry, you're too old to go to The Ball Room. $15.00 an hour for a table? Who's hustling whom? Pose like your favorite member of the Melrose Place cast. Imagine yourself at the Hollywood Athletic Club (which is, of course, a pool hall, in case your *People* magazine got lost in the mail). Try to hear a little music above the din. Feel pretty. Have a ball.

## LIVE MUSIC

Sometimes it seems as if every garage band in Houston has a club date, and there *are* places that give newcomers a chance. (How do you think Lyle Lovett and ZZ Topp were discovered?) But there are other venues that emphasize quality live music played by qualified live musicians. Listen up at:

### ALE HOUSE

**2425 West Alabama • Central • 521-2333 • Live music Fri and Sat Cover varies • Over 21 • Open daily; Cr.**

The Ale House has many identities. Downstairs, Rice grad students, writers, and less-compulsive business types can enjoy an atmosphere of funky Anglophilia. Upstairs, local bands entertain on weekends and sometimes during the week. There's even an Open Mike night. (Call for details.) Everyone can enjoy the multitude of beer brands and the tree-shaded garden in which to drink them.

### ANDERSON FAIR

**2007 Grant • Central • 528-8576 • Open Fri & Sat nights only Cover varies**

Here in this tiny, back-street time warp off Montrose Boulevard (behind Texas Art Supply), it has been 1968 for more than a quarter of a century. The last survivor of the once-thriving Montrose hippie scene, the Fair has helped launch the careers of hundreds of local musicians, including such big national names as Nanci Griffith and Lyle Lovett. Still committed to the music scene that gave it birth, Anderson Fair features accoustic and folk music by Texas singers and songwriters.

### STUDIO 59

**9301 Bissonnet • Southwest • 270-6602 • Open daily; Cr. • 18 to get in, 21 to drink**

Rock and roll seven nights a week! Sometimes you hit it lucky and see featured rising bands with national recording contracts. Folks with strong eardrums enjoy the sometime battles of the bands. The crowd is mostly over 21, but the attitude is young. Shorts and really casual dress okay.

## BLACK LABRADOR PUB

**4100 Montrose • Central • 529-1199 • Open nightly; V, MC, AE Live music • No cover • Under 21 admitted**

The Black Lab has the feel of a homey British pub in a university town. Located in the attractive, red-brick Campanile Center near the former church that now houses the Montrose Public Library, it is a neighborhood fixture. Low-ceilinged, wood-floored, with plank tables and pub grub, beers, and ales, the Lab attracts university intellectual types and the Montrose art crowd. Outdoor seating and a garden chessboard are attractions, as is the bluegrass, Celtic, and other acoustic music. Dress ranges from casual to academic rumpled.

## THE FABULOUS SATELLITE LOUNGE

**3616 Washington Avenue • Central • 869-2665 • Live music Thu, Fri, Sat, sometimes Sun; Cover; Cr. • Generally closed Mon–Wed**

Love the latest? Try the Satellite. Among other things, it plays host to CD release parties for both local and regional bands. This is also your chance to see some groups you may actually have heard of—and some you'll hear of soon—in a club setting.

## FITZGERALD'S

**2706 White Oak • Central • 862-3838 • Open Wed–Sat • Cover varies for live entertainment; AE, MC, V • W variable**

The old Polish Hall in the Heights, housed in a rambling white wooden building on White Oak, is one of the granddaddies of the Houston live music scene. When many other, fancier venues failed, Fitz hung in there, surviving the roller coaster ride of the economy. It still offers great rock, blues, reggae, and more. Zelda's, its sister club downstairs, features mostly popular local talent. Upstairs is for serious dancing when both local and nationally known groups play.

## KENNEALLY'S IRISH PUB

**2111 South Shepherd • Central • 630-0486 • Open daily; often live music Wed–Sat • No cover; AE, MC, V**

One of Houston's favorite old-style pubs, Kenneally's offers darts, sports talk, serious drinking, and traditional Irish folk music,

often featuring well-known acts direct from Boston, New York, or
the auld sod itself. And the food—especially the pizza and the
famous do-it-yourself steak barbeque—is just fine, too.

## LAST CONCERT CAFE

**1403 Nance • Central • 226-8563 • Mon–Fri lunch and dinner; Sat
dinner only; closed Sun • Reservations suggested on Friday and
Saturday • Cover varies • AE, MC, V, DC**

Though better known as a Tex-Mex restaurant than as a club,
The Last Concert features some surprisingly fine music. This diffi-
cult-to-find, one-time whorehouse still requires patrons to knock
on the unmarked door that's a relic of Prohibition, but these days,
it features good local musicians, and the jukebox is as Latin-fla-
vored as the margaritas. Call for directions unless you're really
familiar with the odd corners of downtown Houston.

## MARKET SQUARE BREW PUB

**809 Congress • Downtown • 222-6925 • Open every day except
Sun.; cover Fri & Sat • AE, V, MC**

Local musicians enliven evenings at Market Square. The big draw
is the homemade beer and ale, but it's worth calling to see who's
playing on weekends. Some have considerable local followings.

## MCGONIGEL'S MUCKY DUCK

**2425 Norfolk • Central • 528-5999 • Closed Sun
Cover varies; Cr.**

Maybe the town's best combination of live music and *lots* of tap
beers. The Duck also offers a pleasant patio and a decent kitchen.
Well-known local and regional musicians. Call for schedule.

## RICHMOND ARMS

**5921 Richmond • West • 977-8635 • Open daily • Occasional live
music; no cover • AE, DC, MC, V • W variable**

Houston Anglophiles and homesick Brits gather here to enjoy
the dart boards, Guinness and Bass on draught, and the real pub
atmosphere. The steak and kidney pie, bangers and mash, and
other pub grub go down just right.

## ROCKEFELLER'S

**3620 Washington • Central • 869-8427 • Days and hours vary depending on performance schedule • Cover varies for live entertainment; AE, MC, V • W variable**

The stolid gray building was once a bank. Like so many Houston banks in the late 1980s, the business it housed went under. Unlike many financial institutions, Rockefeller's managed to reopen. Now it once again plays host to rock, blues, and jazz acts—some with real national reputations. Local bands also are showcased here. Rockefeller's has a small dance floor, but even that is taken up with tables when the club is packed.

## RUDYARD'S PUB

**2010 Waugh Dive • Central • 521-0521 • Live music often, usually rock and roll, sometimes jazz • Open every day; no credit cards**

Nothing fancy, but a long-time survivor of the local club scene. Rudz offers darts, local musicians, bikers, artists, and the feeling that only a true, worlds-colliding Montrose neighborhood bar can produce.

## SAM'S BOAT

**5720 Richmond Avenue • Richmond Strip • 781-2628**

**3002 NASA Road 1 • Clear Lake • 335-7267 • Open daily; Cr.**

## SAM'S PLACE

**5710 Richmond • Richmond Strip • 781-1605 • Open daily; Cr.**

Side by side on the "Richmond Strip" (from 610 to Hillcroft), these two clubs help anchor Houston's liveliest entertainment district. Both feature cover bands and local talent, but the people-watching is a major attraction, especially when the Harley-riding contingent convenes for parking lot parties.

## SHAKESPEARE PUB

**14129 Memorial Drive • West • 497-4625**
**Open every day, but no live music Mon. • MC, V, Dis.**

Improbably located in the far reaches of Memorial, The Shakespeare offers decent live music that tends toward R&B. Sometimes it's cheap, and sometimes it's actually free.

## THE VELVET ELVIS

**3303 Richmond • Central • Open daily; live blues Thu, Sat, Sun; cover varies • 520-0434**

Back, just like The Man himself! The Velvet now boasts a cigar room, full kitchen, and entertainment that varies in quality but not in enthusiasm. If you remember where you were when you heard about the King's "death," this is not the club for you. The crowd was born after Elvis left the building. Most are college age with a sprinkling of mid-20s.

---

# BLUES

---

Some of the greatest blues musicians in history were nurtured in Houston. The early practitioners found inspiration in the pre-integration Wards, and even in the tough times that followed. While created by African-American artists, the blues has a home in any place and any time that people struggle to get by. It's like B.B. King says, "The blues was like that problem child that you may have had in the family. You was a little bit ashamed to let anybody see him, but you loved him. You just didn't know how other people would take it." Some Houston blues bars have taken that problem child and dolled it up until it's almost unrecognizable. These are the places that seem too joyful for the blues, but if you really listen, the root music is still there—somewhere. Other locations stick to the basics. Give them a try.

## BILLY BLUES BARBECUE

**6025 Richmond at Fountainview • Richmond Strip • 226-9294 Open daily, live music daily, cover; Cr. • W**

It's the saxophone most people remember. Outside the club is a gigantic, blue saxophone (note that the bottom of the piece is an upside-down Volkswagen bug) that the city tried to claim was a "sign" that violated an ordinance. The club owners countered that the sax was sculpture, and, backed by noisily partisan patrons, won the battle of the beholders. Inside, the music ranges from the best of the local bands to some well-known national figures.

## THE BIG EASY SOCIAL AND PLEASURE CLUB

**5731 Kirby • Central • 523-9999 • No cover**

The location has had many incarnations, but this one seems likely to stick. The music tends toward New Orleans-flavored jazz and blues with more than a soupçon of Zydeco.

# JAZZ

The all-American art form has had a checkered career in Houston. There is a hard core of support for the music, and from time to time its popularity breaks out into the mainstream as in the days of the long-gone but not forgotten La Bastille, which hosted some of the nation's greatest jazz artists. Nowadays, there are a number of club that feature fine local talent and a few that showcase national names.

## CEZANNE

**4100 Montrose (above The Black Labrador) • Central**
**867-7992 • No cover; Cr.**

A lovely, intimate spot for listening to some of the local best. If you want a quiet evening of good music, this is the place.

## CHELSEA PUB

**2525 Rice Boulevard • Central • 523-3509 • Open daily; Cr.**

The Chelsea Pub is an unlikely jazz venue. The place is your basic, English-style pub, complete with noisy dart games and pints of ale, but on Saturday nights—sometimes other nights as well—you can listen to local musicians offering more-than-creditable jazz stylings. Go figure.

## CODY'S JAZZ BAR & GRILL

**2450 University Boulevard • Central • Closed Sun and Mon**
**Live music Tue–Sat, cover Fri & Sat • 520-5660**

Cody's has a considerable history as a jazz venue that's followed it from the erstwhile, Montrose Boulevard location. The newer club, in the heart of the Rice Village shopping area, seems an unlikely location for a night spot. Nevertheless, it offers jazzy, urban-contemporary stylings by better local groups. The crowd is young professional and tends to be dressy, especially on weekends.

**MONROE'S GALLANT KNIGHT**

**2337 Holcombe • Central • 665-9762**
**Closed Sun • Live music Wed–Sat • No cover; Cr.**

One of Houston's hidden treasures, this long-time institution offers, perhaps, the best live jazz lineup in town. How the Knight manages to prosper in its unlikely location on Holcombe, not far from the Houston Medical Center and West University, remains a mystery. Make an expedition. It's worth the trip.

## OLDER CROWD

If you know absolutely nothing about most of the groups on MTV—and you have no desire to learn—folks in the club business consider you part of the "older crowd." Lowering as this thought may be, it seems better to follow Jean Paul Sartre's advice and "be of your time" than to try to cultivate an interest in the latest video sensation. And so we offer a selection of establishments catering to those who prefer comfortable music. These are not genre-specific places like jazz or blues clubs, and they aren't designed specifically for dancing, but they may offer any or all of the above.

**BISTRO VINO**

**819 Alabama • Central • 526-5500 • Open Mon–Sat**
**No cover; reservations suggested; Cr. • Under 21 admitted**

Downstairs there is a very nice Italian-Continental style restaurant with a fireplace to make it cozy in winter, and a green, secluded outdoor deck for cooling summer evenings, but upstairs is one of Houston's very nicest small piano bars. Just right to end the evening.

**LA CARAFE**

**813 Congress • Downtown • 229-9399 • Open daily**
**No cover; no cr.**

La Carafe is located in the oldest building left in Houston. At one time this was a stagecoach stop, and before the Civil War there were slave quarters in the back. Now this strange little hole-in-the-wall off Market Square attracts a weird mixture of artistic types, street people, Rollerbladers, lofties, and downtown lawyers. Some say the ancient jukebox has the best playlist in town. It certainly has the most eclectic.

## MAGIC ISLAND

**2215 Southwest Freeway • Central 526-2442**
**Closed Sun • Cover includes meal; MC, V • W**

There is nothing like Magic Island this side of Las Vegas—and maybe not even there. That strange building on the Southwest Freeway near Shepherd, the one with the huge Egyptian head on top, is not a Southwest Freeway-induced hallucination. And in fact, the interior decor makes the head look tame. The Island is a kind of dinner theater at which the admission fee includes your choice of entree, but—caveat emptor—not your drinks, dessert, tax, or tip. The magic shows, comedy acts, and disco are included, however. While none of the acts are really big names, they are dependably professional. This is a great place to take out-of-town visitors or to plan a special occasion.

## MARFRELESS

**2006 Peden • Central 528-0083 • Open daily**
**No cover; AE, DC, MC, V • W variable**

To find Marfreless, walk east from the entrance of the Landmark River Oaks Theatre, turn into the parking lot of a small bank, and look for the door under the metal fire stairs. It's across the street from Biraporetti's restaurant on West Gray. The entrance is unmarked, and the bar's ambiance is decidedly low-key. There is no entertainment as such, just classical music on the sound system, and good conversation from the movie-buff regulars (note the poster with an iconoclastic list of Houston's 100 top films of the year). The pronunciation of the name, by the way, is mar-FRAY-less, and the long-winded explanation of its meaning, found on printed sheets near the bar, makes no sense whatsoever. FYI: The dim alcoves, especially the tiny back room on the second floor and the nook under the stairs make this Houston's hottest adult make-out spot.

## MUNCHIES

**1617 Richmond • 528-3545 • Open daily, no cover • AE, MC, V**

This is the place for the way cool and the culture vultures who like to party. Folk music and poetry slams are regular features. Great goofy open stage evenings include everything from all-tuba concerts and Mozart on a harp to lawyers singing Nelson Eddie's greatest hits. Games on the tube, a great selection of beers, and surprisingly good deli sandwiches, too, are on the Munchie's bill of fare. Picnic tables outside recall the never-forgotten Bissonnet location's patio.

## OVATIONS

**2536 Times Boulevard (at Kirby) • Central • 522-9801**
**Open daily; Cr.**

Almost as hard to find as the deliberately obscure Marfreless, Ovations is tucked into a deco-period building on one of the less-traveled streets in the Rice Village shopping area. Once you've navigated the narrow hallway, the space opens up into a surprisingly lovely two-story club that features some of the best in sophisticated lounge entertainment. Although minimally talented Las Vegas singers have given the term a bad name, the lounge act *is* an honorable genre and Ovations offers some of its better local and national practitioners. The club is also one of the few places in town offering sophisticated entertainment on Sunday nights. Always check the schedule, though.

## SPORTS BARS

Houston sports fans are all over the map. When the local teams are winning, all kinds of folks turn up at sports-themed establishments. When the Aeros, Astros, Hotshots, Oilers, or Rockets are having a bad season, the crowd thins considerably. Still, sports bars are a fun place to knock back a couple of brews, share razzing the ref with perfect strangers, or follow an out-of-town team.

### BIG JOHN'S NEIGHBORHOOD SPORTS BAR

**6150 Wilcrest • West • 498-3499 • Open daily; Cr.**

Just what it says: a neighborhood sports bar, which is kind of nice. During playoffs and other big events, the crowd can get intense. Be prepared. (Open air.)

### DAVE & BUSTERS

**6010 Richmond Avenue • 952-2233 • Open daily; Cr.**

This is part of the latest in clubbing—the mega club. In addition to those who come for the monster game arcade in the back, D&B's

attracts lots of sports fans, many of them young professionals, especially during a hot pennant race or the basketball playoffs. Radio sports call-in shows sometimes use the venue for live broadcasts.

## GRIF'S

**3416 Roseland • Central • 528-9912 • Open daily; No cover; Cr.**

Grif's is a neighborhood sports bar so good that *Esquire* magazine once named it one of the 100 best bars in America. It is still sports maniac heaven. There are a couple of video games, a dart board, and a pool table in the back, but they don't count. The secret of Grifs success is the deck full of picnic tables and the funky, indoor booths—they are filled with serious sports fans talking serious sports talk. The bar is the traditional sponsor of various "Armies" of fans who travel en masse, complete with bagpiper, to Houston pro teams' important games.

# COMEDY CLUBS

## LAFF STOP

**1952-A West Gray • Central • 524-2333**
**Closed Mon. • Reservations necessary; Cover charge; AE, MC, V**

The Laff Stop is part of a nationwide chain of clubs that are on the comedy circuit. The comics you'll see here aren't ready for the *Tonight Show* or *Comedy Central* yet, but some of them will be soon. The show usually consists of a comic MC and three comedians who appear in increasing order of competence. Some of the material is pretty raunchy. Check on the rating before booking your reservations.

## SPELLBINDERS

**10001 Westheimer • West • 266-2525 • Closed Mon. • Reservations necessary on weekends; Cover charge; Cr.**

Spellbinders, too, is part of a national comedy club circuit. The headliners are sometimes comics you've already heard of, and the middle-segment guys are on the way up, but like all comedy clubs, the opening acts are still paying their dues. Even during the week when reservations aren't necessary, it's a good idea to call and check on the nature of the material.

# HOTELS

No matter what you need—be it a pampered weekend away from the kids and the chinch bugs, or a place that'll make out-of-town relatives and that old college roommate feel comfortable—Houston's hotels have something to offer. There are more than 30,000 hotel rooms in the Houston area; one of them will surely fit your needs.

Of course there are representatives of all the national chains, from Motel 6 and Holiday Inn through all the variations of Hilton, Marriott, and the others. These can be reached through their national reservation numbers.

The Houston Convention and Visitors Bureau also offers a reservation and information line through which you can find the hotel room of your choice. Just call 1-800-4-HOUSTON, give them the arrival date and a price range, and they'll give you a rundown of what's available as well as make a reservation, if you'd like.

The hotels listed here are special in some way. Most are high-end, and priced to match during the business week, but almost all offer tremendous package deals on weekends and holidays. Sometimes there are even unadvertised weekday specials. It pays to call around.

**KEY TO SYMBOLS**
Inexpensive $ (under $55)
Moderate $$  ($55–$75)
Expensive $$$   ($75–$125)
Very Expensive  $$$$ ($125–plus)
W Wheelchair accessible

## ASTRODOME HOTEL COMPLEX
**South Loop at Kirby • South • 748-3221 • $–$$$$ • W variable**

The Astrodome Complex includes the Sheraton Astrodome, a Days Inn, and a Holiday Inn super convenient to the Astrodome and Astroworld. In fact, if you don't mind a hike through acres of parking lot, you can walk. All the facilities here are perfectly adequate, with the garden rooms near the pool the best of the lot. The real attraction, however, is the Celestial Suite in the Sheraton Astrodome. Built back in the 1960s by judge Roy Hofheinz, the entrepreneur par excellence who built the Dome, this dozens-of-rooms suite is supposedly America's most expensive. It is certainly America's weirdest, with circus-themed rooms, jungle rooms, and a mini baseball diamond. Although no longer available for the night, the Sheraton Astrodome offers at least part of it for events. Great for parties.

## ADAM'S MARK
**2900 Briarpark Drive at Westheimer • West
978-7400 • $$$–$$$$ • W**

The Mark's vast atrium lobby, which is more inviting than most with a piano bar, a fountain, and, of course, glass elevators, makes the hotel an asset to west Houston. Its restaurants and lounge frequently attract shoppers from the nearby Carillon West shopping center. The location near the Beltway is also convenient to many parts of southwest Houston. Conventions and meetings account for much of the traffic (a 14,800-square-foot exhibition center is adjacent to the hotel). Exercise facilities include a weight room, a sauna, tennis courts, and an indoor-outdoor swimming pool.

## ALLEN PARK INN

**2121 Allen Parkway • Near downtown • 521-9321 • $$–$$$ • W**

The appeal of the Allen Park Inn rests almost entirely in its reasonable prices and its location, which is convenient to downtown, but without any of the downtown parking hassles. The rooms tend to be small and dark, but it does boast a 24-hour restaurant and all-night room service. It does have a lovely outdoor pool and patio, a small gym, and easy access to the Allen Park jogging trail. Best of all, the clientele is fascinating. For obscure reasons, the Allen Park is the hotel of choice for Hollywood movie companies filming in town. You never know who you're going to meet in the bar or at the pool.

## DOUBLETREE GUEST SUITES

**5353 Westheimer • Galleria Area • 961-9000 • $$$–$$$$ • W**

This is a suite-hotel targeted at business executives. It isn't really geared to families, although there are some in eveidence especially on weekends. Suites come with a bedroom, a living room, a dining area, and a microwave. Some have a fully equipped kitchen. The location—withing walking distance of the Galleria mall complex—is another attraction. For business types, there is good freeway access to nearby U.S. 59, which can take you downtown in minutes.

## DOUBLETREE HOTEL AT ALLEN CENTER

**400 Dallas • Downtown • 759-0202 • $$–$$$$ • W**

Once upon a time, this was the French-built Meridian. The building's interior still maintains a European touch of class in its Doubletree incarnation. Centrally located for business travelers, the hotel is connected to Allen Center by a glass overhead ramp and to much of the rest of downtown via the tunnel system. Many of the luxe rooms and suites overlook a fountain garden. Amenities indude concierge service, 24-hour room service, a fine restaurant, and a lobby lounge as well as complimentary downtown transportation.

## DOUBLETREE HOTEL POST OAK

**2001 Post Oak Boulevard • Galleria Area**
**961-9300 • $$–$$$$ • W**

The building was designed by renowned architect I. M. Pei, and it is one of the ornaments of the "Uptown" Post Oak district. The rooms and suites are as spacious and elegantly appointed. Many feature balconies with a view of the Houston skyline. There is food and beverage service at the pool. The concierge service, the restaurants, and the lobby lounge all are first class.

## EMBASSY SUITES

**9090 Southwest Freeway • Southwest • 995-0123 • $$–$$$ • W**

For family groups or for anyone planning a long stay, this is still one of the better hotel bargains in town. While it isn't luxe deluxe, the Embassy Suites does have an enclosed atrium surrounded by the guest quarters, and all of the suites contain a master bedroom, a living room, and a kitchenette with stove and refrigerator. There is a small swimming pool with sauna near the atrium. If your business is on the southwest side of town, the location (between Gessner and Bissonnet) is fine. Otherwise, the commute downtown is difficult; rush-hour traffic on the Southwest Freeway can be brutal.

## FOUR SEASONS HOTEL

**1300 Lamar • Downtown • 650-1300 • $$–$$$$ • W**

The Four Seasons is posh by almost any standard, with quietly elegant guest rooms. Its multilevel lobby frequently is graced by visiting celebrities. Watch for them on the grand staircase leading to the conference rooms and ballroom. All guests have access to the Houston Center Club (an athletic and dining club), the swimming pool, and the Park, an upscale mall connected to the hotel via an enclosed aboveground walkways. One of Houston's best restaurants, the de Ville, is located on the premises.

## HOUSTONIAN HOTEL AND CONFERENCE CENTER

**111 North Post Oak Lane • Southwest • 680-2626 • $$$–$$$$ • W**

When President George Bush was in the White House and this was his voting address, rumor had it that his space was permanently booked by a Republican political organization after local Democrats staged a media event in it. Now that the president has his own home, all rooms at the Houstonian are once again available, which is good news for those who enjoy this lovely, secluded spot just minutes from the Galleria. On a hard-to-spot country lane, the Houstonian offers a wooded jogging track and some of the city's best health club facilities. Weekend specials make this an ideal getaway.

## HYATT REGENCY

**1200 Louisiana • Downtown • 654-1234 • $$$–$$$$ • W**

The patented Hyatt atrium is 30 stories high, the glass elevators are a kick, and the place is almost always festive with some kind of event. The Hyatt has almost a thousand rooms, several restaurants, and an almost always crowded lobby bar. Because it's in the heart of downtown, the Hyatt is popular with business travelers who can reach nearby office buildings via air-conditioned overhead bridges and the tunnel system. Conventions, meetings, and special events—such as the Houston Marathon—are frequently headquartered at the Hyatt. So, if small and restful is your notion of the ideal hotel, look elsewhere.

## L'HOTEL SOFITEL

**18700 Kennedy Boulevard • Intercontinental Airport**
**445-9000 • $$$–$$$$ • W**

This hotel is the last word in European style, with fine French cuisine offered in the restaurants. The location is convenient to the Hardy Toll Road, which, despite the 25-mile-plus distance, makes for a quick trip downtown. It is also just minutes from Greenspoint Mall. The fitness club, pools, and sauna are much appreciated by the business folks, who are the main clientele. Weekend package deals include a romantic getaway special.

## LA COLOMBE D'OR

**3410 Montrose • Central • 524-7999 • $$$$**

There is nothing else like this in Houston and few places like it in the world. On Montrose Boulevard in the Museum District, the mansion built by W. W. Fondren, founder of Humble Oil, has been converted into the most exclusive hotel in town. Housing only five suites and an ultra-luxurious penthouse suite, this elegant historical landmark is renowned as the "World's Smallest Luxury Hotel."

The service and the appointments—antique and flower-filled rooms each with its own private dining room—match the $200–$600 per-night price tag. The world-class gourmet restaurant offers some of the city's very best French-accented cuisine. Bookings for holiday periods must be made many months in advance.

## LANCASTER HOTEL
### 701 Texas • Downtown • 228-9500 • $$$$ • W

The Lancaster is one of Houston's best. With no more than nine rooms per floor, this luxurious 93-room hotel emphasizes stellar personal service. Lavishly furnished in the manner of an English country house with antiques, brass fixtures, and imported Italian marble, the Lancaster pampers visitors and international business types. Twenty-four-hour room and valet service go a long way toward dealing with jet lag. Located in the heart of the theater district, near the Wortham Center, Jones Hall, and the Alley Theatre, the Lancaster is ideal for weekend getaways. The small, quiet Bistro Lancaster sees much power breakfasting, and the menu frequently delights visiting restaurant critics.

## OMNI HOTEL HOUSTON
### 4 Riverway (off Woodway) • West • 871-8181 • $$$–$$$$ • W

This luxurious gem is improbably hidden away on the fringes of the chaotic Galleria area. Sitting amid acres of woods, it seems miles from the city with its reflection pond (home to a flock of rare black swans), lush thickets, and a trickling bayou. The two enormous swimming pools, tennis courts, and a fully equipped health club create a resort-like atmosphere. This is a favorite hideaway for celebrities and those who demand the very best in service. The Omni's La Reserve, one of Houston's best gourmet restaurants, offers world-class French cuisine.

## RITZ-CARLTON
### 1919 Briar Oaks Lane • Galleria Area • 840-7600 • $$$$ • W

The Ritz is River Oaks society's home away from home. When Houston's bold-faced types need a quiet, expensive, super-ritzy place to entertain visitors, this is it. Located in a wooded 45-acre park five minutes from the Galleria, the Ritz specializes in pampered elegance. The lobby is cool and quiet, as are the spacious rooms and ultra luxe suites. The small, tasteful lounges and restaurant are superb. Afternoon tea is much frequented by socialites shopping at nearby Pavilion Center, and the Sunday brunch is splendid. Getaway weekends here are a special treat.

## STOUFFER RENAISSANCE HOUSTON HOTEL

**6 Greenway Plaza East (Southwest Freeway at Edloe)**
**Southwest • 629-1200 • $$–$$$$ • W**

Located in Greenway Plaza and connected by tunnels to the surrounding complex of corporate headquarters, shopping areas, dining, entertainment, and sports facilities, the Stouffer Renaissance emphasizes convenience and business amenities rather than charm. Sports teams and rock stars performing at the Summit arena next door are frequent guests. Night views from the rooftop lounge attract big before-and-after-event crowds.

## SHERATON GRAND HOTEL

**2525 West Loop • Galleria Area • 961-3000 • $$–$$$$ • W**

A good price for the location is the Grand's big claim to fame. While it is not inexpensive, the whole Galleria complex is within easy walking distance. Not as luxurious as the Ritz or the hotels in the mall, the Grand offers pleasant if somewhat colorless rooms. Business travelers appreciate the office area and the chance to schmooze with like-minded others in the Grand Bar and Grille. A number of good eating places are also within easy walking distance, a rare circumstance in car-happy Houston.

## WESTIN OAKS

**5011 Westheimer • Galleria • 623-4300 • $$$–$$$$ • W**

## WESTIN GALLERIA

**5060 West Alabama • Galleria • 960-8100 • $$$–$$$$ • W**

Big and bustling, these Westin hotels are connected to the famous Galleria business and shopping complex. Hundreds of stores, restaurants, art galleries, and an indoor ice-skating rink are at your feet. Thanks to their unusual location, the Westins attract an interesting mix of business folks and shoppers. Holidays find the hotels crowded with families, many from Central and South America, which adds to the Galleria's generally festive air. Because there are dozens of nearby restaurants to choose from, you might end up overlooking the hotel cuisine, which is quite good. Each Westin also features a rooftop nightclub with a fine panorama.

## WOODLANDS INN RESORT
**2301 North Millbend Drive • Far north • 367-1100 • $$$–$$$$ • W**

Designed as a conference center, this is an ideal place to combine business and pleasure. The Woodlands Inn is surrounded by some of Houston's finest sports facilities. Championship golf courses, an Olympic-sized pool, indoor and outdoor tennis courts, an ice rink, health clubs, and even a small lake for sailboarding and windsurfing keep conference-goers and their families occupied. The rustic setting in a pine forest some 27 miles north of the city is an attraction in itself. For those with business downtown, the commute is probably a bit much, but for those who take advantage of the extensive conference facilities, the setting couldn't be better.

## WYNDHAM WARWICK
**5701 South Main • Central • 526-1991 • $$$–$$$$ • W**

Old-fashioned luxury with a European flavor is the Warwick's stock in trade. *And* the hotel boasts one of Houston's spiffiest locations. Set at the edge of verdant Hermann Park, it is convenient to both downtown and the Medical Center. Directly across the street from the Museum of Fine Arts, it is also within walking distance of the Contemporary Arts Museum, Rice University, and boutiques and restaurants on Montrose Boulevard. In April, it is the headquarters for WorldFest/Houston International Film Festival. Movie stars and directors may be seen in the quietly elegant Lobby Lounge.The Sunday brunch, which is served on the 12th floor with a panoramic view of the city, is lavish, and the Hunt Room restaurant serves some of Houston's best steaks.

# BED & BREAKFAST

The growing popularity of this homey alternative to hotels has made bed & breakfasting an option for more and more travelers. Even some adventurous business types are giving it a try. There are dozens of these establishments in the Houston area; one of them might be right for you.

## BED AND BREAKFAST SOCIETY OF TEXAS
**Numerous locations in Houston • 771-3919**

This is an idea whose time has come. The society is an association of private homes and small inns that offer reasonably priced bed & breakfasts in the manner of a European pension. For a nominal fee the society will send you a booklet that lists its Houston—and other Texas—members. Call for details.

## DURHAM HOUSE BED AND BREAKFAST
**921 Heights Boulevard • Houston, Texas 77008 • 868-4654**
**Open daily; AE, MC, V**

This lovely Queen Anne Victorian building, which is listed on the National Register of Historic Places, is located just five minutes from downtown Houston. The proprietors have filled the six rooms with antiques. Adding to the atmosphere is a player piano, a solarium, and a turn-of-the-century-style gazebo. There's even a a bicycle built for two available! The Durham is a favorite of romantic Houstonians in need of a weekend getaway. Reservations are essential. This is the full breakfast to end all full breakfasts; and, if you're lucky, the House will be hosting one of its popular murder-mystery dinner parties.

## THE LOVETT INN
**501 Lovett Boulevard • Houston, Texas 77006 • 522-5224; (800) 779-5224 • Open daily; AE, MC, V**

The Lovett Inn, which is located in the Montrose area on the southwestern edge of downtown, looks like a vintage Federalist-style mansion. The building was actually a family home built in the 1920s when the area was an attractive, upper-middle-class suburb. Now the seven-room inn, furnished with lovely 19th-century reproductions, hosts a charmingly eclectic group of visitors. The location is convenient to the attractions of the Museum District, downtown Houston, the Galleria, the Houston Medical Center, and the gay nightlife of Montrose. The breakfast is continental, but unlike most bed & breakfast establishments, the Lovett Inn boasts a pool and features color TV in each room.

## THE OAKS COTTAGE BED & BREAKFAST
### 1118 South Shepherd • Houston, Texas 77019 • 520-0226

At the edge of posh River Oaks and within easy walking distance of dozens of nifty restaurants and shops, this is one of Houston's best locations. The cottage is literally that, a cottage attached to the garage behind the owners' private home. There is only one suite, complete with private bath and sitting area. It is reasonably priced, and breakfast can be anything you'd like. As you can imagine, with inducements like these, The Oaks books up fast. Call well in advance.

## THE PATRICIAN BED & BREAKFAST INN
### 1200 Southmore • Central • 523-1114 • $$–$$$ • W variable

Located in the Museum District close to the MFA, Contemporary Arts Museum, and Rice University, this lovely three-story mansion dates back to 1919. The four bedrooms, each with private bath, are furnished with period antiques, and some of the baths even boast claw-foot tubs. During the week, this is a favorite of business travelers. On weekends, visitors—or Houstonians in need of a romantic getaway—enjoy the Patrician's relaxed elegance.

## SARA'S BED AND BREAKFAST INN
### 941 Heights Boulevard • Houston, Texas 77008
### 868-1130; (800) 593-1130 • Open daily; Cr.

When Victoria was queen, this beautiful old historic mansion housed a large family. Now the 13 rooms play host to a fascinating collection of visitors. The Queen Anne-style building, complete with turret and widow's walk, is only six blocks from I-10 (the Katy Freeway) in Houston Heights. Downtown Houston is only four miles away, but what makes this an especially nice place to stay is the neighborhood, one of the few in Houston boasting historic homes, some of which are on the National Historic Register. The bedrooms are furnished with pieces true to the period, and there are singles, doubles, and family rooms. The Balcony Suite is really nifty. There are two bedrooms, two baths, as well as a full kitchen and a sitting room. Sara's serves continental breakfast each morning, and complimentary tea and soft drinks in the afternoon.

# GET OUT OF TOWN

What are you going to do when you've got a bad case of the blahs and there's no hope of an vacation any time soon? Why not play tourist close to home? There's no need to make elaborate plans, and—unless you want the break—no need to stay overnight. Each of the following is a location well worth visiting that's close enough to home for an easy weekend getaway. Enjoy!

## ALABAMA-COUSHATTA RESERVATION

The Alabama-Coushatta reservation sits deep in the piney woods of the Big Thicket near Livingston. These members of the Southern forest tribes have lived here since time immemorial, and Sam Houston himself helped to ensure that their land would stay in the family. After Sam's death and Texas' anexation, the U.S. Congress ordered all native tribes in Texas to move to Indian Territory in Oklahoma, but the Alabamas and Coushattas peacefully refused to go. Much political hoo-ha ensued, but in the end the natives triumphed. And for decades now the tribe has successfully used its reservation to introduce visitors to its rich heritage. Here many of the old ways continue. All tribal council and intertribal meetings are conducted in the native language. And the old way of life is lovingly preserved.

A visit to the reservation is well worth the two-hour trip from Houston and makes for a wonderful getaway from urban life in general.

Leave the city behind. Take the little train that chugs slowly through the deep shade as it winds its way through the forest, where the air is full of the sharp, crisp scent of the pines, tempered with the seductiveness of honeysuckle. In the spring, there are bluebells, Indian paintbrushes, and black-eyed Susans crowding clearings in the old-growth forest; and year round, there are birds in abundance.

In addition to the train ride, there are narrated tram tours of the reservation and walking tours through the "living Indian village," where people wear traditional costumes and demonstrate traditional skills such as sewing, weaving, and making arrows. There are also performances of songs in the Alabama and Coushatta languages, as well as daily performances of native dances performed in elaborate traditional costume.

There are camping facilities at 26-acre Lake Tombigbee, where the fish are always jumping, and the visitors' center includes the Inn of the Twelve Clans, featuring a restaurant where the menu emphasizes traditional and American Indian cuisine. At the cultural center there is a museum exhibition of traditional Indian artifacts as well as a gift shop offering native crafts and modern Alabama-Coushatta artwork. Be on the lookout for the world-famous, handmade baskets made from the needles of local long-leaf pines and woven so tightly that they actually hold water. These are made by true artists. No two baskets are alike.

Visitors should note that tribal law prohibits alcohol, firearms, fireworks, and narcotics—as well as unleashed pets—on the reservation property, and that no boats with gasoline engines are allowed on the lake. During the summer, the reservation is open seven days a week. Call  (800) 444-3507 for open dates after Labor Day.

## ANAHUAC

To some, Anahuac is known only via the Austin Lounge Lizards' wonderfully goofy song of the same name. To others, it is, as it advertises, "The Gator Capital of Texas," but to birders and others who love the primeval beauty of coastal east Texas, Anahuac means the Anahuac National Wildlife Refuge, one of the most amazing places within easy driving distance of Houston.

Inside the 30,000-acre reserve administered by the U.S. Fish and Wildlife Service, it's easy to imagine that dinosaurs still roam the earth. This is definitely NOT a place for those who demand amenities, which are all designed for the inhabitants: alligators, snakes, and snapping turtles; Roseate Spoonbills, egrets, and Great Blue Herons; to say nothing of insects, insects, and more insects.

The refuge, which does have some 12 miles of rough road, is a combination of coastal marsh and salt-grass prairie. The marshes are the incubators. Shrimp and crab, as well as some finfish, get their start in the warm, shallow estuaries and bays where they feed happily on "plankton soup" and one another. As these critters get bigger, migrating wading birds, geese, and ducks see the refuge and the rice fields nearby as one big fast food joint. Some 75,000 Snow Geese, several other species of geese, and 22 species of ducks stop by to feast from October through March. And after the long-distance travelers come the songbirds, who show up faithfully every spring. All in all, some 255 species consider part of the refuge home, at least temporarily.

There are gravel roads and the critters are used to seeing cars, so you'll have a chance to see them. Hiking trails are in short supply, and it's OK to walk along the roads—but be on the lookout for snakes and alligators. The mosquitos will be on the lookout for you, and they outnumber people about 100,000 to 1; wear repellant, especially if you plan to attend the annual Texas Gatorfest. (See September Calendar listing.)

## BOLIVER

Across the entrance to Galveston Bay lies the Bolivar Peninsula, one of the Houston area's great hidden treasures. Just a little over one hour away at the far end of the Gulf Freeway in Galveston are the ferries that make the trip to Bolivar every 20 minutes or so. Operated by the Texas Highway Department, it is *free*, and one of the best spirit-lifting things you can do for yourself and your family.

Get out of your car and head for the bow. Let the breezes blow over you and the sea birds circle, laughing, overhead. If you're lucky, dolphins will play around the the prow as you cut through the water. See the giant tankers moving majestically in the channel as you cross between them, feeling removed to another world.

On a good (read uncrowded) day , the round trip takes about 45 minutes. On a bad day (most summer weekends) the wait for the boat can last from an hour to two hours. But if you don't mind walking, you can park your car near the landing and walk onto the ferry—but be warned, the walk to the beach on the other side can take half an hour or more.

If you have the time, Bolivar is a wonderful getaway destination. About all it has to offer is peace and quiet. So, if you like tranquility when you go to the beach instead of boom boxes and beer coolers, this is the place for you. You can just kick back and do as little as possible. In fact, Boliver likes to claim that *that's* its claim to fame: It is famous for nothing.

While you're soaking up rays, the kids can play at being pirates. Because Jean Lafitte is supposed to have rolled his barrels of pirate treasure over the narrow stretch of Boliver beach to the bay on the other side, the locals called it Rollover Pass. True or not, it's a good story, and folks with metal detectors pretend to take it seriously enough to sweep the beach. It's unlikely that you'll find pirate gold, but you will find some of the best shells in this part of the Gulf. There are no giant conchs, but there are whole sand dollars, and lots of small "fighting conch" shells and cat's eyes.

After a peaceful day on the beach, take the twilight ferry back to Galveston as magic hour lighting turns the whole sky to gold. (See Galveston section.)

## FORT BEND

Fort Bend County these days is best known as a nice place to live and a convenient bedroom community for Houston, but there's more to Fort Bend than meets the eye. It has an interesting place in Texas's story. In 1822, some of Stephen F. Austin's "Old Three Hundred," the original colonists, built a fort at a bend of the Brazos River, later, an ex-Virginian named it Richmond, and the rest, as they say, is history.

While most folks in Fort Bend, which became a county in 1837, just minded their own business and grew cotton or cane or other crops, a few local residents went on to make names for themselves.

Those of us who neither slept nor flirted our way through Texas History in high school might remember Jane Long. The textbooks used to call her the "Mother of Texas"—and the kids a lot worse. In fact, she was the mother of the first Anglo child born in Texas and lived out most of her long life in Richmond.

Deaf Smith, who probably wasn't completely, but who was Sam Houston's famous scout, lived there, too, as did his fellow veteran of San Jacinto, plantation owner Mirabeau B. Lamar. Lamar went on to become the second president of the Republic, much to his political enemy Sam Houston's disgust.

A lot of saloon keepers were disgusted with Richmond's own Carry Nation. Before she took to bustin' up bars with an ax on behalf of the Temperance society, she kept a hotel in Fort Bend. All these characters—and more—may be found in the Fort Bend Museum and the nearby Long-Smith Cottage, and John M. Moore Home in Richmond.

In addition to a collection of the household goods pioneers carried with them to Fort Bend, and the agricultural implements used by early settlers, the museum tells the story of the Brazos River bottomland cotton and sugar cane plantations, as well as of the planter families and the slaves who worked them.

The Civil War was the great divide for Fort Bend County as it was for the rest of the nation. The museum exhibits include newspapers of the period, original photographs of local Confederate soldiers, their letters home, their uniforms and weapons.

The end of the war didn't mean the end of hostilities, and many of the battles resumed locally. Folks outside of Fort Bend County probably don't know anything about it, but the "Jaybird-Woodpecker War" of 1889 was a really big deal at the time. The Jaybirds faction represented the the Old South of the newly defeated Confederacy. The Woodpeckers were Reconstructionists allied with the freed-slave vote. The long-simmering hostilities ended in a Wild West style shootout in front of the County courthouse in Richmond. Things got so crazy, the state militia had to be called in to restore order. The museum depicts the shootout in a diorama, a suitably 19th-century style of presentation.

The restored Long-Smith Cottage, next door to the museum proper, was built in 1840. Jane Long lived here for 22 years and much of the furniture—including a piano, a spinning wheel and sewing table, and a rope bed with rag quilt—belonged to her. The 1883 John M. Moore Home, which is still in its original condition, is used to house traveling historical and folk art exhibits, and Morton Cemetery, a short drive away, is the resting place of Long, Smith, Lamar, and other early Texans. (See September Calendar listings.)

# LAKE CONROE

It's the wet escape few Houstonians think of. Generally, when folks want to head out of town for a day, they go south to the Gulf. For a pleasant change, try north to Lake Conroe for a wonderful weekend on the water.

Located in the rolling hills (yes, there are some near Houston) west of I-45 near the town of Conroe, the lake is set in the heavily wooded countryside spreading out from the San Jacinto River. Many believe that Conroe is the most beautiful man-made lake in Texas—and just about all Texas lakes *are* man-made. The natural beauty of the lake is actually a kind of lagniappe. The area has a practical function. It is part of the master plan to supply the surrounding counties with water for industrial, agricultural, and municipal use. The fact that it's lovely, and a major getaway location—to say nothing of a great fishing lake—is a happy secondary function.

The primeval beauty of the Sam Houston National Forest surrounds 50 miles of Lake Conroe's 150 mile shoreline. The winding forest roads, many with unexpected views of the lake, are a treat in themselves. But the best views of the water are from FM 1097 and FM 1375 where they bridge the upper reaches of the lake. The numerous resorts and marinas such as April Sound, Bentwater, and Del Lago offer recreational facilites for golfers, boaters, sailors, and other weekend escapees.

Fishing is the really big deal, though. Ever since the Aggies figured out how to import the super fish that finally ate the hydrilla plants that spent most of the 1970s killing every inch of the lake, the place has been an anglers paradise. Lake Conroe is stocked with millions of Texas and Florida bass, hybrid bass, catfish, hybrid perch, and crappie fry and fingerlings each year to ensure the supply of game and table fish.

Because it's only 32 miles north of Intercontinental Airport, the lake is especially convenient for those in the FM 1960 area and The Woodlands, but it's worth the trip from no matter where you live in the Houston area. Call (800) 283-6645 for visitor information.

# GALVESTON

Galveston is Houston's elder sibling—and as with all siblings, there is rivalry. These days Houstonians see Galveston as a charming, somewhat funky resort town 50 miles south. It is "our beach." But Galvestonians look at it another way. They have a strong sense of their own history. Outside of San Antonio, Galveston was the most civilized city in Texas in the days of the Republic. When the govenment chose to locate the capital at Houston, the islanders were appalled, calling the village up the bayou a "mudhole populated by thieves." At the time, they weren't far wrong.

Houston's size and economy now dwarf those of Galveston, but the island has qualities we will always find fascinating. It has that special insular charm that defines islands the world over. Simultaneously freewheeling and constricted, elegant and decayed, it is like nothing else in this part of the country. Many people who were born on the island (the self-styled BOIs) never leave it and scornfully refer to towns a few miles north across the bay as "The Mainland." Galveston can be a self-contained universe, but it is also heavily dependent on tourism, and this creates a certain dynamic tension. While recognizing the importance of attracting visitors, islanders can sometimes be heard to complain among themselves, "Tourists come here with five dollars and a dirty shirt. They don't change either one."

The original inhabitants, the Karankawas, were themselves tourists of a sort. Nobody's exactly sure of where they came from originally. All anthropologists are sure of is that by about 1400 A.D. they were well established in the area. Improbably, they spent their winters on the island and summered in the then-dense woods on the mainland, where it was hotter than hell. But year-round they did paddle their magnificent 25-foot-long dugouts across the bay to hunt and fish on the island. They also knew how to farm, but didn't do it. Instead, maybe for ritual reasons or maybe just because they liked it, they ate one another.

The Karankawa men were physically beautiful people with genetically perfect teeth. Close to 6-feet tall when European men were about 5'3", they all wore their hair waist-length, covered themselves with tatoos, did body piercing with reeds, and constantly chewed the tar balls they found on the beach as if they were cud. The tribe also used boards to flatten babies' foreheads because they thought it looked good, and everyone went around naked. This fashion statement had its drawbacks, though. Whenever they spent time on the island, the Karankawas had to cover themselves with mud and alligator grease to ward off the clouds of mosquitoes that infest the bayside swamps.

By the time Spaniard Cabeza de Vaca arrived in 1528, after being shipwrecked, the Kronks, as later settlers would call them, already had a bad reputation. Other, more easygoing tribes thought they had an attitude and left them alone on their inhospitable island. The desolate stretch of sand was low to the Gulf water, which completely washed over it during every storm. In summer, the heat haze was so intense it was impossible to see more than a few feet ahead.

Cabeza de Vaca wasn't exaggerating when he named the place the "Isle of Misfortune." It took him six years to get away from his captors, and once away he never came back.

Other shipwreck victims were the only European visitors for the next 250 years. Finally, someone came to Galveston on purpose. His name was Jose Evia and he was surveying the coast of Texas for his boss, Count Bernardo de Galvez, the royal governor of then-Spanish Louisiana. As he neared the island, Evia noted that heat was awful, the insects were worse, and his crew was terrified of hurricanes. The Spaniard made a few quick charts, named the bay for his boss, took one look at the Karankawas and left pronto. Galvez himself never even saw the place.

The same things that scared off the Spanish surveyor probably attracted pirate Jean Lafitte, who came to live on the island in 1817. Although he'd made a brief attempt to go straight, he seems to have found the honest life a bore. He had done his patriotic duty when it really counted in the War of 1812. He had helped

Andrew Jackson defeat the British in the battle of New Orleans. But that excitement was long over and he was restless. Reverting to type, he cashed in his marker with the fledgling U.S. government and got permission to seize "enemy" vessels. His definition of enemy and theirs proved to be quite different. Which may be why he decided to make remote Galveston island the base for his privateering operations.

Lafitte's headquarters, a large, well-built house called Maison Rouge, was supposed to have been visible for miles out in the Gulf. Legend says his treasure still lies buried somewhere in the island sands. There are those who claim that Lafitte's men packed their loot in barrels and rolled them across the sands from the Gulf side to the bay via what's now called Rollover Pass. Both there and elsewhere hunting for pirate treasure with metal detectors is a favorite Galveston pastime.

After Sam Houston won at San Jacinto and the viability of Texas was assured, Galveston boomed. Most of what is now the city—as well as a couple of miles' worth of coast—had been purchased by Michael B. Menard for a total of $50,000. Suddenly, it was worth a whole lot more. Not only was Galveston now a major gateway to Texas for European immigrants (many of the state's first families first saw their new world here), it was also the port from which the farm products of interior Texas departed for the east coast and Europe.

As a result, the port grew and prospered. When Houston was little more than a landing on Buffalo Bayou, Galveston was the wealthy and thriving Queen City of the Southwest. National firms built their offices in Galveston during the golden era from 1875 to 1900 when Galveston, Texas, was the world's leading cotton port, by far the most important city in Texas, and, per capita, the second-richest town in the entire United States of America.

The wealth that poured into the island city resulted in a remarkable architectural outpouring. Merchants, many of whom had branch offices in England, commissioned the best in the business to design commercial buildings for them in the manner of England's famous Strand. The area quickly became known as the "Wall Street of the Southwest," and architects note that some of the most remarkable commercial iron-front structures in America still line its streets.

The renaissance ended abruptly in 1900. On a sultry weekend in September, the Gulf began to look more than usually rough. From out of the West Indies, where it had already wreaked terrible distruction, a killer hurricane bore down on the island. Trapped between the bay and the fast-rising waters of the Gulf, the island was helpless. The 1900 storm is still the worst natural disaster ever to strike North America. It killed some 6,000 people in one night and swept much of the city out to sea. Galveston, a low-lying barrier island vulnerable to every passing storm, seemed doomed to follow the earlier Texas ports of Indianola and Baghdad into oblivion.

To save the city and ensure its future security, two massive engineering projects were undertaken, each remarkable for its time. The first was the building of a massive seawall 17 feet tall and 10 miles long. (Trivia buffs take note: The work was under the direction of the same Major Roberts who wrote the U.S. Congress' Rules of Order.) The second project sounds impossible, but the Galvestonians did it—with a lot of help from the Army Corps of Engineers. They actually propped every building up on stilts and then raised every bit of land behind that seawall from four to 17 feet above the previous level.

These projects took seven years. Then came the test. In 1915 a second killer hurricane, even more powerful than the first, swept over the island. Thanks to the seawall, fewer than three hundred people were killed. But what the hurricane didn't accomplish, the politicians up the road in Houston did. The successful completion of the Houston Ship Channel began to draw off the cream of the port trade, and Galveston's economy never recovered. Ultimately, the beleaguered port degenerated into one of the wildest red-light towns in the state, with local mobsters and the owners of illegal gambling casinos practically running the city.

During Prohibition, ships from Europe loaded down with liquor anchored in international waters just off the island in what came to be known as "rum row." There, crews offloaded booze onto fast speed boats owned by rival criminal gangs for the run to the beaches. The well-organized Galveston gangsters supplied speakeasies as far away as Ohio and Michigan. They also supplied the local cops with plenty of work. Shootouts in the streets of Galveston in the 1920s were far more numerous than such events ever were in the days of the wild west.

Out of this chaotic atmosphere emerged the Maceo brothers, Rosario (Rose) and Sam. They gradually took almost complete control of Galveston's illegal enterprises. They oversaw the red light district on Postoffice Street (in the 1930s and 1940s there were more prostitutes per citizen in Galveston than in wide-open

Shanghai.) Although Prohibition was repealed in 1933, liquor by the drink was illegal in Texas until 1971—and gambling was strictly prohibited. The Maceos were happy to supply the forbidden pleasures. Their world-famous Balinese Room nightclub and gambling joint, built on pilings out over the Gulf, attracted top Hollywood performers.

These colorful days came to an end when the Texas Rangers raided some of the more famous spots and finally brought law and order to Galveston.

After that, for more than a quarter of a century the island slumbered along as a rather seedy seaside resort. But like Sleeping Beauty in the fairy tale, Galveston awakened in the early '80s and began the transformation that today makes it an absolute must-see.

Much of this remarkable metamorphosis can be traced to the actions of one man, Galveston native son George Mitchell. A visionary developer who had made a fortune in oil and natural gas, he has spent the past several decades transforming the face of his birthplace. Riding the wave of national interest in historical preservation, the island had established the Galveston Historical Foundation in 1973, and had used the funds available for such things during the national bicentennial in 1976 to begin preservation work. Soon George Mitchell and his wife, Cynthia, were working with the city parents and the Moody Foundation to renovate many of the historic buildings in the Strand district.

These renovations sparked others. The East End "Silk Stocking" area, where many of the city's wealthy merchants lived during the Golden Age, has undergone a major face-lift. In fact, the number of preserved and restored period buildings has prompted some to call the district a Victorian era-version of Colonial Williamsburg.

With the island's face-lift has come huge growth in the hotel and convention sector. This in turn has sparked fresh capital investment, and Galveston is now a thriving town with a wealth of year-round attractions.

## WHAT'S HAPPENING

Some kind of festival or event is almost always going in Galveston. To get listings of house tours and other historical events, contact:

**THE GALVESTON HISTORICAL FOUNDATION**
**2016 Strand • Galveston, TX 77550**
**(409) 765-7834 or (713) 488-5942**

If you're planning an island vacation, call or write:

**GALVESTON CONVENTION AND VISITORS BUREAU**
**2106 Seawall Boulevard • Galveston, TX 77550 • (409) 763-4311;**
**(800) 351-4236 inside Texas, or (800) 351-4237 from out of state**

The bureau has brochures and schedules for all the major festivals and attractions. It also offers a free book of discount coupons good for reduced rates on accommodations, attractions, and restaurants, but this can be obtained only by mail. (There are no listings for January or November.)

## FEBRUARY

**Valentine Sea Turtle Open House.** Some of Galveston's marine neighbors, the Kemp's Ridley sea turtles, are in danger of extinction. So, each Valentines Day the island's National Marine Fisheries Service releases hundreds of turtle hatchlings into the Gulf in the hope that they will live long and prosper. To celebrate, the fish folks sponsor a day of festive events including name-the-turtle contests, food, kids' games, and demonstrations. It's all at the National Marine Fisheries Service on Avenue U at 50th Street. Call (409) 766-3523 for dates and details.

**Mardi Gras.** Moving up fast as the island's biggest event, Mardi Gras has a truly international flavor. It is celebrated in many nations (Brazil, the Carribean, southern Europe) and its starting date varies with the Easter moon. The real Fat Tuesday is always 41 days before Easter Sunday, but for celebratory purposes the calendar of Mardi Gras events usually kicks off in late February and runs for several weeks. Unlike the rowdy, drunken New Orleans version, most of Galveston's Mardi Gras is festive family fun—and it keeps getting bigger every year. In fact, to detail everything the Mardi Gras offers would take pages. Best bet is to contact the Convention and Visitors Bureau for a schedule of events. Admission to most events is free. Call (800) 351-4236 or (409) 763-4311.

## MAY

**Texas National Handcar Championship.** Cheer on the team from your favorite local business or civic organization as it competes for bragging rights on the trolley tracks in the Strand District. The winners get the chance to compete in the national championships held later in the year in California. The entry fees benefit the Railroad Museum. Spectator admission is free. Call (409) 765-5700 for information.

**Galveston Historic Homes Tour.** Some of the loveliest historic homes on the island are open to the public during the tour. These range from simple bungalows to elaborate Victorian splendor. The Galveston Historical Foundation, which sponsors the event, provides information at its headquarters on the Strand. Tickets may be purchased at each of the participating homes during the tour, at the Strand Visitors Center, or at Ashton Villa. Admission is about $15. Call (409) 762-TOUR for details.

## JUNE

**Bay Day.** Sylvan Beach Park in LaPorte hosts this fest designed to increase public awareness of Galveston Bay. Featured events include music, a carnival, a gumbo cook-off, and exhibits that introduce fest-goers to the ecology of the area. The weekend-long shindig ends with fireworks above the bay. Admission is about $2-$4/less for kids and seniors. Call (713) 868-3383 for details and directions.

**Caribbean Carnival Extravaganza.** From one island culture to another, Galvestonians and their neighbors across the water know how to *celebrate*. There are colorful costumes and costume contests, steel bands, reggae and calypso music, as well as a parade and a marketplace for arts and crafts, and drinks and island eats. Call (409) 942-9042 for further information.

**Open-air musicals.** The Mary Moody Northen Amphitheatre becomes the southwestern end of the Great White Way every summer. This major family attraction includes performances of *The Lone Star*—a rousing musical version of Texas' battle for independence that has less to do with history than with giving the audience a good time—and popular musicals such as *Oklahoma, West Side Story,* and *The King and I.*

## JULY

**Fourth of July.** There's something for everyone from a traditional band concert and a parade to the gorgeous beachfront fireworks display. There are free events in all the public parks, and a special patriotic concert and a children's parade in the plaza behind historic Ashton Villa. Moody Gardens hosts a party at the Oleander Bowl on the grounds. Call (800) 582-4673 for info. The fireworks display over the water is best seen from Seawall Boulevard, but the annual Independence Day Parade is on Broadway from 6th Street to 24th Street. Call (800) 351-4236 for parade and fireworks info.

## AUGUST

**Muscle Beach Extravaganza.** Strike a pose in the Moody Civic Center! This annual event attracts bodybuilders from all categories and weight classes, and it frequently features a top-ranked guest poser. Muscle freaks of all descriptions turn out for this, and the same vicarious enjoyment that professional wrestling produces makes it worthwhile even for couch potatoes.

## SEPTEMBER

**Labor Day Weekend.** It's time for that one last beach party. There are special activities geared to the family crowd all over town. Remember, except for designated areas, all beaches are alcohol free. The Strand hosts musical events throughout the weekend, and Moody Gardens gets into the act with evening activities. Many activities are free, but Stewart beach parking is $5. Call (800) 351-4236 for info.

## OCTOBER

**Octoberfest.** Celebrate the island's diverse cultural heritage with food, dancing, and music at the annual Octoberfest. Ethnic dancers and German bands entertain under the oaks at Kempner Park. Festival-goers can sample a wide range of ethnic foods and browse through arts-and-crafts booths. There are children's activities, too. Admission $1. Call (409) 763-4311 for details.

**Galveston Island Jazz Festival.** This musical extravaganza on the waterfront boasts the best in jazz as well as arts and crafts, food and general merriment. Admission runs $5 per day/less for kids and seniors. Call (800) 351-4236 for days and times.

**Galveston's Great Pumpkin Party.** Moody Mansion is the ideal setting for Halloween ghost stories. There are also trick-or-treating and other games for children. Admission is free. Call (409) 762-7668.

## DECEMBER

**Dickens Evening On The Strand.** This was the first festive event in the Galveston revival. It is still the biggest, though Mardi Gras is moving up fast. Generally the first weekend in December can be counted on to produce a London-style pea-soup fog that adds to the 19th-century atmosphere in the historic Strand district. Residents of the whole island, as well as lots of mainlanders, enjoy the atmosphere as the Strand shops turn back the clock to Victorian times in honor of Charles Dickens. Shopkeepers, visitors, and members of the Galveston Historical Foundation dress in Victorian garb and feast on vintage eats like roasted chestnuts, wassail, scones, and plum pudding. All the local attractions such as the 18th-century sailing ship *Elissa,* historic Ashton Villa, and the various museums get into the act. It's a wonderful way for families to kick off the holiday season. Adults in Victorian costume, and kids under 12 get into the festival area free. Civilians pay about $9 each day. Call (713) 280-3907 or (409) 765-7834 for dates, times and directions.

**Galveston's "Victorian Christmas" Home Tour.** Early in December, the East End Historical District Association sponsors a tour of appropriate-period private homes. Each is decorated in Victorian holiday style. You can even hire horse-drawn carriages for the trip from site to site. Along the route, Christmas carolers add to the holiday atmosphere, and Ebenezer Scrooge himself often puts in an appearance. The number of tickets (about $13) is severely limited. Get them in person at the Grand 1894 Opera House, 2020 Postoffice, or charge them by calling (409) 765-1894 or (713) 480-1894.

## ATTRACTIONS

### The Beach—all 32-plus miles of it

Beachgoers in Galveston have a lot of options. The decisions start after you cross the causeway from the mainland on I-45 and see the directional signs for East and West beaches.

East Beach is essentially the town beach. West Beach starts where the Seawall ends and the road becomes FM 3005. Vehicular traffic on the beaches is restricted year-round. Much of West Beach is still untamed. Though residential development continues at an alarming rate, hurricanes periodically persuade builders to slow down by wiping out whole sections of subdivisions. Even with all the building, the area remains quiet—ever wilder—as you go west.

West beach is long and uninterrupted, great for walking, running, and just enjoying nature. When you need the amenities, there are three beach parks on FM 3005, operated by Galveston County. Each has changing rooms, showers, food concessions, playgrounds, and picnic areas, and is backed by protected natural dunes. Horseback riding, parasailing, windsurfing, and other commercial beach activities often are available nearby during warm months.

For people who prefer a bit more action, on East Beach in town, there are numerous small beaches tucked between the jetties along Seawall Boulevard. These are periodically expanded by pumping millions of pounds of sand onto the rocky shore. Some are reserved exclusively for surfers. Otherwise, surfing near the jetties is prohibited.

Stop along the Seawall to watch dolphins play in the offshore swells, and then walk out onto the jetties and chat with the fishermen. There also are several places to rent roller skates, bicycles, or pedal surreys, and the wide sidewalk along the top of the Seawall is a favorite promenade.

The boulevard curves at the east end of the island and intersects Broadway at Stewart Beach. This city-run stretch of sand is popular with families—and teenagers—because it is Galveston's version of Coney Island, complete with games, rides, lifeguards, a bathhouse, lockers, parking, and concessions.

R. A. Apffel Park is a multimillion-dollar development located at the extreme end of East Beach. It is a favorite with fisherfolk and families as well as teens. It has excellent boating and fishing facilities and a huge recreation center, which includes a bathhouse and concessions. Galveston Island State Park, west of downtown Galveston on FM 3005 at the intersection of 13 Mile Road, is another beach facility with picnicking and camping. This 2,000-acre state park also offers birdwatching from observation platforms and nature trails along its north boundary, which faces protected Galveston Bay.

Palm Beach at Moody Gardens (Ten Hope Boulevard off 61st Street, (409) 744-7256), a Disneyesque version of a tropical beach, is man-made. The white sand was imported from Florida at great expense and installed amid extensive landscaping, which includes artificial rocks, a boardwalk, and a freshwater swimming pool. Concessions are available, and lifeguards are on duty, but no food, beverages, or lawn chairs may be brought in. Hours vary with the seasons. Admission is not cheap.

## OTHER ATTRACTIONS

### ANTIQUE DOLLHOUSE MUSEUM
**1721 Broadway • (409) 762-7289.**

This collection of beautiful and rare dolls is located in a pre-Civil War cottage. Both kids and collectors find it fascinating. Schedule varies; but it is always closed in January.

### AUDIO TOUR
**Strand Visitors Center • 2016 Strand • (409) 765-7834**

Take a 40-minute walking tour of the Strand historic district. The narration reflects a knowledge of Galveston history that is both encyclopedic and fascinating. Open daily 10 to 4.

### BOATS FOR PARTY FISHING
**Galveston Party Boats • (409) 763-5423 or (713) 222-7025**
**Williams Party Boats • (409) 762-8808 or (713) 223-4853**

Boats for either Bay fishing or Gulf deep-sea fishing leave early in the morning from Pier 19 on the bayfront. A Texas fishing license is required for everyone between the ages of 17 and 65, unless you are fishing at least 10 miles offshore. Check to see if a license is required when you make your reservations. Common Gulf catches include red snapper, sailfish, pompano, marlin, ling, king mackerel, bonito, and dolphin. Take some seasick pills before you go; the Gulf can get rough.

## BOLIVAR FERRY
### End of Second Street

This is one of the best free deals in Texas. From the slip at Second Street (turn north from Broadway), the car ferries of the Texas Highway Department cross regularly from Galveston to Bolivar. There's nothing much to do on the other side, but some people like it that way. Best bet is to park in the lot near the landing and walk aboard for 15 minutes of sea air, wonderful sights, and gulls begging for a treat. Kids love daytime; sweethearts prefer the evening cruises. A caveat: Do not try to do this at prime time on summer weekends unless you love to wait.

## CARRIAGE RIDES
### Strand Visitor's Center • (409)763-4666 or (713) 280-3980

Authentic horse-drawn surreys leave daily during tourist seasons on 30- and 60-minute tours of the Strand and other historic districts. This is the ideal way to see the Victorian city. Schedules and fees vary. Call for info.

## THE COLONEL
### Moody Gardens • (409) 740-7797 or (713) 280-3980

Take a trip into the past aboard this modern reconstruction of a historic paddlewheeler. It leaves for two-hour narrated island cruises. There are also dinner, jazz, and moonlight dance cruises. Hours vary with the season. Call for times and fees.

## COLONEL BUBBIE'S
### 2202 Strand

This place defies description. It is definitely an attraction of some sort—but *what* sort? Ostensibly a military surplus store, the hot warehouse is crowded to the ceiling with the strangest collection of junk this side of your garage. Need an original World War II hymnal? No problem. Iraqi Air Force pants? Sure. Dog tags? *Luftwaffe* mess kits? Korean War vintage K-rations? You never know what you'll find. It's worth braving the crowds and the heat just for the flat-out strangeness of it all. Open seven days.

## DAVID TAYLOR CLASSIC CAR MUSEUM
### 1918 Mechanic • (409) 765-6590

The collection includes everything from vintage roadsters to hot rods. There are more than four dozen lovingly restored vehicles in the museum, with new ones being added all the time. The exhibition is housed in several historic buildings. Open daily. Call for hours and group rates.

## THE ELISSA
### Pier 21 • (409) 763-1877

Just one block north of the Strand at the Texas Seaport Museum is the oldest ship in Lloyd's Register of Shipping. This beautifully restored 1877 square-rigged barque still sails the Gulf several times a year and is one of the oldest merchant ships afloat anywhere. The acquisition of the ship and its restoration, stories in themselves, are detailed in the *Elissa* film at the Strand Visitors Center. Visitors can roam the restored after-cabins, the hold (self-guided), and the decks. Alongside, but on land, is a pint-size playship for children and the Sail Loft museum shop. Open daily, unless she is at sea. Call for schedule and admission charges.

## FISHING
### Gulf and Bay

Whether you want to try your luck off the rock jetties along the Seawall or from the commercial fishing piers at 25th, 61st, and 90th streets, the fishing on Galveston can be great. For a change of pace try Seawolf Park on Pelican Island. Also, surf fishing is allowed along most of the open beaches. Common catches are speckled trout, flounder, catfish, and redfish.

## GALVESTON COUNTY HISTORICAL MUSEUM
### 2219 Market Street • (409) 766-2340 for hours

The County Museum is located in the restored 1919 City National Bank Building, which is worth seeing in itself. The exhibits range from the lens from the historic South Jetty Lighthouse to the culture and traditions of the Karankawas and Atakapas, Galveston County's first inhabitants. Admission is free. Open daily, except New Year's Day, Thanksgiving, Christmas Eve, and Christmas Day.

## GRAND 1894 OPERA HOUSE
### 2020 Postoffice • (409) 765-1894 or (713) 480-1894

This is the historic theatre where Sarah Bernhardt, Paderewski, and Anna Pavlova performed. There's nothing else like it in the state of Texas. Where else have John Philip Sousa, William Jennings Bryan, the Marx Brothers, George Burns and Gracie Allen, Helen Hayes, Ramsey Lewis, Sarah Vaughan, Lionel Hampton, and the Vienna Choir Boys all appeared? Open daily for self-guided tours: Monday-Saturday 9–5, and Sunday Noon–5. Call for admission charge.

## THE GREAT STORM
### Pier 21 • (409) 763-8808

This panoramic, multi-media documentary uses eyewitness accounts, historic photographs, and sound to recreate the 1900 hurricane that wiped out the island. The storm inflicted terrible devastation and is still the deadliest natural disaster in United States history. Open daily except Thanksgiving and Christmas Day. Call for hours and admission.

## LONE STAR FLIGHT MUSEUM
### 2002 Terminal Drive • (409) 740-7722

The museum houses one of the nation's finest collections of restored aircraft. A commemorative collection of World War II vintage planes, the museum showcases fighters, bombers, and reconissance aircraft. It also houses an exhibition of the history of aviation. These are not just museum pieces. They are fully restored and in flying condition. It's well worth the trip to see the planes that won "The Good War." Open daily. Call for times and admission prices.

## MARDI GRAS MUSEUM
### 2211 Strand, third floor • (409) 763-1133

The good times roll all year long at the Mardi Gras Museum, which is located in Old Galveston Square. The collection includes historic costumes, as well as the elaborate masks, crowns, and scepters of the Mardi Gras royalty. It also describes the history of the event from the Island's first Fat Tuesday celebration just after the Civil War through today's family-oriented citywide celebration.

Open Wednesday through Sunday only. Closed Thanksgiving and Christmas Day. Call for hours and admission charge.

## MARY MOODY NORTHEN AMPHITHEATRE

### Galveston Island State Park, FM 3005 at the intersection of 13 Mile Road • (409) 737-3440

In the 1,700-seat outdoor arena, you can watch outdoor musicals such as *The Lone Star,* a rousing version of Texas' fight for independence, as well as Broadway favorites. Tickets may be purchased at Houston ticket centers and at the gate. Dinner is available before the performance. Schedule varies with the season. Call for times and prices.

## MOODY GARDENS

### Ten Hope Boulevard, near the Galveston Municipal Airport (409) 744-HOPE

On the banks of Offatts Bayou, the Moody Foundation has constructed a mini wonderworld. It includes the truly fabulous Rainforest Pyramid, an IMAX theater, and Palm Beach (see Beaches), as well as various lavishly landscaped gardens. Call for schedule and fees.

## THE RAILROAD MUSEUM

### Rosenberg Street at the Strand • (409) 765-5700

Officially, it's known as the Center for Transportation and Commerce, but this island favorite is better known as the railroad museum. Located in the former Santa Fe station on the Strand, it houses dozens of railway cars from the steam era and an opulent private car from 1929. Sound and light shows detail the history of the island. Open daily. Call for fees and special events.

## SEAWOLF PARK

### Pelican Island • (409) 744-5738

The park's location on Pelican Island provides an unusual view of Galveston's busy harbor. Kids love the playground and scrambling over naval exhibits that include an airplane, a destroyer escort, and a submarine. Also here is the *Selma,* one of the ill-fated cement ships built as an experiment during World War II. It ran aground here years ago. Fishing pier. Open daily. Call for admission charge and special events.

## TROLLEY CARS

**Convention and Visitors Bureau • (409) 763-4311**

**Strand Visitors Center • (409) 765-7834**

The system's 4.7 miles of track connects the Strand Historic District with the Seawall in 1890s-to-1920s style. More than 50 designated points of interest along the route are accessible via trolley stops. Hours vary with the season, but there are schedules posted along the route. Admission.

## HISTORIC GALVESTON

Start with the Strand. It once was called the Wall Street of the Southwest, with considerable justification. Thanks to Galveston's long decades of economic slumber, the Strand is left with one of the largest and best collections of 19th-century iron-front commercial buildings in America. Architects come from all over the world to study and marvel, but most tourists are more interested in the shops, galleries, businesses, and restaurants. For information and maps, stop by the Strand Visitors Center, 2016 Strand, open daily year-round and run by the Galveston Historical Foundation in the restored **Hendley Row (1856-1860).** A free 12-minute film will orient you to the town. Brochures outlining walking and biking tours are also available here, and audio-guide equipment for tours may be rented.

The **1871 League Building** on Strand at Tremont showcases one of the nicest restorations in the city and houses several interesting shops, including the Wentletrap (see Restaurant listings).

The **Marx and Kempner Building** in the 2100 block of the Strand sports a clever *trompe l'oeil* mural. The original detailing of this building was removed decades ago, and what looks like several ornate, original facades actually are hand-painted artwork.

The **1882 H. M. Trueheart-Adriance Building** at 210 Kempner was designed by noted Galveston architect Nicholas J. Clayton and is one of the most ornate and distinctive structures in the area. Its restoration in 1970 sparked the Strand's renaissance.

The **East End Historical District,** though still a bit spotty in the process of restoration, is known as the Victorian equivalent of

Colonial Williamsburg. This is where the merchants who worked in the Strand lived back in the Golden Age. Even semi-restored, this special area, which includes 40 blocks of Victoriana in the general area bounded by Broadway, Market, 19th, and 11th streets, is well worth a look. It can be driven or walked, but the best way to see the most in the least amount of time is by bicycle. The Galveston Historical Foundation runs a homes tour in early May (see Calendar of Events).

**The Bishop's Palace** at 1402 Broadway got its name from its one-time use by the Catholic bishop of Galveston. It is now the only home in the East End Historical District open to the public on a regular basis. This massive place was built between 1887 and 1892 for the Walter Gresham family. Designed by Nicholas J. Clayton, it is considered one of the 100 most-outstanding residential structures in America. Even more interesting than its turreted rococo exterior are the details and furnishings inside. Call for tour schedule, which varies with the season, and for admission prices from September through June, (409) 762-2475.

The **Silk Stocking Historical District** is a nine-block area loosely bound by Rosenberg, J, and N avenues, and Tremont Street. When Galveston was the Queen of the Gulf, this is where the Queen's court lived. Brochures on the most interesting homes open to the public are available at the Strand Visitors Center, the Galveston Island Convention and Visitors Bureau, and at Ashton Villa.

**Ashton Villa** at 2328 Broadway is an Italianate gem built in 1859 of bricks made on the island. It survived both a disastrous island-wide fire in 1885 and the great 1900 storm. During the grade-raising, the ground floor was buried, which accounts for its somewhat stumpy look. Now restored as the showplace of the Galveston Historical Foundation, it hosts many of the foundation's functions. Tours begin in the carriage house with an excellent film on the city and the 1900 storm, and an interesting urban archaeological dig exposes a small portion of the home's original first level. Open daily, but the schedule varies with the season. Call for ticket information, (409) 762-3933.

**The 1839 Samuel May Williams Home** at 3601 Bernardo de Galvez, a.k.a. Avenue P, is one of the two oldest structures in Galveston. It was built in 1839 in Saccarappa, Maine, then disassembled and shipped to Galveston in pieces. This charming restoration now looks as it did in 1854. Tours include audio dramas that tell the

Williams family story as you move from room to room. Open daily; fee, (409) 765-1839.

**John Sydnor's 1847 Powhatan House** at 3427 Avenue O is the home of the Galveston Garden Cub, which is appropriate for this handsome mansion with its oak-studded gardens. Picture books in each room help visitors to conjure up the elegance of the city's golden era. No high heels, please; they damage the remarkable pine floors. Open afternoons only during most of the year. Call for times and prices, (409) 763-0077 or (409) 744-7431.

## SHOPPING

Galveston has the most incredible array of tourist junk shops in the Western world. Along the Seawall you can buy every kind of kitsch the mind can conjure. Need a life-sized inflatable mermaid? They've got it. Green nose zinc? No sweat. And the T-shirts . . . don't get me started on the T-shirts. In the tonier precincts of the Strand, the junk and fun stuff is mixed in with some really nice boutiques and specialty shops. The Strand Visitors Bureau has brochures detailing who sells what where.

# HOTELS

Because Galveston has been a resort town for so long, it has aquired an encrustation of accommodations. There is something here to suit every taste and pocketbook—from Motel 6 to expensive high-rise condos and luxury resorts. Just about every hostelry on the island has a schedule of prices that varies with the season. Unlike Houston hotels, Galveston's are generally more expensive on weekends, but offer some good midweek and off-season bargains.

**KEY TO SYMBOLS**
**Inexpensive $ (under $55)**
**Moderate $$ ($55–$75)**
**Expensive $$$ ($75–$125)**
**Very Expensive $$$$ ($125–plus)**
**Wheelchair access W**

## FLAGSHIP HOTEL

**2501 Seawall Boulevard • (409) 762-8681 • $$$; Cr. • W variable**

Built on a pier over the Gulf, the Flagship is periodically wrecked by hurricanes, but it is always rebuilt promptly because it is such a popular spot. Each room has a balcony with a view of the water and the city—pretty stunning on a clear night.

## HOTEL GALVEZ

**2024 Seawall Boulevard • (409) 765-7721**
**$$$–$$$$; Cr. • W variable**

This was the symbol of the city's resurrection from the awful devastation of the 1900 storm. Finished in 1910, it was then the height of elegance, and Franklin Roosevelt, among others, stayed here. After a long period of decay, the Galvez was restored in the late '70s. Now a bit overshadowed by newer, posher establishments, the Galvez still embodies the spirit of the island better than anyplace else.

## HARBOR HOUSE

**No. 28 Pier 21 • (409) 763-3321 or (800) 874-3721 • $$$$; Cr.**
**W variable**

A nautical addition to the Strand district, some of the rooms at Harbor House have a stunning view of the Bay. It's small, only 42 rooms, and guests are invited to moor their boats in one of the hotel's 10 slips. It's also within easy walking distance of all the Strand area attractions.

## THE SAN LUIS HOTEL

**53rd at Seawall Boulevard • (409) 744-1500 or (800) 392-5937 in Texas or (800) 445-0900 outside the state • $$$$; Cr. • W variable**

This is the luxe deluxe of island accommodations. The San Luis, imaginatively constructed over the site of old Fort Crockett, is a top-notch resort hotel with all the amenities.

## TREMONT HOUSE

**2300 Ship's Mechanic Row • (713) 480-8201 • $$$$; Cr. • W variable**

The Tremont House, the crown jewel in the Strand's restoration, is one of the finest smaller hotels in America. Artfully taking advantage of its 19th-century shell, the Tremont provides every luxury for its pampered guests.

## THE VICTORIAN

**6300 Seawall • (409) 740-3555 or (800) 231-6363**
**$–$$$; Cr. • W variable**

Facing the Gulf in a location close to town, this condo development with the Victorian gingerbread offers a good deal to families on vacation. There are fully equipped kitchens and living space as well as bunk beds for the kid. During the off-season, it offers some really inexpensive midweek packages.

# RESTAURANTS

## KEY TO SYMBOLS

| | |
|---|---|
| **AE** | **American Express** |
| **CB** | **Carte Blanche** |
| **DC** | **Diners Club** |
| **MC** | **Mastercard** |
| **V** | **Visa** |
| **Dis** | **Discover** |
| **Cr.** | **All of the above** |
| **W** | **Wheelchair access** |

**Dinner for one, exclusive of drinks and tips.**

| | |
|---|---|
| **$** | **Inexpensive Under $7** |
| **$$** | **Moderate $7-$15** |
| **$$$** | **Expensive $16-$29** |
| **$$$$** | **Very Expensive $30 and up** |

## DINNER ON THE DINER

**Center for Transportation and Commerce, 25th and Strand**
**(409) 763-4759 • Open seven days; reservations suggested**
**$$–$$$; Cr. • W variable**

If you have never clackety-clacked along across the country on the Super Chief or its counterparts, you can make up for it here with a meal in a real Silver Hours Club Car, circa 1940. Special railroad-style lunches and dinners are served Monday through Saturday; Sunday brunch. Reservations advised. Bar.

## GAIDO'S

**39th and Seawall • (409) 762-9625**
**Open seven days • $$–$$$; AE, MC, V • W variable**

Dine on seafood in a setting that is part of Galveston's days of old. You might feel pretty old yourself by the time you get a table for a weekend dinner. Still, many don't mind the mind-boggling lines. Fried, broiled, or boiled, the fresh seafood here is excellent, and the dressings and sauces are made from scratch. Daily specials change with the catch. Bar.

## HILL'S PIER 19

**Pier 19 at Port Industrial • (409) 763-7087**
**Open seven days • $$$; AE, MC, V**

It isn't fancy, but it is almost always crowded. This is one of the places in town for fresh fish, salads, gumbo, and more, all served cafeteria style. You can eat inside or up on the top deck overlooking the boat basin. Beer and wine.

## THE MERCHANT PRINCE

**Tremont House Hotel • 2300 Ship's Mechanic Row**
**(409) 763-0300 • Open seven days • $$$–$$$$; Cr.**

The beautifully restored setting and the superb food make this one of Galveston's classier dining spots. Power breakfasters abound during the week. Evenings are elegant. Best to reserve early for summer and special-event weekends. Bar.

## THE WENTLETRAP

**2301 Strand • (409) 765-5545 or (713) 225-6033**
**Mon-Sat lunch and dinner only; Sunday brunch • $$$-$$$$; Cr.**

Not a few Texans consider this the finest restaurant in the state. Housed in the historic League Building, which was built in 1871, the Wentletrap (the name comes from a seashell) boasts an inventive menu; upscale, dressy patrons; and lovely decor.

# CLEAR LAKE AND
# THE NASA AREA

This is another of those marvelous Houston misnomers. Clear Lake is neither clear nor a lake. It is shallow, muddy-brown, and a salty arm of Galveston Bay. I suppose it was named by the same folks who dubbed an area barely inches above sea level Mount Houston. In any event, Clear Lake has become an important part of metropolitan Houston.

And like Houston itself, it started off as a . . . how shall we put this . . . . complex? real estate deal. In the early 1960s when it became clear that the United States was about to commit big bucks to the space race, NASA was looking around for a place to build its new headquarters. Congressman Albert Thomas (with able assistance from Lyndon Johnson, no doubt) made them an offer they couldn't refuse. The oil company now known as Exxon had a parcel of swampland south of Houston it wanted to unload on the government, and Thomas fixed it up so that everybody involved benefitted.

First, he got the oil company to "donate" the land to Rice University. Then Rice donated the land to NASA, which purchased some more—but not the parcel Exxon had kept for itself right on the edge of the Space Center campus.

Of course the government spent gadzillion dollars building the installation, which was nice, but then they had to man it. Eureka! Exxon just happened to have a home-building subsidiary,

Friendswood Development, that had a planned community, Clear Lake, all set to go right next door to NASA!

So in the end, the government got the free land. Rice got good oil company largesse and government grants. Exxon got a tax break *and* a pool of buyers for its planned community. Down the road a few years, amid much howling, weeping, and gnashing of teeth, the City of Houston, which annexed a none-too-thrilled Clear Lake, got the tax base—and we all lived happily ever after.

That's not a joke. Clear Lake makes a lot of Houston-area residents happy. For water sports, everything from jet boats to windsurfers, it's hard to beat. The area is already home to the nation's third-largest fleet of pleasure craft, with their numbers growing daily. Many of the subdivisions around the water emphasize their nautical flavor, and some even offer boat slips outside your back door along with garages. Because Clear Lake is only 25 miles from downtown—less than an hour from most parts of Houston—it makes for a wonderful weekend getaway.

South of Houston, off I-45, is NASA Road 1, the main drag through the Clear Lake/Bay Area, which includes the towns of Texas City, Seabrook, and Kemah. NASA is high-tech; the beach towns are like something out of a Jimmy Buffett ode to Margaritaville. All are fascinating.

## WHAT'S HAPPENING

**The Clear Lake Convention and Visitors Bureau,** 1201 NASA Road 1, Houston, TX 77058, (713) 488-7676, has a wealth of information about annual events as well as lists of all boat ramps, bait and fuel spots, and marinas, and their hours of operation. The bureau also staffs a desk in the NASA Visitors Center and places brochures in the lobby of area hotels that detail dozens of area events and attractions. (There are no listings for September.)

### JANUARY

**Winter Star Party.** Johnson Space Center Astronomical Society helps to sponsors this family event at Challenger 7 Park near NASA. It's designed to introduce party-goers to our celestial neighbors. Spectacular views of the moon, Jupiter, and other planets may be seen through the society's telescopes, and there are videos, games, and prizes for the kids. Admission is free. Call 332-5157 for dates and details.

## MARCH

**The Clear Lake area's annual St. Patrick's Day parade** is always fun. Generally, the festivities include a rowdy Irish Stew cook-off as well. Spectating is free, but there's an entry fee for the cook-off. Call 488-7676 for information.

## APRIL

**The Spring Fling and Boating Festival** brings thousands to the water. The U.S. Triathlon has become a major attraction for those crazed enough to swim, bike, and then run improbable distances. This is also the time of year for the Texas Boat Show at Clear Lake and the month when the Chamber of Commerce sponsors its annual Epicurean Evening.

## JULY

**Clear Lake Fourth of July.** There's a parade in Crosby, and a carnival in Clear Lake Park, but the really big show is the fireworks shot off from the middle of the lake. As the bombs burst in air, a local radio station simulcasts patriotic music. It's a wonderful effect. Best viewing is from Clear Lake Park on NASA Road 1. Call 488-7676 for details.

**Lunar Rendezvous Festival and Space Week.** In honor of the first landing on the moon in July 1969, the NASA area celebrates with various parades, contests, and high-tech activities, frequently attract visiting celebrities. Call 488-7676 for dates and locations.

## AUGUST

**Ballunar Liftoff Festival.** Perhaps the most beautiful festival of the summer takes place at Rocket Park, next door to Space Center Houston. Dozens of huge, gorgeously colored hot-air balloons lift off in various competitions. In early evening, when all of them take off at once, it is an absolutely spectacular sight. After dark comes the "Balloon Glow" event in which the pilots fire up the propane jets inside their balloons, which are still tethered to the ground, creating what looks like dozens of huge candles. There are also activities for kids, live entertainment, arts and crafts, lots of food, and aviation equipment displays. Admission is free. Parking at Space Center Houston is $2. Call 244-2105 for dates and details.

**The Blessing of the Fleet.** Once upon a time the blessing was little more than a prayer for a bountiful catch, the safety of the sailors and the boats, and that there might be enough fish left in the ocean to reproduce for the following catch, now it's a festival as well. This Kemah/Seabrook extravaganza offers parades on both land and water, arts and crafts, lots of food, a street dance, and a carnival midway. The blessing itself takes place on Sunday afternoon as boats parade through the Clear Creek channel. Call 488-7676 for dates and details.

**World War II vintage planes** are the major draw at the Confederate Air Force's annual show. And the huge Houston in-the-water Boat Show gives enthusiasts a chance to get a feel for the latest equipment.

## OCTOBER

**Armand Bayou Nature Center's Fall Festival** celebrates the most visually beautiful time of year at the nature reserve. The City of Seabrook also stages its annual civic celebration in October.

## DECEMBER

**Christmas Boat Parade.** Floating along the lake, more than 100 boats of all sizes are decorated in the best holiday fashion. At dusk, the moving lights reflected in the water create a spectacular effect. Spectators can just line the shore to watch the parade move from South Shore Harbour Marina in League City to the Clear Lake channel, where it passes beneath the Seabrook-Kemah bridge, then out into Galveston Bay before it circles back. The hotels, restaurants, and clubs along the lake, as well as those along Clear Creek channel in Kemah, offer special Christmas Parade package deals. Just watching from shore is free. Call 488-7676 for date and time.

# ATTRACTIONS

### ARMAND BAYOU NATURE CENTER

**Bay Area Boulevard approximately 20 miles southeast of Houston**
**Exit Interstate 45 at Bay Area Boulevard, head east approximately**
**12 miles • 474-3074 • Open Wed–Sun; closed Mon–Tues**
**Free • W variable**

Armand Bayou lets you see the Houston area as it was before civilization. In the 2,000 or so acres of reserve are forest, prairie, and marsh environments, with educational material available on each. In addition to the trail system, boating on the bayou is popular. Visitors can either bring their own boats or take advantage of a free group ride.

### LYNDON B. JOHNSON SPACE CENTER

**NASA Road 1, three miles east of Interstate 45 (25 miles**
**southeast of Houston) • 483-3111 • Open daily 9–4 • Free • W**

This is the number one attraction in the Houston area. While the Disney-built Space Center Houston gets most of the attention these days—and it certainly is well deserved—take time to visit Rocket Row, where you can see the actual craft that took America into space. Of special interest is the *tiny* Mercury-program rocket and the first space capsules, which were dubbed (with complete accuracy) the Man in a Can. Virgil I. Grissom, who was one of the original seven Astronauts, flew in a Mercury can. When asked, as a guy with the "Right Stuff," if he'd been scared, he is supposed to have said: "How would you feel sitting on top of 3 million separate parts, each one made by the lowest bidder?" See for yourself what he was talking about. There is nothing else like NASA—except perhaps for Star City in the former USSR, and it's a lot easier to get to Clear Lake.

### SPACE CENTER HOUSTON
**Nasa Road 1 at Second Street (on the Johnson Space Center campus) • (800) 972-0369 or 244-2100 • Open 10–5 Tue–Fri; 10–7 Sat–Sun; Closed Mon (except during school holidays) Admission • W**

This is the really big show. It's magic. It's a treat for the imagination. Houston is a city based on imagination—it was, after all, imaginary when the founders advertised for residents—but the Space Program was the ultimate act of imagination, and Space Center Houston's design, by Walt Disney Imagineering, does the voyage out from Earth proud. The exhibitions take visitors through the past, present and future of NASA's Manned Space Program through spectacular interactive exhibits, and IMAX giant-format films. You can interact with real, live astronauts and see demonstrations of the latest equipment. You can also take a behind-the-scenes tram tour of Johnson Space Center, and see the podium President John F. Kennedy used when he made his "Go To the Moon" speech. Wear a space helmet. Land an 85-ton orbiter. Touch a rock brought back from the moon by one of our neighbors. Inspire the future astronauts in your family. Inspire *yourself*. Go!

### SCHOONER MORNING STAR
**Nassau Bay Hilton • 335-1292**

Feeling romantic? The schooner does two-hour sunset cruises around the lake year-round except in bad weather.

## SPORTS & FITNESS

**Canoeing.** With a map from the Armand Bayou Nature Center in hand, take a water trip through the wilderness. You'd never believe you're so close to civilization. You can put in at Bay Area Park and at the NASA Road 1 bridge at Clear Lake Park, 5001 NASA Road 1. Canoes are available to members at Armand Bayou Nature Center, but otherwise you're pretty much on your own.

**Gulf Coast Sailing Center,** 1206 FM 2094 on the south side of Clear Lake, offers full- and half-day sailboat rentals. If you have always wanted to sail but don't know how, these folks offer a quickie in-the-water course on weekends that will have you sailing on your own in a day. Course reservations required. They take credit cards. Call 334-1722 for info.

**Golf Courses** include public facilities, such as the Bayou Golf Club in Texas City, (409) 948-8362, the private Clear Lake Golf Club in Clear Lake, 488-0250, and South Shore Harbour Golf Club in League City, 334-0521.

**The Water Sports Center** of Clear Lake is in Harris County Park, 5001 NASA Road 1. Open daily 10 until dark, the center offers sailing lessons and rents sailboats, 16-foot Hobie Cats, and canoes by the hour. Credit cards are accepted. Call 326-2724.

**Club Nautico** at the Nassau Bay Hilton has catamarans, sunfish, and 18-foot Wellcraft motor runabouts for rent year-round. Reservations advised for weekends. Credit cards honored. Call 333-1495 for information.

**Sculling.** Ivy League types who used to row the Thames at Yale or the Charles at Harvard have long touted sculling as the only way to row. Now Houstonians are skimming across Clear Lake. Learn the fundamentals with group or private lessons from the Houston Rowing Club at South Shore Harbor. 334-3101.

**Canoeing Dickinson Bayou.** Roughly parallel to FM 517, both west and east of 1-45, this splendidly wild place is best in late fall. There's a good place to put in (as well as parking) at the T-3 bridge in Dickinson, and then you have your choice of take-outs: either a carry out at the FM 646 crossing (3.5 miles) or at Cemetery Road.

## HOTELS

Along NASA Road 1 are many of the major chain hotels and motels. These offer something for just about every price range. As a rule, the farther away from the tonier South Shore, the less expensive.

**KEY TO SYMBOLS**
**Inexpensive $ (under $55)**
**Moderate $$ ($55–$75)**
**Expensive $$$ ($75–$125)**

**Very Expensive $$$$ ($125–plus)**
**Wheelchair access W**

## BED AND BREAKFAST ON THE BAY
**Eleventh Street, Seabrook • 771-3919 • $**

The last house at the end of the street is more than one of the neighbors: It is a member of the Bed and Breakfast Society of Texas (see Houston Hotels) and does indeed boast a spectacular view of the bay. Guests have the use of two swimming pools, and the boat parade through the channel is right outside the door. There are also excellent spots for crabbing and fishing in the channel under the bridge.

## NASSAU BAY HILTON AND MARINA
**3000 NASA Road 1 • 333-9300 • $$–$$$; Cr. • W variable**

One of the spiffier places along the lake, this is where the big honchos stay when there's a major event at NASA. Look for Dan Rather in the lobby. The view on the lake side is just wonderful. You'll find entertainment in the lounge and parties on the deck in fine weather. For those who sail instead of drive, the marina out back has all the facilities.

## SOUTH SHORE HARBOR HOTEL
**Fed. 2094, League City • 334-1000**
**$$ weekends; $$$–$$$$ weekdays; Cr. • W**

This is the last word in nautical elegance. The conference center attracts plenty of business types to the booming Clear Lake area, and the South Shore puts them up in style, offering fine dining in several restaurants and dancing in the club.

# RESTAURANTS

Many of the same chain restaurants found up the road in Houston have locations in Clear Lake as well, such as the Black-eyed Pea, plus an infinity of Chinese eateries and barbeque joints. But the area's proximity to the water creates some wonderful opportunities for seafood lovers. So forget about NASA 1 and head for Kemah and Seabrook. That's where the good eats are.

**KEY TO SYMBOLS**

| | |
|---|---|
| **AE** | **American Express** |
| **CB** | **Carte Blanche** |
| **DC** | **Diners Club** |
| **MC** | **Mastercard** |
| **V** | **Visa** |
| **Dis** | **Discover** |
| **Cr.** | **All of the above** |
| **W** | **Wheelchair access** |

**Dinner for one, exclusive of drinks and tips.**

| | | |
|---|---|---|
| **$** | **Inexpensive** | **Under $7** |
| **$$** | **Moderate** | **$7–$15** |
| **$$$** | **Expensive** | **$16–$29** |
| **$$$$** | **Very Expensive** | **$30 and up** |

Several of the restaurants on the Kemah side of the channel have gotten together to promote themselves as "Houston's Waterfront." It's not a bad idea. The row of eating and drinking establishments makes for a fun pub prowl and the nearby tony marina means that at least some of the crowd will be upscale.

## BRASS PARROT
**Second and Kipp, Kemah • 334-1099 • $$–$$$; Cr.**

The shrimp and other seafood dishes are flavored with Carribean touches. The boat parade goes by, and you have a front row seat if you choose to sit out on the Clear Lake area's largest open-air deck.

## FLYING DUTCHMAN RESTAURANT & OYSTER BAR
**505 Second Street, Kemah • 334-7575**
**Open daily • $$–$$$; AE, DC, MC, V**

Second Street, which faces the channel, is a little difficult to find because it requires a looping turn off the 146 bridge, but it's worth whatever trouble it takes to reach. If you're a shrimp lover, this is close to paradise. The Dutchman and other seafood restaurants face the channel with its endlessly fascinating parade of boats. Bar.

## LANDRY'S AT JIMMY WALKER'S

**Kipp and Second Streets, Kemah • 334-2513**
**Open daily • $$–$$$; Cr. • W variable**

When it was Jimmy Walker's this was more high-tone than most of the seaside establishments, but now as Landry's it's saltier. The Louisiana-flavored seafood dishes are just fine, and the shrimp offerings and broiled fish are better than fine. The view of the channel and Galveston Bay is the best in the area. At sunset on a good day it's absolutely enchanting. Bar.

## JOE LEE'S SEAFOOD RESTAURANT

**Second and Kipp, Kemah • 334-3711 • Open daily, lunch and dinner only • $–$$; Cr.**

Done in by Hurricane Jerry back in the late 1980s, Joe Lee's rebuilt version has recreated the casual indoor and outdoor dining on good Gulf seafood that made the place famous. The oyster bar has long been a local favorite, as is the outdoor deck overlooking the boat parade from the lake to the bay.

## REGATTA RESTAURANT

**Seabrook Shipyard • Seabrook • 474-3432**
**Open daily • $$–$$$; Cr.**

In what was once a yacht club, the Regatta maintains the air of a private facility. The intimate setting in this hard-to-find gem provides a tree-shaded view of a back channel to Clear Lake and is one of the most restful places around. The food is well-prepared middle-of-the-road seafood. Bar with one of the city's best wine lists.

## S. W. TOOKIE'S

**1202 Route 146 (Bayport Boulevard) • Seabrook**
**474-3444 • Open daily, lunch and dinner only • $; No cr.**

When you want a change from seafood, try Tookie's. It can be found in a brightly painted old barn on the east side of Route 146 serving up some of the best hamburgers in town. Tookie's grinds its own meat and slices real, thick, sweet onion rings. Even the iced tea is freshly brewed. Simple and satisfying.

# KEMAH AND SEABROOK SIGHTS

NASA Road 1 East dead ends at the Route 146 intersection in Seabrook and turns into the graceful Seabrook Bridge. From the center of the high span, Galveston Bay stretches out to the left as far as you can see. Fleets of dazzling white sailboats skim over dark water. Freighters move in stately procession up the Houston Ship Channel in the distance. The towns of Kemah and Seabrook bound the bridge itself and stretch off toward the water.

These former fishing villages are heaven for shrimp lovers and boat watchers. Because the channel under the bridge is the only passage from Clear Lake into Galveston Bay, the water traffic can be prodigious on summer weekends.

The Seabrook side is still a good place to buy relatively inexpensive fresh shrimp and fish from the dockside fish markets that cluster in the shadows of the bridge; shop around for the best price. The shrimp usually come "head on." Bring your own ice chest.

Much of what was once the funky little fishing village of Kemah across the channel was leveled in the 1980s by Hurricane Alicia. The whole south end of the bridge is now devoted to the tony Lafayette Landing Motel and Marina complex. Shrimpers and other indigenous water folk have largely abandoned the Kemah side to small shops and boutiques that now occupy the few houses that survived the 1983 storm. The area has become a kind of nautically flavored Old Town Spring (See Houston Attractions).

# ATTRACTIONS

Party Boat Fishing on Galveston Bay. The Judy Beth, a 65-footer holding up to 80 passengers, has operated out of the Kemah docks for more than a decade. The boat takes anglers for an afternoon of fishing off Redfish Island, the Houston Yacht Club, and the entrance to the Houston Ship Channel, and around oil-rig platforms where the big ones hide. Tackle and bait are available, and your catch can range from flounder and sand trout to croaker, whiting, or black drum, depending on the season. There are year-round departures, but the schedule varies with the season. Weekends are always crowded, and reservations are necessary. Winter weekdays are open, but in summer it's best to reserve well in advance. Beer, wine, sandwiches, and junk food available on board. No credit cards. For reservations, call 334-3760.

# READ MORE
# ABOUT IT

There are hundreds of books about our town, and most of them can be found in the Texas Room of the downtown public library. These are a few of the most interesting, informative, or useful.

## 175 BOOKS ABOUT HOUSTON AND HARRIS COUNTY
### Houston Public Library • Houston

A reprint of an informative pamphlet first printed in 1967. It indexes many of the early works on Houston that are available in the Texas Collection. When it's available, the booklet is free at any branch of the library.

## ALLEN'S LANDING
### Ralph E. Dittman • A. C. and J. K. Allen Publishing

Ostensibly, this is a novel. In reality, it is a somewhat confusing version of the lives of the Allen brothers who founded Houston. It was written by one of their descendants, who seems to have had access to unpublished family papers. Perhaps as a result, the whole tone is worshipful.

## M.D. ANDERSON: HIS LIFE AND LEGACY

**Texas Gulf Coast Historical Association • William B. Bates • 1956**

It's always nice to know something about the city's parents. This is certainly not objective, but it is interesting.

## ARCHITECTURE OF JOHN F. STAUB: HOUSTON AND THE SOUTH

**Howard Barnstone • University of Texas Press • Austin**

In the 1920s, Staub was Houston society's favorite architect. He designed many of the homes in Shadyside and the then-new River Oaks. This book is a coffee-table gem with wonderful photos of some of Houston's finest homes.

## BOB'S GALVESTON ISLAND, TEXAS READER

**Bob Nesbitt • Self-Published • Galveston, TX**

One of the greatest eccentric works extant on Galveston Island. "Bob" gives his own idiosyncratic view of everything from the weather to the food.

## CLAYTON LIBRARY (CENTER FOR GENEALOGICAL RESEARCH)

**5300 Caroline • Downtown • 524-0101**
**Open Mon–Wed 9–9; Thurs–Sat 9–5; Closed Sun • W**

With an enormous collection of town records from all over Texas and many resources from the rest of the United States, this is one of the finest genealogical libraries in the country. The knowledgeable staff can help you trace your family tree.

## ENVIRONMENTAL GEOLOGY ATLAS OF THE TEXAS COASTAL ZONE

**Galveston-Houston area**

Not light reading. This isn't just a book of maps.

## ETHNICITY IN THE SUNBELT:

**A History of Mexican Americans in Houston**
**Arnoldo de Leon • University of Houston**

From the very first Mexican settlers in Houston to the present era, this book by a UH professor gives detailed accounts of the community's growth and increasing cultural importance.

## GALVESTON:
### A History of the Island • Gary Cartwright • Atheneum

Gary Cartwright is a long-time *Texas Monthly* writer who has also written a number of novels and the famous true-crime thriller *Blood Will Tell* about the Cullen Davis case. He knows how to tell a good story, and the history of Galveston certainly is that. If you want to read an entertaining account of the entire story of the island, this is what you're looking for.

## A GUIDE TO THE TEXAS MEDICAL CENTER
### Clyde W. Burleson and Suzy Williams Burleson • University of Texas Press • Austin

For anyone who is planning to check into one of the Medical Center facilities—as well as for friends and family members—this paperback guide is invaluable. It gives detailed maps and directions for finding your way through the labyrinth of buildings, and it supplies visiting hours, phone numbers, parking information, and short histories of each institution.

## THE HANDBOOK OF TEXAS
### Walter Prescott Webb, editor • Volumes 1, 2, and Supplement
### The Texas State Historical Association • Austin, TX • 1952

Nobody can write about Texas without the *Handbook*. It is an amazing collection of information, though very much of it's Eisenhower-era time. Very few women or minorities are profiled (and in the cases of African-Americans, there is much emphasis on Anglo ancestors, if any). Despite these omissions and a worshipful tone in its discussion of Texas' "captains of industry," the *Handbook* remains indispensable.

## IMA HOGG: FIRST LADY OF TEXAS
### Louise Kosches Iscoe • The Hogg Foundation for Mental Health
### Houston, TX • 1976

This is an interesting monograph on the life of Miss Ima. It's a bit hagiographic, but the pictures are fascinating.

*HOUSTON CHRONICLE*

**Daily and Sunday • By subscription or on a newstand near you**

The "Cronk" is now Houston's only daily newspaper. It's a big responsibility, and the reporters and editors take it seriously. Of special interest are *Texas Magazine,* and the *Zest* entertainment sections, both of which come out on Sunday.

**HOUSTON BY STAGES**

**Sue Dauphin • Eakin Press • 1981**

Written by a woman who covered the Houston theater scene for many, many years, this book is encyclopedic. The author's numerous newspaper features are augumented with theater history and profiles of local theater figures.

**HOUSTON ENVIRONMENTAL GEOLOGY: SURFACE FAULTING, GROUND SUBSIDENCE, HAZARD LIABILITY**

**Houston Geological Society**

This certainly isn't light reading, but much of the worthwhile info comes under the heading of "who knew?"

**HOUSTON FOR FREE**

**Joel and Peggy Bloom • Follett Publishing Company • Chicago**

This early 1980s book is out of print and somewhat out of date, but it still supplies fascinating bits of information and can be helpful when the kids are home during the summer. You can often find it in secondhand bookstores.

**HOUSTON: A HISTORY**

**David G. McComb • University of Texas Press • Austin**

McComb is a fine historian. His works on Texas, Galveston, and several editions of this 1969 work all are worth reading.

**HOUSTON: A HISTORY OF A GIANT**

**Houston JayCees • Continental Heritage, Inc.**
**Houston, TX • 1976**

As you can imagine, a book published by the Junior Chamber of Commerce gives our history a decidedly positive spin, but this one also provides lots of useful information about the early days of Houston, and it is extremely well-illustrated.

## HOUSTON: THE ONCE AND FUTURE CITY

### By George Fuermann • Doubleday and Company • New York

Fuermann is a wonderful writer. His views of the city, though particular to an earlier time, are lots of fun. The book is also illustrated with fascinating photos of early Houston.

## *HOUSTON PRESS*

### Weekly (Thursdays) • Free in newsboxes all over town

This feisty tabloid weekly has great listings of events as well as some of the nation's best restaurant reviews.

## THE HOUSTON SHIP CHANNEL

### John Leslie Dickson • Thesis, George Peabody College for Teachers • 1929

An interesting glimpse of a world gone by. Even before Houston became one of the world's busiest ports, the ship channel was crucial to the economy.

## HOUSTON SURVIVAL HANDBOOK

### Chase Untermeyer • Bayland Publishing • Houston

Now out of print and somewhat dated, the book contains valuable info about things like obtaining building permits and influencing politicians. Untermeyer, then a state representative, went on to become a bigwig in the Bush administration, so he must know what he's talking about. Look carefully in Half Price Books and Paperbacks Etc. They'll sometimes have copies.

## IMPERIAL TEXAS: AN INTERPRETIVE ESSAY IN CULTURAL GEOGRAPHY

### D. W. Meinig • University of Texas Press • Austin

As you can tell from the title, this isn't for casual readers. Still, if you're serious about finding the whys and wherefores of Houston, the book offers some excellent insights. Look for it in academic secondhand bookstores.

## IN TIME

### Patrick J. Nicholson • Gulf Publishing Company • Houston

If you come across this one at a garage sale or in a secondhand bookstore, buy it just for fun. Nicholson was a longtime University of Houston official who is perhaps best known in these parts for compiling the society "Blue Book" (an address book for the *right* people). He takes the university very seriously.

## KUHF-TV (CHANNEL 8)
### University of Houston • PBS

Obviously, this isn't a publication, but it is a good source of information about Houston. KUHF is the nation's oldest public television station and depends almost entirely on its viewers for financial support. Because they are less likely to find many "buyers" among other PBS stations, programs with local themes must be financed locally—and they are terribly expensive to produce. So, if you'd like to see more programming about Houston, SEND MONEY!

## THE LAST AMERICAN CITY: AN INTREPID WALKER'S GUIDE TO HOUSTON
### Douglas Milburn • Texas Chapbook Press • Houston

This is still my favorite guide to Houston. The author, Doug Milburn, is a well-known teacher, and he's also a wonderful writer. He wrote this some years ago, but it remains the best completely idiosyncratic version of Houston attractions I know of. Imagine a Gray Line tour conducted by the old *Monty Python* TV troupe and you're in the right ballpark. Unfortunately, the book is long out of print and difficult to find even in secondhand stores. The Heights branch still has a couple of copies, though, and will send them out on inter-library loan.

## LONE STAR: A HISTORY OF TEXAS AND THE TEXANS
### T. R. Fehrenbach • Collier Books

Fehrenbach is probably the best-known historian in the state. His works are always detailed, extremely well-researched, and highly readable.

## MAKE WAY FOR SAM HOUSTON
### Jean Fritz • G. P. Putnam's Sons • New York • 1986

This is a young adult book that gives the basics of Sam Houston's career in a clear, straightforward fashion. If you need to know the basics, you could do a lot worse.

## NATIVE HOUSTONIAN: A COLLECTIVE PORTRAIT

**Ann Quin Wilson • Houston Baptist University Press • Houston**

This is easy reading with an emphasis on the colorful personalities who shaped the city.

## THE PORT OF HOUSTON: A HISTORY

**Marilyn McAdams Sibley • University of Texas Press • 1968**

In more ways than most of us ever realize, the story of the Port is the story of Houston. This does a good, if factually overwhelming, job of telling its story.

## *PUBLIC NEWS*

**Weekly (Midweek) • Free in shops and restaurants**

An alternative weekly that does the best job in town of covering the club scene. If four-letter words offend you, do NOT pick it up.

## RAY MILLER'S HOUSTON

**Ray Miller • Gulf Publishing Company • Houston • 1992**

Ray Miller, who practically invented television journalism in Houston, has written histories of Houston and Galveston, and a whole series of guidebooks describing different parts of Texas. Each is written in his own distinctive, personal voice. It's like watching him describe a place on TV.

## ROADSIDE GEOLOGY OF TEXAS

**Darwin Spearing • Mountain Press • 1991**

Aimed at the interested layperson, this book gives anyone a different perspective on those road-cuts between here and Austin.

## SAM HOUSTON: AMERICAN HERO

**Ann Fears Crawford • Eakin Press • Austin, Texas • 1988**

Let me tell you the secret of the research universe. Always read a kid's book first. They're like outlines of the information you're after. They point the way toward areas to research in depth. If you're researching the life of Sam Houston, this is a good place to start.

## SAM HOUSTON: MAN OF DESTINY
### Clifford Hopewell • Eakin Press • Austin, Texas • 1987

Sam Houston's life was too strange to have been invented. This detailed biography does a good job of presenting the facts and doesn't get bogged down in speculation about why he did what. You can do your own fantasizing about that.

## THE TEXAS NORTHER
### Edward Hake Phillips • The Rice Institute Pamphlet
### Volume 41 • Houston, TX • 1955

Unlike the storms its describes, this is pretty dry. It's not fun reading, but the information is intrinsically interesting.

## TEXAS TRIVIA
### Ernie and Jill Couch • Rutledge Hill Press • Nashville

Only part of the Q&A stuff applies to Houston, but all of it is just so darn silly that the book is worth reading. Often found at Half Price with the Texana or at Paperbacks, Etc. in the comedy section.

## TOMLINSON'S LONE STAR BOOK OF TEXAS RECORDS
### Lone Star Books • Fort Worth

This out-of-print book is filled with strange information. Enough of it is about Houston to make it fascinating.

## TRUE STORIES OF OLD HOUSTON AND HOUSTONIANS
### Dr. S. O. Young • Houston

The author was born in 1848, and his book was published in 1913, so these are *really* old Houstonians we're talking about. Young's descriptions of the city and its citizens from the founding until its 75th birthday make fascinating reading. Though the The Texas Room of the downtown library has copies of the book, which was reprinted in 1974, copies sometimes turn up in bookstores.

## WPA GUIDE TO TEXAS
### Federal Writers Project • Texas Monthly Press • Austin • 1940

The past is indeed another country. In 1940, when this book was published, Houston was another planet, segregated, un-air conditioned, and filled with drive-in restaurants. The period of the Great

Depression comes alive in this 1986 reprint, which is still available in most bookstores.

## BOOKSTORES

After years of Houston's being unjustly labeled a "bad book town," booksellers from around the nation have finally snapped to the fact that people here actually READ! As a result, dozens of megastores have sprung up in the past few years with more to come. There are now good bookstores within easy driving distance of just about everywhere, but there are also some very special places that—for true book lovers—are well worth a trip across town. All are worth visiting.

### B. DALTON
#### 11 Locations including Galleria II • 960-8191

Dalton's offers a complete range of titles with a fine selection of travel and computer books. Each store has a wide spectrum of paperbacks with genre emphasis varying from location to location. All major credit cards are accepted and there is a mailing service available.

### BARNES & NOBLE
#### Several locations including 3003 W. Holcombe • 349-0050

Long a mainstay of book discounting in the Northeast, Barnes & Noble is making a splash in Houston with its huge selection. The travel section is particularly good.

### BOOKSTOP
#### 8 Locations including 2922 South Shepherd • 529-2345

Bookstop's flagship location in the old Alabama Theater on the western edge of Montrose is a wonderful place preserving much of the art deco moviehouse feel. There is now a coffee bar in the balcony and a massive magazine rack where the screen used to be. Homage to the building's history aside, the Bookstop's strengths are the latest bestsellers, discounted, and a huge selection of cooking and gardening books.

## BORDERS
### Several locations including 9633A Westheimer • 782-6066

Borders is another recent entrant in the Houston megastore sweepstakes. Offering a coffee bar, CDs, and videos as well as a large selection of paper and hardback books, Borders wants to attract the whole family.

## BRAZOS BOOKSTORE
### 2421 Bissonnet • 523-0781

More than half of the Brazos Bookstore is devoted to literature, fiction, poetry, drama, belles lettres, and literary criticism. Owner Karl Killian and his employees, many of them graduate students at the University of Houston or nearby Rice, have a good knowledge of contemporary literature, and even when the store is crowded, they take time with each customer. This is also one of the few places in town that offers readings by some of the biggest names on the literary circuit.

## BRENTANO'S
### Several location including Galleria III • 961-1091

The famous chain's Galleria location still has something of the private club about it, what with its elegant hunter-green facade and brass fixtures. Though not as big as the megastores, it does offer one of the widest ranges of choice in town.

## CROWN AND SUPER CROWN BOOKSTORES
### Several locations including 4714 FM 1960 West • 580-2167

This is the chain that brought serious discounting to Houston, and it has prospered in strip centers and smaller malls all around town. The format stays the same with the highlights including coffeetable books and the ever-popular bargain racks. Crown now offers a selection of audio books and a few CDs as well.

## FUTURE VISIONS
### 10570 Northwest Freeway • 682-4212

*Star Trek* fans, comic-book collectors, and science fiction, fantasy, and horror readers of all description love this place. The staff knows more bizarre trivia about science fiction books, comics, and films than seems humanly possible.

## HALF PRICE BOOKS

### Several locations including 2537 University Boulevard
### 524-6635

You never know what's going to turn up here. The store claims to buy everything printed. Maybe. Sellers beware. You're not going to get rich on the rock-bottom prices paid here. Still, in addition to the usual paperbacks and discontinueds, the ever-changing collection includes everything from auto-repair manuals for 1969 Volkswagen bugs to some genuine collectors items. Keep trying, that's half the fun.

## MUNCHKIN MABLIES'

### 2530 Times • 522-3911

*Babar the Elephant, Curious George, Danny and the Dinosaurs* and just about every other kids' book you've ever heard of and more crowd this colorful store that is completely devoted to children's literature. They even offer readings by kid-lit biggies. Your children will love it.

## MURDER BY THE BOOK

### 2342 Bissonnet • 524-8597

Martha Farrington was a mystery fan who couldn't find enough of her faves in regular bookstores, so she opened Murder by the Book, which is devoted entirely to mystery, suspense, espionage, true crime, and detective fiction. The shop has expanded considerably and now offers one of the biggest, most diverse collections anywhere. The top names in the field make a pilgrimage to Bissonnet whenever they tour a new book to meet with the faithful. Part of the fun has always been reading the hand-written reviews posted along the shelves by loyal customers. Mystery paraphernalia—coffee mugs, T-shirts, old radio shows on tape, party games—are also for sale.

## PAPERBACKS, ETC.
### 3210 South Shepherd • 521-1020

A tiny, crowded shop of the sort book lovers crave, Paperbacks offers a wide range of used books—everything from philosophy and classical drama to romance novels—as well as a few hardbacks and audiobooks, but only if they're particularly interesting to the owner, Saul Levinson. He is such fun to talk to, and knowledgeable about so many things, that folks from all over town come to chat and stay to trade. Well worth a visit anytime.

## RIVER OAKS BOOKSTORE
### 3270 Westheimer • 520-0061

This is one of the finest bookstores in Houston. Owner Jeanne Jard emphasizes personal service, and her small staff is both friendly and tremendously knowledgeable. If they don't have it, they'll get it for you pronto. Located in the same small shopping center as Andre's Confiserie (opposite Lamar High School), the River Oaks is elegant without being stuffy. The strength of the collection is one of Houston's best selections of gardening, cooking, and armchair travel books.

## THIRD PLANET
### 2718 Southwest Freeway • 528-1067

The Dungeons and Dragons crowd, to say nothing of collectors of the latest underground comics and science fiction buffs love this place. In addition to books and 'zines, it offers a huge selection of posters, T-shirts, and collectors cards. Third Planet also has a subscription service.

## WALDENBOOKS
### 15 locations including West Oaks Mall • 558-2585

Best-sellers and leading-category paperbacks make up the bulk of the collection, but Walden also stocks lots of computer titles and kids' books. There are several promotional book clubs for fans of various fiction genres. Gift certificates, phone orders, and mailing services are available at all locations.

# INDEX

Adam (movie), 134
Aeros (hockey team), 154
Air Show, 112
Airline Farmers Market, 169
Alabama-Coushatta, 98, 238–239
Allen Brothers, 27–30, 39, 41, 276
Allen, Eliza, 13
Alley Theatre, 144
American Cowboy Museum, 45
Anahuac, 239–240
Anderson Fair, 218
Anderson, M.D., 76
Annual Events: Clear Lake,
    266–268
  Galveston, 249–252
  Houston, 80–123
Antique Rose Emporium, 165
Apollo 13 (movie), 136
Apple, Max, 81
Arboretum: Houston, 62
  Mercer, 67
Armand Bayou Nature Ctr., 47,
    272
Armstrong, Neil, 22
Art in Downtown, 124–129
Art League of Houston, 136
Art Car Parade, 90
Arts, 124–151

Ashton Villa, 260
Asian-American Festival, 112
Astrodome, 47
Astros (baseball team), 153
Astroworld, 48
Attractions: Clear Lake, 269–271
  Galveston, 254–261
  Houston, 44–79
Audubon, John James, 10
Austin, Moses, 26
Austin, Stephen F., 14, 15, 26
Austin, town of , 32
Azalea Trail, 86, 167

Ball, Tom, 71
Ballunar Liftoff Festival, 105
Barthelme, Donald, 92
Bates, Alan, 93
Battleship Texas, 48
Bay Day, 98
Bayou Wildlife Park, 51
Bayou Bend, 49
Bayou Place at Albert Thomas, 49
Bishop's Palace, 260
Blaffer Gallery, 137
Blessing of the Fleet, 106
Blue Norther, 2

BOI's, 244
Boliver, 240–241, 255
Borden, Gail, 30
Bradbury, Ray, 43
Brazos Bookstore, 285
Brown, George R., 53
Brown, Rosellen, 83
Buck-a-Book Sale, 91
Buffalo Bayou, 6, 8–10, 27–29
Buffalo Bayou Regatta, 91
Bulb Mart & Plant Sale, 109, 167
Burke Baker Planetarium, 52
Butterfly Center, 54

Can Castle Competition, 116
Caribbean Weekend, 108
*Challenger* (Space Shuttle), 43
Channel 13 (television station), 79
Channel 8 (television station), 281
Cherokee, 12–14
Children's Museum, 54
Christmas Bird Count, 122
Christmas Boat Parade, 122, 268
Cinco de Mayo, 92
Clayton Library, 277
Clear Lake, attractions, 269
Clear Lake, events, 266–268
Clear Lake, history of, 265–266
Clubs & Pubs, 216–227
College Sports, 155–156
Confederate Museum, 54
Connally, John, 41
Conrad Hilton Archives, 59
Conroe Cajun Catfish Fest, 112
Contemporary Arts Museum, 137
Cornelius Nursery, 163
Cullen, Hugh Roy, 84
Cynthia W. Mitchell Pavilion, 101
Czech Fest, 111

de Menil, Dominique, 137,
    140–141
Dean, James, 39

Dickens Evening on the Strand:
    Galveston, 119, 255
Diverseworks, 146
Dobie, J. Frank, 5

*Eagle, The* (Spacecraft), 22
Earthquakes, 8
Edith Moore Nature Sanctuary, 67
8-F Crowd, 40
Eureka Heights Fault, 8
Egyptian Festival, 109

Fannin Street Flower Market, 169
Farm Fall Festival, 116
Ferber, Edna, 39
Fiestas Patrias, 109
Film Festival (see WorldFest)
Fire Museum, 62
*For All Mankind* (movie), 136
Fort Bend, 241–242
Fort Bend Museum, 55, 242
Freedom Fest, 100
Fulshear Follies, 104
Funeral Service Museum, 45

Galleria, 55
Galveston Beaches, 253–254
Galveston, events, 249–252
Galveston, history of, 244–248
Gar, 9–10
*Garden Book for Houston*, A, 165
Garden Centers, 162–165
*Gardening Newsletter,* 166
Gatorfest, 110, 243
George Observatory, 57
*Giant,* (novel and movie), 39
Gilbert & Sullivan Society, 146
Golf Hall of Fame, 74
Golf, 89, 158, 271
Goyens, William, 46
Great Storm, 35, 247, 257
Greek Festival, 111
Green Houston, 162–170

Gulf Coastal Plain, 5
Gulf Greyhound Park, 59
Gumbo soil, 5

Hanukkah Adventure, 121
Harris, John Richardson, 27
Health Clubs, 158–160
Hermann Park, 59
Hermann, George, 60
Hofheinz, Judge Roy, 40
Hofheinz, Mayor Fred, 42
Hogg, Miss Ima, 50, 278
Holocaust Education Center, 61
Hotels: Clear Lake 271–272
  Galveston 261–263
  Houston 228–237
Hotshots (indoor soccer team),
  155
Houston Ballet, 131
*Houston Chronicle*, 165, 279
Houston Community College, 147
Houston Grand Opera, 141
Houston International Festival, 89
Houston International Jazz Fest,
  106
*Houston Post*, 28, 97
*Houston Press*, 280
Houston Shakespeare Festival, 106
Houston Symphony, 142
Houston, area of, 1
Houston, history of, 22–43
Houston, population of, 1
Houston, Sam, 11–21
Houston's Birthday, 107
Hughes, Howard, 58
Hurricanes, 4

Inn of the Twelve Clans, 239
Intercontinental Airport, 36
International Quilt Festival, 116

Japanese Garden, 64
*Jason's Lyric* (movie), 134
Jaybird-Woodpecker War, 242

Jesse H. Jones Park, 64
Jewish Book Fair, 116
Jingle Bell Run, 119
Johnson, Lyndon Baines, 40, 41,
  74
Jones, Jesse H., 64
*July 20, 1969*, 22
Juneteenth, 96, 98

Karankawas, 22–24, 244–245
Katy Rice Harvest Fest, 113
Kennedy, Jackie, 41
Kennedy, John F., 41
Kiddie Wonderland, 66
King, Martin Luther, Jr., 81
King's Orchard, 66
KNUZ Radio, 170
KPRC Radio, 166
KSEV Radio, 166
KTRH Radio, 166
KTRK-TV, 79
KUHF Radio (public), 142
KUHT-TV (public), 281
Kuumba House, 147

La Carafe, 224
Laffite, Jean, 24, 245
Lake Conroe, 102, 243
Lamar, Mirabeau B., 56
Latitude, 1
*Laura M.* (steamboat), 33
Lea, Margaret, 18
Leland, "Mickey," 37
Leydon, Joe, 133
Lights in the Heights, 120
Lilypons Water Garden, 165
Livestock Show & Rodeo, 85
*Local Hero* (movie), 135
Long, Jane, 25, 241
Longitude, 1
Lowry, Beverly, 107
Lucia's Garden, 163
Lunar Rendezvous Festival, 267
Lynchburg, 26

"Magnolia City," 36
Marathon, 82
Mardi Gras, 86, 249, 257
McCarthy, Glenn, 88
Mediterranean Festival, 108
Menil Collection, 137
Mexico City, 17, 26
MFA Film Program, 132
Montgomery County, 59, 243
Moon Day, 104
Mosquito Festival, 103
Murder By the Book, 286
Museum of Fine Arts (MFA), 138
Museum of Natural Science, 62
Museum of Printing History, 67

NASA (see Space Center)
NASA/Clear Lake Area, 265–275
Nation, Carry, 242
Nature Discovery Center, 68
New Orleans, 17, 27
Newspapers 279, 280, 282
Nutcracker (ballet), 120

Oilers (football team), 154
Old Town Spring, 68, 103
Open Air Musicals, 253
Orange Show, 69

Paperbacks, etc., 287
Park People, The, 170
Pasadena Historical Museum, 69
Pasadena Strawberry Festival, 91
Pasadena Historical Museum, 69
Pin Oak Charity Horse Show, 95
Police Museum, 70
Port of Houston, 70
Public Television (Channel 8), 281
Public Radio (88.7 FM), 142

Raven's Bride, The (novel), 13
Reinert, Al, 136
Renaissance Festival, 110
Restaurants: Clear Lake, 272–274

Galveston, 263–264
Houston, 171–215
Rice Media Center, 132, 138
Rice Hotel, 41
Richmond, 241
River Oaks Bookstore, 164, 287
River Oaks, 38
Rocket Row, 66, 272
Rockets (basketball team), 153
Rollover Pass, 241
Rothko Chapel, 139
Round-Up Rodeo, 71

Safari-Land of Texas, 72
Sam Houston Park, 72
San Jacinto, Battle of, 11, 16–17, 28
San Jacinto Monument, 73
Sanders, Doug, 89
Santa Anna, Antonio Lopez de, 15, 27
Schjeldahl, Peter, 126
Scott, Emmett J., 96
Shamrock Hotel, 39, 43
Shange, Ntozake, 86
Ship Channel, 36
Ships: Elissa, 256
    Morning Star, 270
    Selma, 258
    USS Texas, 48
Sidekicks (movie), 135
Shamrock Hotel, 39
Slavic Heritage Festival, 105
Smith, Erastus (Deaf), 241
Society for the Performing Arts, 149
Southern Empress, 73
Space Week, 267
Space Center Houston, 74
Spindletop, 139
Splashtown, 74
Sports Museum, 63
Sports, 152–161
SWAMP, 133

Teas Nursery, 164
*Telegraph & Texas Register,* 28
Tennis 90, 159
*Terms of Endearment* (movie), 135
Texas Medical Center, 75
Thanksgiving Day Parade, 117
*The Martian Chronicles,* 43
The Woodlands, 101, 243
Theatre Under the Stars, 150
Thomas, Albert, 52
Thomas, Lorenzo, 101
Tranquility Base, 22
Tranquility Park, 75
Transco Tower, 75
Tunnel System, 54

Vaca, Cabeza de, 23

Velodrome, 44
Vera Cruz (Mexico), 1

Waller County Museum, 77
Waterwall, 75
Waterworld, 77
Westheimer Art Festival, 111
"White Gold," 33
Whitmire, Kathy, 42
Wood, Susan, 104, 115
WorldFest (Film Festival), 92, 133
Wortham IMAX Theater, 77
Wortham, Gus, 78

Zindler, Marvin, 79
Zoo, 63